全国普通高等教育"十二五"重点建设规划教材
普通高等学校少数民族预科教育系列教材

英语基础语法汇编与练习

主　编　陈　燕　巫　莉
副主编　李　华　赵留美　陆艳云
参　编　周轶文　温　颖　何　毅
　　　　莫双赫　王　筱

北京理工大学出版社
BEIJING INSTITUTE OF TECHNOLOGY PRESS

版权专有 侵权必究

图书在版编目（CIP）数据

英语基础语法汇编与练习/陈燕，巫莉主编. —北京：北京理工大学出版社，2018.9
（2018.10 重印）

ISBN 978-7-5682-6328-3

Ⅰ. ①英… Ⅱ. ①陈… ②巫… Ⅲ. ①英语-语法-高等学校-教学参考资料
Ⅳ. ①H319.35

中国版本图书馆 CIP 数据核字（2018）第 211489 号

出版发行 / 北京理工大学出版社有限责任公司
社　　址 / 北京市海淀区中关村南大街 5 号
邮　　编 / 100081
电　　话 / （010）68914775（总编室）
　　　　　（010）82562903（教材售后服务热线）
　　　　　（010）68948351（其他图书服务热线）
网　　址 / http://www.bitpress.com.cn
经　　销 / 全国各地新华书店
印　　刷 / 涿州市新华印刷有限公司
开　　本 / 787 毫米 × 1092 毫米　1/16
印　　张 / 13.5　　　　　　　　　　　　　　　　　责任编辑 / 梁铜华
字　　数 / 310 千字　　　　　　　　　　　　　　　文案编辑 / 梁铜华
版　　次 / 2018 年 9 月第 1 版　2018 年 10 月第 2 次印刷　责任校对 / 黄拾三
定　　价 / 39.00 元　　　　　　　　　　　　　　　责任印制 / 李志强

图书出现印装质量问题，请拨打售后服务热线，本社负责调换

编 委 会

广西民族大学预科教育学院
预科教材编审指导委员会

主任委员　林志杰

委　　员（按姓氏笔画为序）

　　　　　吴胜富　杨社平　周国平　唐德海　容学德

　　　　　黄永彪　覃炳荣　樊爱琼　樊常宝

序 言

  普通高校少数民族预科教育是指对参加高考统一招生考试、适当降分录取的各少数民族学生实施的适应性教育，是为少数民族地区培养急需的各类人才而在高校设立的向本科教育过渡的特殊教育阶段。它是为加快民族高等教育的改革与发展，使之适应少数民族地区经济社会发展需要而采取的特殊有效的措施；是中国特色社会主义高等教育体系的重要组成部分，是高等教育的特殊层次，也是我国民族高等教育的鲜明特色之一。其对加强民族团结、维护祖国统一、促进各民族的团结奋斗与共同繁荣具有重大的战略意义。

  为了贯彻落实"为少数民族地区服务，为少数民族服务"的民族预科办学宗旨，建设好广西少数民族预科教育基地，适应普通高等学校少数民族预科教学的需要，近年来，广西民族大学预科教育学院在实施教学质量工程以及不断深化教育教学改革的过程中，结合少数民族学生的实际情况，组织处在民族预科教育教学一线的教师编写了《思想政治教育》《阅读与鉴赏教程》《写作实训教程》《微积分基础》《英语写作口语教程》《计算机基础》《计算机基础实验教程》《基础物理》《大学预科物理实验》《普通化学》《八桂乡情》等十多种教材，形成了颇具广西地方特色的、适用的少数民族预科教材体系。广西少数民族预科系列教材的编写和出版，成了我国少数民族预科教材建设中的一朵奇葩。

  本套教材以国家教育部制定的各科课程教学大纲为依据，以民族预科阶段的教学任务为中心内容，以少数民族预科学生的认知水平及心理特征为着眼点，在编写过程中力求思想性、科学性、前瞻性、适用性相统一，尽量做到内涵厚实、重点突出、难易适度、操作性强，真正适合民族预科学生使用，从而使学生在高中阶段各科教学内容学习的基础上，通过一年预科阶段的学习，能够对应掌握的学科知识进行全面的查漏补缺，进一步巩固基础知识，培养基本能力，达到预科阶段的教学目标，实现"预与补"的有机结合，为其一年之后直升进入大学本科学习专业知识打下扎实的基础。

百年大计，教育为本；富民强国，教育先行。教育是民族振兴、社会进步的基石，是提高国民素质、促进人的全面发展的根本途径，教育寄托着千百万家庭对美好生活的期盼，而少数民族预科教育作为我国普通高等教育的一个特殊层次，是少数民族青年学子由以进入大学深造的"金色桥梁"，承载着培养少数民族干部与技术骨干、为少数民族地区经济社会发展提供人才保证的重任。本编委会祈望，本套教材在促进少数民族预科教育教学中能够发挥其应有的作用，在少数民族高等教育这个百花园里大放异彩！

林志杰

2018 年 4 月

前 言

　　《英语基础语法汇编与练习》是根据高等院校人才培养的目标和要求，以广西少数民族预科学生的英语知识水平为基础组织编写的一套语法教材。它旨在为学生提供适合其学习水平的语法内容，使其通过学习语法，掌握英语语言的规律，提高其语言知识水平和语言运用能力，从而为本科院校输送合格的人才，满足时代对人才的需求。

　　本书共分为十八章，每一章都由语法知识讲解与配套练习组成。语法知识讲解通过突出重点和难点、精选例句，帮助学生理解并掌握语法知识。配套练习有选择和改错两种题型，旨在通过强化训练，加强学生对语法的理解和掌握，巩固其所学的语法内容。

　　本书为高等院校预科文科、理科班、工科班、医科班等的英语语法教材，也可作为其他有志于学习英语语法知识、提高语法运用能力的广大学习者的参考用书。

　　本书的编写分工为：李华编写第一章，王筱编写第二章，赵留美编写第三、四章，陆艳云编写第五章至第七章，周轶文编写第八、十一章，温颖编写第九、十章，莫双赫编写第十二章，陈燕编写第十三章至第十五章，巫莉编写第十六章，何毅编写第十七、十八章。

　　由于编者水平有限，书中如有错误和不妥之处，恳请同行专家与广大读者批评指正。

编　者
2018 年 4 月

目 录

第一章 英语的基本句型 ······ 1

 第一节 句型的概念 ······ 1
 第二节 六种基本句型的内涵 ······ 1

第二章 动词的时态与语态 ······ 11

 第一节 动词时态（Verb Tense） ······ 11
 第二节 语态（Voice） ······ 22

第三章 主谓一致 ······ 27

 第一节 主谓一致的概念 ······ 27
 第二节 主谓一致的用法 ······ 28

第四章 情态动词 ······ 39

 第一节 情态动词的概念 ······ 39
 第二节 情态动词的用法 ······ 40

第五章 名词 ······ 51

 第一节 名词的定义与分类 ······ 51
 第二节 名词的数与所有格 ······ 52
 第三节 名词的功能 ······ 55

第六章 冠词 ······ 59

 第一节 冠词的定义与分类 ······ 59
 第二节 冠词的用法 ······ 59

第七章 代词 ······ 65

 第一节 代词的概念 ······ 65
 第二节 代词的分类及用法 ······ 65

第八章　数词 ······ 75

第一节　数词的定义及表示 ······ 75
第二节　数词的语法功能 ······ 81
第三节　数词学习要点 ······ 82

第九章　形容词 ······ 90

第一节　形容词的定义与分类 ······ 90
第二节　形容词的构成与用法 ······ 91

第十章　副词 ······ 97

第一节　副词的定义与作用 ······ 97
第二节　副词的分类与构成 ······ 98
第三节　副词的用法 ······ 101
第四节　副词的比较等级 ······ 102

第十一章　介词 ······ 106

第一节　介词的定义及用法 ······ 106
第二节　介词的区分与辨别 ······ 111
第三节　常用介词短语 ······ 115
第四节　省略介词的几种情况 ······ 117

第十二章　非谓语动词 ······ 125

第一节　非谓语动词的定义与句法作用 ······ 125
第二节　非谓语动词的分类及用法 ······ 125

第十三章　名词性从句 ······ 145

第一节　名词性从句的定义与连接词 ······ 145
第二节　名词性从句的分类及用法 ······ 145

第十四章　定语从句 ······ 151

第一节　定语从句的定义与结构 ······ 151
第二节　定语从句的用法及注意问题 ······ 151
第三节　非限定性定语从句 ······ 154
第四节　同位语从句与定语从句的区别 ······ 154

第十五章　状语从句 ······ 158

第一节　状语从句的定义 ······ 158
第二节　状语从句的分类及用法 ······ 158

第十六章 虚拟语气 167
第一节 虚拟语气的定义 167
第二节 虚拟语气的用法 167

第十七章 倒装句 178
第一节 倒装句的定义与结构 178
第二节 倒装句的用法及注意问题 179

第十八章 感叹句 190
第一节 感叹句的定义与结构 190
第二节 感叹句的用法及注意问题 191

参考文献 199

第一章

英语的基本句型

第一节　句型的概念

句型（Sentence Patterns），即句子的结构类型，包括构成句子的语词的不同类别、序列、搭配方式等。英语句子看上去纷繁庞杂，但仔细观察不外乎六个基本句型。从这六个基本句型出发可以演变出多种复杂的英语句子。换言之，绝大多数英语句子都是由这六个基本句型生成的。掌握好这六个基本句型，就可以为运用英语这门语言打下良好的基础。这六种基本句型分别为主语+谓语（SV），主语+系动词+表语（SVP），主语+谓语+宾语（SVO），主语+谓语+间接宾语+直接宾语（SVoO），主语+谓语+宾语+宾语补足语（SVOC），There be 句型。

第二节　六种基本句型的内涵

一、主语+谓语（SV）

在"主语+谓语"句型中，谓语动词为不及物动词或者是不及物动词词组。例如：
The boy runs very fast.
The sun is rising from the top of the hill.
I'll try again.
Did you sleep well last night?
Unfortunately, the engine of our car broke down.

二、主语+系动词+表语（SVP）

在"主语+系动词+表语"句型中，除了系动词 be 之外，还有一些动词可以充当系动词，例如，表示状态的系动词：appear, seem, keep, remain, stay, prove, continue, stand 等；表示感觉的系动词：look, feel, smell, sound, taste 等；表示转变的系动词：become, fall, get, go, grow, turn 等。例如：

My grandmother is still in good health.

The most important thing for us to do now is to decide when to leave.

She appears younger than her age.

The weather continued fine.

He looks much happy today.

It sounds interesting to go cycling around the countryside.

He became mad after that.

His brother grew rich within a short time.

Seeing is believing.

三、主语 + 谓语 + 宾语（SVO）

（1）谓语动词为及物动词。例如：

He sold his house in the countryside and moved his family to the city.

Many people believe that exercise can help people keep fit.

He smiled a strange smile.

Sometimes I can't express myself in English.

The little boy really enjoys reading in the sun.

I really don't know what we are going to do next.

（2）谓语动词后面跟不定式作宾语。例如：

We can't afford to pay such a high price.

He decided to move to Chicago.

The Customs officer demanded to see my passport.

We tried to kill two birds with one stone.

She liked to dance on the stage.

（3）谓语动词后面用"连接副（代）词 + 不定式"作宾语。例如：

I didn't know how to get to the subway station.

I forgot what to say.

You should learn how to be patient.

Many students wondered where to apply for jobs.

（4）谓语动词后面用动名词作宾语。例如：

The government official avoided answering our questions.

Would you mind waiting a minute?

The young man kept looking at the beautiful girl.

It has stopped raining.

（5）有些谓语动词既可跟不定式，也可跟动名词作宾语，但两者意思差别不大。例如：

What do you propose doing/to do next?

It started raining/to rain.

（6）有些谓语动词既可跟不定式，也可跟动名词作宾语，但意义不同。

①动词 forget，remember，regret 等接不定式时，表示非谓语动词的动作发生于谓语动词的动作之后；接动名词作宾语时，表示非谓语动词的动作发生于谓语动词的动作之前。例如：

I forgot to tell you about it.

我忘记告诉你那件事了。

I remembered giving the money to him, but he said I didn't.

我记得我把钱给他了，但是他说我没有给。

另外，动词 forget，remember，regret 等接动名词的完成式或不定式的完成式作宾语时，意义相同。例如：

I regretted to have broken the rules of our class.

= I regretted having broken the rules of our class.

我后悔违反了班规。

②mean 接不定式作宾语时，表示一种意图，意思是"打算做，想要做"；接动名词作宾语时，表示解释，意思是"意味着，意思是"。例如：

I didn't mean to hurt your feeling.

我本不想伤害你的感情。

What he said means going there on foot.

他的意思是走着去那儿。

③try 接不定式作宾语时，表示一种决心，意思是"设法做，尽力做"；接动名词作宾语时，表示尝试，意思是"试着做"。例如：

I'll try to catch up with my class.

我将尽力赶上同学们。

I tried reading the novel without consulting my dictionary.

我试着不查词典来阅读这本小说。

④need, require, want, deserve 后接不定式或动名词时表示的语态不同。need, require, want, deserve 等表示"需要"，后接另一动词作宾语时，该动词用不定式或动名词均可。但是其语态不同，即动名词用主动形式表示被动意义，而不定式则用被动形式表示被动意义。例如：

The flowers need watering every day.

= The flowers need to be watered every day.

花儿需要每天浇水。

注意：若 need, require, want 后接动词为句子主语所发出的动作，则只能用不定式，不能用动名词。例如：

He needs to water the flowers every day.

他需要每天给花浇水。

⑤can't help 后接不定式时，意思是"不能帮忙做某事"；接动名词作宾语时，意思是"禁不住做某事，情不自禁做某事"。例如：

I'm very busy now, so I can't help (to) clean the house.
我现在很忙,因此不能帮助打扫房子。
The girl couldn't help crying when she saw her mother again.
当小女孩再次看到母亲时,她情不自禁地哭了起来。
⑥stop 接不定词作宾语时,表示停下正在做的事以便去做另一件事;接动名词作宾语时表示停下正在做的事。例如:
The boy was watching TV just now. When he heard his father come into the room, he stopped to do his homework.
刚刚男孩正在看电视。当听到他父亲走进房间时,他马上停下来,然后去做作业了。
The students stopped talking immediately when they saw the teacher come in the classroom.
看见老师走进教室,学生们立刻停止了讲话。

四、主语+谓语+间接宾语+直接宾语(SVoO)

在"主语+谓语+间接宾语+直接宾语"句型中,及物动词后跟双宾语,即指人的间接宾语和指物的直接宾语。例如:
My Chinese teacher asked me a very difficult question.
He gave me his address.
I'll show you around my hometown when you come to see me.
The famous company offered him a well-paid job.
My father told me a white lie.
但若要先说出直接宾语(事物),后说间接宾语(人),则需要借助于介词 to 或 for。用 to 侧重于指动作的方向,表示朝着、向着、对着某人;用 for 侧重于指动作的受益者,表示为了某人、替某人。
需借助 to 的动词有:bring, give, lend, hand, offer, pass, pay, return, send, teach, tell, write, ask 等;需借助 for 的动词有:buy, call, cook, draw, find, get, make, order, sing, save, spare 等。例如:
He brought a cake to me.
My friend bought a cute dog for me.
Please return the bag to its owner.
The old soldier always tells stories about the heroes to the children in the Long March.
Can you order some drink for me?
Her father bought a dictionary for her as a birthday present.

五、主语+谓语+宾语+宾语补足语(SVOC)

"主语+谓语+宾语+宾语补足语"句型中的"宾语+补语"统称为"复合宾语"。宾语补足语的主要作用是补充、说明宾语的特点、身份,或者是表示让宾语去完成的动作等。在一个句子中担任补语的常常是名词、形容词、副词、介词短语、分词、动词不定式等。例如:

She wanted me to give her some money. （不定式）

I found the begger lying dead on the road. （现在分词）

Many towns had their water supply cut off because there was no electricity. （过去分词）

He pushed the door open. （形容词）

The parents named their baby "Maomao." （名词）

This left them without a ray of hope. （介词短语）

I won't let you in. （副词）

When he woke up, he found himself being looked after by a kind old woman. （现在分词的被动式）

Why did you leave the light on? （副词）

六、There be 句型

1. There be 句型的概念

There be 句型由 "there + be + 主语 + 状语" 构成，用以表达某种存在关系，可以称为 "……有……" 句型。There be 句型其实是倒装的一种情况，主语位于谓语动词 be 之后，there 仅为引导词，并无实际语意。有时，此句型不用 be 动词，而用 appear, live, stand, come, go, lie, remain, exist, arrive 等动词。例如：

There stands a big tree in the middle of the park.

Once upon a time there lived an old king in the town.

There appears to be no doubt about it.

There lies a mountain behind our college.

There exist many ancient temples in the country.

2. There be 句型的时态与情态变化

在 There be 句型中，be 与其后的主语在人称和数量上保持一致，且有时态和情态的变化。

（1）there is/are，表示现在有。

There is a cherry tree in the garden.

There are two men waiting outside the room.

（2）there was/were，表示过去有。

There was no one waiting for us.

There were too many people in the park yesterday.

（3）there will be、there is/are going to be，表示将来有。

There will be a huge crowd at the New Year's Eve party, won't there?

There is going to be a football game in the afternoon.

（4）there has/have been，表示现在已经有。

There has been a small church in the town.

There have been many such accidents here.

（5）there might be，表示可能有。

There might be something wrong with your television.

（6）there must be/there must have been，表示肯定有。

There must be a reason for his weird behavior.

There must have been an answer to the difficult question.

（7）there used to be，表示过去曾经有。

There used to be a library in this area.

（8）there seems/seem/seemed to be，表示似乎有。

There seems to be a man sitting on that fence.

（9）there happen/happens/happened to be，表示碰巧有。

There happened an old friend in the bank who helped me solve the problem.

3. There be 句型否定式的表达方式

there be 句型的否定句有两种表达法：

（1）在 be 后面加 not。例如：

There isn't a man under the tree.

There are not any books on the table.

（2）通过 no 来表达，此时的 no 相当于 not any。例如：

There is no milk in the bottle. = There isn't any milk in the bottle.

There are no pictures on the wall. = There aren't any pictures on the wall.

4. there be 与 have 的异同

（1）There be 和 have 都可以表示"有"，此时，两者的用法可以相互转化。例如：

There are many beautiful houses in the ancient town.

此句可转化为：

The ancient town has many beautiful houses.

（2）there be 能用来表示"存在"，侧重表达某地有某物，而 have 没有此用法。例如：

There are some trees in front of the house.

此句不能转化为：

In front of the house has some trees.

5. there be 句型的非谓语形式

（1）there being 结构在句子中主要用作状语或是介词宾语。例如：

There being nothing to do, I went to sleep.

There being no taxi available, we had to walk home.

What's the chance of there being an election this year?

No one would have dreamed of there being such a good place.

（2）there to be 结构用作动词宾语。能够使用该结构的动词不多，常见的有 like, prefer, hate, want, mean, intend, expect, consider 等。例如：

I don't want there to be any more trouble.

Students hate there to be too much homework.

6. "there be + 名词 + 非谓语动词"结构

在此结构中，非谓语动词可以为现在分词、过去分词，以及不定式形式。例如：

There are some children playing football in the field. （现在分词）
There is a table standing against the wall. （现在分词）
There was nobody injured in the car accident. （过去分词）
There is nothing written on it. （过去分词）
There was so much to lose that we couldn't take any risks. （不定式）
There was nobody to ask for help. （不定式）

7. "There is no + 动名词"结构

（1）表示否定，意思是"不可能……""无法……"。例如：

There is no getting over the difficulty.

这个困难无法克服。

There is no knowing what the boss will do next.

无法知道老板下一步要干什么。

（2）表示不允许。例如：

There is no photographing here.

这里不允许拍照。

Sorry, there is no smoking in the waiting room.

对不起，等候室不允许吸烟。

8. "There is no + 名词 + in doing sth."结构

例如：

There is no difficulty in finding his home.

找到他家一点都不费劲。

There is no harm in your coming early.

你早到没有害处。

There is no point in wasting time.

浪费时间没有意义。

There is no sense in making him angry.

惹他生气是没有道理的。

There is no use in complaining.

发牢骚没用。

 Exercises

Ⅰ. Choose the best answer to complete each sentence.

1. Once upon a time, there _____ an old queer man in the city.
   A. has B. is C. lived D. lives
2. There is an old man _____ besides the sea.
   A. lived B. lives C. live D. living
3. There _____ no going to college if you don't study hard.

A. is   B. are   C. was   D. were
4. These bananas taste _____ and sell _____.
   A. well; well   B. good; good   C. good; well   D. well; good
5. John _____ his father about his failure in the exam.
   A. dares not tell   B. dare not tell   C. dares not to tell   D. dare not to tell
6. How long will it take you _____ the repairs?
   A. complete   B. completed   C. completing   D. to complete
7. The hijackers are demanding _____ to the representatives of both governments.
   A. speak   B. speaking   C. to speak   D. spoke
8. They didn't mean _____ her, but talking like that means _____.
   A. to hurt; to hurt   B. to hurt; hurting
   C. hurting; hurting   D. hurting; to hurt
9. Have you sent your parents an E-mail _____ them you arrived safely?
   A. telling   B. to tell   C. tells   D. tell
10. Do you know the boy _____ under the big tree?
    A. lied   B. lain   C. laying   D. lying
11. There's not much news in today's newspaper, _____?
    A. is there   B. isn't there   C. is it   D. isn't it
12. I don't know _____.
    A. where lives she   B. she lives where   C. where she lives   D. where does she live
13. There _____ a table and four chairs in the room and the couple _____ doing some cleaning.
    A. is; is   B. is; are   C. are; is   D. are; are
14. Don't leave the water _____ while you brush your teeth.
    A. run   B. ran   C. to run   D. running
15. It is her _____ I saw yesterday.
    A. who   B. whom   C. which   D. that
16. The boss made me _____ a nail into the table.
    A. driven   B. drove   C. drive   D. to drive
17. The cloth _____ soft and _____ well.
    A. feels; sells   B. is felt; is sold   C. feels; is sold   D. is felt; sells
18. There used to be a big fire in the city, ____?
    A. wasn't there   B. didn't there   C. didn't it   D. used not to there
19. I often hear the ABC song _____, but I have never heard Alice _____ it.
    A. to be sung; to sing   B. being sung; sang
    C. sang; singing   D. sung; sing
20. _____ he thought about is _____ will hold the meeting.
    A. What; who   B. That; who   C. What; where   D. That; where
21. He was advised _____ an operation at once since his leg was broken in a skiing accident.

A. made B. making C. make D. to make

22. The twins look _____ in almost everything.
    A. like B. alike C. as D. same
23. As Mr. Smith lay in bed, the weather _____ colder and colder.
    A. become B. becomes C. became D. has become
24. One of the hobbies of his little sister is _____.
    A. collect B. to collect C. collecting D. collected
25. When we live in the field, we should have the fire _____ all night.
    A. burn B. to burn C. burning D. burnt
26. He never dreamed of _____ a chance for him to be sent to China very soon.
    A. being B. having C. there is D. there being
27. About twenty-three centuries ago, _____.
    A. there lived in Greece a great thinker who called Aristotle
    B. a great thinker lived in Greece calling Aristotle
    C. lived there in Greece a great thinker called Aristotle
    D. there lived in Greece a great thinker named Aristotle
28. _____ no need for us to discuss the problem again since it has already been settled.
    A. There is B. It has C. It is D. There has
29. _____ appeared to be a war between his heart and his mind.
    A. There B. It C. What D. Where
30. _____ by bike will take us half an hour.
    A. Get there B. To get there C. Getting there D. Gets there
31. _____ without practice is no good.
    A. To learn B. Learn C. Learning D. Learns
32. We think _____ important for us to learn a foreign language well.
    A. that B. there C. which D. it
33. I suggest _____ our summer vacation in a seaside town.
    A. to spend B. spending C. to be spent D. being spent
34. Have you forgotten _____ her in Beijing airport?
    A. meet B. to meet C. meeting D. meets
35. We regretted _____ you that all of you are not invited to attend the party.
    A. to tell B. telling C. tell D. being told
36. My chief purpose is _____ the difficulties of the matter.
    A. to point out B. pointing out C. to be pointed out D. being pointed out
37. Would you like me _____ your regards to Mary?
    A. give B. giving C. given D. to give
38. They make the students _____ too much homework every day.
    A. to do B. doing C. done D. do
39. He has arranged for a car _____ the guests at the airport.

  A. pick up B. picking up C. to pick up D. picked up
40. The hospital _____ by the end of next year.
  A. will have been finished B. has finished
  C. will have finished D. has been finished

Ⅱ. Identify the mistake in each sentence and then correct it.

1. There are a lot of people are waiting for the bus to come.
2. There is used to be plenty of water in this river before.
3. I don't want it to be a war between these two countries.
4. I enjoy meeting Chinese people and travel around the country.
5. She wants to make this clear that she loves her children very much.
6. The food in that restaurant tastes really well.
7. In recent years the house prices in Beijing have been rise greatly.
8. Can you tell me how can I get to the railway station?
9. He saw a little boy beg in front of a store while he was walking across the street.
10. We found the great hall is full of students and teachers listening to an important report.

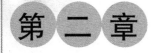

动词的时态与语态

第一节 动词时态（Verb Tense）

一、动词时态的定义

动词时态表示动作或状态发生的时间，例如，表示动作刚结束、已停止或反复出现等的时间。

二、动词时态的结构

英语中，有十六种时态，常见的为十二种：一般现在时、现在进行时、现在完成时、现在完成进行时、一般过去时、过去进行时、过去完成时、过去完成进行时、过去将来时、一般将来时、将来进行时、将来完成时等，如表 2-1 所示。

表 2-1 英语的十二种时态

时态	一般时	进行时	完成时	完成进行时
现在时	I find	I am finding	I have found	I have been finding
过去时	I found	I was finding	I had found	I had been finding
将来时	I will find	I will be finding	I will have found	
过去将来时	I would find			

三、动词时态的用法

鉴于汉语动词没有时态形式上的变化，英语的时态对于中国学生来说，是学习英语的一个难点。汉语用特定的词汇来表示动作或状态发生的不同时间，如"正在""着""了""过"等，而英语则用词形变化来表示。例如：

The students are studying in the library.
学生们正在图书馆学习。
He has already read the story.
他已读过这个故事了。
下面就英语中常见的十二种时态，展开详细阐述。

（一）一般现在时（The Simple Present Tense）

1. 一般现在时的定义
一般现在时用于表示现在一段时间内经常发生的动作或存在的状态。
2. 一般现在时的结构
一般现在时的结构为"be/have/行为动词原形"。
3. 一般现在时的用法
（1）表示经常发生的动作或现在的存在状态，常和副词 often，usually，always 与 frequently 连用。例如：
She gets up at seven every day.
I always take a walk after dinner.
（2）表示主语的特征、性格、能力。例如：
She is good at playing piano.
Mary speaks French well.
（3）表示客观事实或永恒真理。例如：
The sun rises in the east.
It rains a lot in the rainforest.
（4）一般现在时表示将来的情况。
①表示安排或计划好的将来动作，句中通常有表示未来的时间状语。例如：
The plane leaves in 8 minutes.
I'm at work this afternoon.
②在时间和条件状语从句中表示将来的动作。例如：
If the weather is fine tomorrow, we will visit the park.
I'll tell him as soon as he arrives.

（二）一般过去时（The Simple Past Tense）

1. 一般过去时的定义
一般过去时用于表示过去的动作或状态。
2. 一般过去时的结构
一般过去时的结构为"be/have/行为动词过去式"。
3. 一般过去时的用法
（1）表示过去某一时间的动作或状态，句中常带有表示过去的时间状语或由 when 等连词引导的时间状语从句。例如：
When I was a child, I was afraid that I failed in the exams.

Jack believed it was not his fault.

（2）表示过去经常或反复发生的动作或存在的状态。例如：

We often played chess on weekends.

The old workers got together chatting.

（3）在时间和条件状语从句中表示过去将来的动作。例如：

She said she would visit her grandfather if she had time.

They wanted to go abroad after they graduated from college.

（三）一般将来时（The Simple Future）

1. 一般将来时的定义

一般将来时用于表示将要发生的动作或情况。

2. 一般将来时的结构

一般将来时的结构为"助动词 shall/will + 动词原形"。

3. 一般将来时的用法

（1）表示将来的动作或状态。例如：

I will come back tomorrow.

The new swimming pool will be open next week.

（2）表示一种倾向或对未来的预见。例如：

Do you think it will be sunny on Saturday?

They will pass the exam for sure.

（3）其他表示将来的说法。

①be going to + 动词原形，表示打算、计划或将来要做的事。例如：

I'm going to the theatre next Friday.

It is going to rain soon.

②be about to + 动词原形，表示即将、正要做某事，强调马上要做。例如：

The meeting is about to begin.

The train is about to leave in five minutes.

③be + 不定式结构，表示安排或计划好的动作。例如：

The competition is to start tomorrow.

You are to stay here till we get home.

④come，go，arrive，leave，start 等表示动作的动词，可用一般现在时表示安排或计划好的事情。例如：

The train leaves at 8 tomorrow morning.

Mr. Johnson arrives on Monday.

（4）用现在进行时表示计划或准备要做的事，意为"意图""打算""安排"。常见动词有 come，go，arrive，start 等。例如：

The students are having a party on Friday night.

He's leaving school next year.

（5）be going to 和 will 的区别：用于条件句时，be going to 表示将来，will 表示意愿。例

如：

If you are going to visit your grandparents, you'd better visit them on Spring Festival next year.

If you will make up your mind to go abroad, we will support you.

（6）be to 和 be going to 区别：be to 表示客观安排或受人指示而做某事，be going to 表示主观打算或计划。例如：

I'm to meet the client tomorrow. （客观安排）

I'm going to meet the client tomorrow. （主观安排）

（7）shall 的用法。shall 多用于第一人称后，如"shall I..." "shall we..."，用于询问对方意见，尤其用于请求或建议。例如：

Shall we play tennis this weekend?

Shall I open the window?

（四）过去将来时（The Future in the Past）

1. 过去将来时的定义

过去将来时用于表示过去将要发生的动作或情况。

2. 过去将来时的结构

过去将来时的结构为"助动词 should/would + 动词原形"。

3. 过去将来时的用法

（1）表示从过去观点看将要发生的事。例如：

We would go into town after we rested for a while.

It was midnight. She would not come.

（2）"would + 动词原形"表示过去的习惯动作。例如：

When in winter, we would go skiing.

When I was a little girl, my parents would take me to the park on weekend.

（3）表示意愿或许诺。例如：

He promised he would never let that happen.

They wished the guy would keep his promise.

（4）过去将来时一般用于宾语从句中。例如：

The students all wanted to know when the result of the exam would come out.

We didn't expect that you would come and visit our family.

（5）其他表示"过去将来时"的用法。

① "was/were going to + 动词原形"，表示过去某时间内计划、打算的动作。例如：

There was going to be sunny soon.

We were going to have a road trip last week, but it was canceled.

② "was/were about to + 动词原形"，表示过去某时正要做某事。例如：

Jack was about to leave the house when the baby began to cry.

I was about to take a shower when the phone rang.

③ "was/were due to + 动词原形"，表示定于将来某时做某事。例如：

The meeting was due to last for a few days.

She was due to deliver a speech tomorrow.

④ "was/were + 不定式"，表示过去某时准备将来做某事。例如：

He was to learn French this summer.

Linda was to go picnicking with families next weekend.

⑤ "was/were + 不定式完成时态"，表示本来打算做某事。例如：

They were to have been married this month, but something happened.

I was to have told you the plan, but the plan changed.

⑥过去进行时也可以表示过去某时将要做某事。例如：

They told me they were leaving soon.

Mr. Thomson was coming to the party tonight.

（五）现在进行时（The Present Progressive Tense）

1. 现在进行时的定义

现在进行时用于表示说话时正在进行或现阶段正在进行的动作。

2. 现在进行时的结构

现在进行时的结构为"助动词 am/are/is + 现在分词"。

3. 现在进行时的用法

（1）表示此时此刻正在进行的动作。例如：

She's cooking dinner right now.

He's playing computer games in the dormitory.

（2）表示现阶段正在进行着的动作，虽然此动作不一定正在进行。例如：

Tom is teaching in a primary school.

Cindy is learning English these days.

（3）用来表示将来的动作，且多指按计划安排好的事。此时，句中通常有一个表示未来时间的状语。例如：

I'm flying overseas tomorrow.

They are spending the weekend in Japan.

（4）表示经常性的动作，常与 always，forever，constantly 等副词连用。此时，句中多含有厌烦、赞美等情绪。例如：

Mary is always making that mistake.

He's constantly forgetting things.

（5）表示刚过去的动作，或表示暂时的情况。例如：

I don't know what you are talking about.

Mary is replacing because she is ill.

（6）有些动词不能用于现在进行时，这些动词包括表示状态和感觉的动词、瞬间动词、系动词等，常见的有 know，love，accept，finish，want，need，remain，see，hear 等。例如：

I need your help.

I accept your apology.

表示渐变的动词可以用现在进行时，常见的有 get，become，turn，go 等。例如：

It is getting colder and colder these days.

She is becoming more and more beautiful.

（7）现在进行时和一般现在时的区别。

①现在进行时表示某一时刻或某段时间内正在进行的动作，一般现在时表示一段时间内普遍或反复发生的动作。例如：

The water is boiling now.

The water boils at 100 degrees Celsius.

②现在进行时表示暂时的情况，一般现在时表示持久的状态。例如：

I'm living with my parents before I get married.

I live in Nanning for a very long time.

③现在进行时表示某一时刻或某段时间内正在进行的动作，一般现在时表示主语的特征、性质、能力等。例如：

She is swimming with her kids.

She is a good swimmer.

（六）过去进行时（The Past Progressive Tense）

1. 过去进行时的定义

过去进行时用于过去某一时刻或某段时间正在进行的动作。

2. 过去进行时的结构

过去进行时的结构为"was/were + 现在分词"。

3. 过去进行时的用法。

（1）过去某一时刻或某一段时间正在进行的动作，往往带有时间状语。例如：

I was preparing for the exam yesterday.

Where were you going last night?

（2）过去进行时可表示一个动作发生时，另一个动作仍在进行。例如：

He lost his wallet when he was playing football with his classmates.

When we reached the top of the mountain, the sun was rising.

（3）表示过去即将发生的动作。例如：

Tom asked when we were arriving Beijing.

Her family wanted to know when she was leaving Beijing.

（4）过去进行时和一般过去时的区别。

①过去进行时表示正在进行的动作，一般过去时表示已经完成的动作。例如：

I was doing my maths homework this morning.

I did my maths homework this morning.

②过去进行时带有一定的感情色彩，此时，句中通常带有 always, constantly 等词。例如：

She was always studying.（有表扬意味）

They were constantly making trouble.（有抱怨意味）

③有时，过去进行时用以表示现在的想法，且语气较为客气委婉。例如：

I was wondering if you could help me carry the box.

I was hoping you could accept my present.

(七)将来进行时(The Future Progressive Tense)

1. 将来进行时的定义

将来进行时用于表示将来某一时刻或某一段时间正在进行的动作。

2. 将来进行时的结构

将来进行时的结构为"shall be/will be + 现在分词"。

3. 将来进行时的用法

(1) 表示将来某一时刻或将来某段时间正在进行的动作。例如:

I will be flying to Tokyo at this time tomorrow.

My boss will be working in the office tomorrow morning.

(2) 表示安排要做的事或预计会发生的事。例如:

We'll be getting in touch with you.

He'll be meeting you this afternoon.

(3) 有时将来进行时与现在进行时换用(多用于口语中)。例如:

I'll be having dinner with Tom tonight.

= I am having dinner with Tom tonight.

When will you be arriving Shanghai on Monday?

= When are you arriving Shanghai on Monday?

(4) 将来进行时不用于表示意志。例如:

I'll be having a talk with Annie later. (×)

I'll be seeing Jack soon. (√)

(八)现在完成时(The Present Perfect Tense)

1. 现在完成时的定义

现在完成时用于表示已发生的事件与现在的情况具有某种联系。

2. 现在完成时的结构

现在完成时的结构为"have/has + 动词过去分词"。

3. 现在完成时的用法

(1) 表示动作到现在为止已经完成。例如:

I have finished my homework.

The plane has taken off.

(2) 表示过去发生的动作,但发生的时间不确切。例如:

Have you ever been to China?

He has just left.

注意:have gone to 和 have been to 区别:have gone to 表示"到某地去了",人还没有回来;have been to 表示"到过某地"。例如:

The kids have gone to the park. (孩子们去公园了)

The kids have been to Europe. （孩子们去过欧洲）

Where has Susan gone? （苏珊去哪里了）

Where has Susan been? —She has been to the library. （苏珊去过图书馆）

（3）表示过去反复发生的动作。例如：

I have done the calculation several times.

I have been to Beijing many times this year.

（4）表示动作发生在过去，并且一直延续到现在，常和 since 与 for 引导的短语或从句连用。例如：

I have worked here since I graduated from college.

We have lived in Nanning for over 20 years.

现在完成时和 since 与 for 引导的从句连用时，需注意以下问题。

①Since 引导的从句一般用过去时，主句谓语用现在完成时。例如：

We've been in Nanning since we moved here ten years ago.

Since I was here, everything has changed.

②当主句中的谓语动词为 be 动词时，Since 引导的从句可用现在完成时。例如：

Since he has been away for some time, his house has been empty.

Since I have been back from abroad, I have been busy with my life here.

③since 和 for 区别。since 用以说明动作起始时间，for 用以说明动作延续时间长度。例如：

I have worked here since 2017.

I have worked here for more than one year.

I haven't heard from him since 1999.

I haven't heard from him for 10 years.

④并非带有 for 时间状语的句子都用现在完成时。例如：

I lived in Nanning for 3 years. （现在我不住南宁了）

I have lived in Nanning for 3 years. （现在我还住在南宁）

（5）现在完成时的动词通常是延续动词，因为现在完成时表示从过去持续到现在的动作或状态，常见的动词有 learn，work，study，know，teach 等。例如：

I have learned English for more than 10 years.

He has taught French in the college for a long time.

有时，现在完成时的动词也可与表示非延续性的动词连用。常见的非延续性动词有 get，go，become，start 等。例如：

They have got married for 20 years.

I have become a teacher since 2008.

另外，现在完成时通常不和疑问副词 when 连用。when 一般与过去时态连用。但现在完成时可以和疑问副词 where，why，how 连用。例如：

Why have you been late?

Where have you been recently?

（6）适用于现在完成时的句型。

①It is the first time that... 句型，从句用现在完成时。例如：
It is the first time that I have learned sky diving.
It is the first time that I have seen this movie.
②This is the... that... 结构，从句用现在完成时。例如：
This is the best time that we have had now.
This is the worst moment that you have met him.

（7）现在完成时和一般过去时的比较。

①现在完成时和一般过去时都表示过去已经发生的事，但现在完成时强调动作与现在的关系，以及对现在产生的结果、影响等；而一般过去时表示动作发生在过去，与现在没有联系。因此，有明确过去时间状语的，只能使用一般过去时。例如：

I have been to the meeting. （强调参加过会议）

I went to the meeting yesterday. （只说明昨天参加会议这件事）

I have had lunch already. （强调已经吃过午餐）

I had my lunch at the dining hall. （只说明吃午餐的地点）

②现在完成时的时间状语模糊甚至没有时间状语；一般过去时的时间状语比较具体、清晰。现在完成时常见的时间状语为 for，since，so far，yet 等；一般过去时常见的时间状语为 yesterday，two days ago，in September，just now 等。例如：

We have been to several countries so far.

We went to several countries in September.

I haven't received your letter yet.

I didn't receive your letter yesterday.

（九）过去完成时（The Past Perfect Tense）

1. 过去完成时的定义

过去完成时用于表示过去某一时间或动作以前已经完成的动作。

2. 过去完成时的结构

过去完成时的结构为"had + 动词过去分词"。

3. 过去完成时的用法

（1）表示过去某一时间前已完成的动作或状态。过去的时间可以由 by，before 等介词或某一时间状语来表示。例如：

We had just finished work when we decided to have dinner together.

I didn't go to the theatre because I had seen it before.

By the end of last month, we had built up so many organizations.

（2）与 hope，intend，mean，think 等动词连用，表示未实现的愿望。例如：

I had hoped to catch the bus but I didn't make it.

I had meant to make it happen, but it didn't work out quite well.

（3）与 when/before/after/until 等连词引导的分句连用，表示过去某一动作之前的动作。例如：

The phone had rang when we opened the door.

The guest had arrived before we came to the meeting.

（4）用于 if, as if, I wish 引导的分句中，表示与过去事实相反的主观设想。例如：

I wish I hadn't hurt you.

She seemed to be happy as if you hadn't said anything to annoy her.

（5）过去完成时常和 for 与 since 构成的短语或其引导的从句连用，表示由过去某时间开始，一直延续到过去另一时间的动作。例如：

I remembered I had given you the advice before the end of last term.

I had known Peter for 3 years before Joe introduced him to me.

（6）过去完成时常见的时间状语包括 by the time, before, until, after, as soon as 等。例如：

By the time we met him, he had done physical exercises in the gym.

I was surprised after all the students had reacted so positively.

（十）将来完成时（The Future Perfect Tense）

将来完成时的定义

将来完成时用于表示将来某一时间之前所完成的动作。

2. 将来完成时的结构

将来完成时的结构为"shall/will have + 动词过去分词"。

3. 将来完成时的用法

表示在将来某一时间之前已经完成的动作。例如：

We shall have finished the study at the end of July.

By the end of this year, we shall have finished the project.

（十一）现在完成进行时（The Present Perfect Progressive Tense）

1. 现在完成进行时的定义

现在完成进行时用于表示过去的动作一直延续到现在并可能继续进行下去。

2. 现在完成进行时的结构

现在完成进行时的结构为"have/has been + 现在分词"。

3. 现在完成进行时的用法

（1）表示一个持续到现在的动作，这个动作可能刚停止，也可能仍在进行。例如：

I have been thinking about my future.

It has been raining for two days.

（2）现在完成进行时常与 how long 状语连用。例如：

How long have you been studying English?

I have been writing my thesis for a whole year.

（3）有时，现在完成进行时可表示动作的重复。例如：

I have been using this desk for almost 9 years.

You have been making the same mistakes.

（4）现在完成时和现在完成进行时的区别。

①现在完成时表示动作到现在为止已经完成,而现在完成进行时表示动作仍继续进行。例如:

I have finished my project. (项目已经完成)

I have been doing my project. (项目还在进行)

②现在完成时强调动作的结果,现在完成进行时强调动作本身,表示过去发生的动作持续进行下去,且带有一定的感情色彩。例如:

I have quit smoking.

I have been playing badminton since last year.

③现在完成时强调动作发生的数量,现在完成进行时强调动作发生持续的时间长度。例如:

I have taken three courses this term.

I have been learning English for 10 years.

(5) 现在完成进行时需注意的方面如下:

①当强调时间长度时,多用现在完成进行时。例如:

She has been sitting in the library for a whole day.

It has been raining for a week.

②静态动词只能用于完成时而不能用于完成进行时。例如:

I have seen him since last week.

They have owned the property for a long time

(十二) 过去完成进行时(The Past Perfect Progressive Tense)

1. 过去完成进行时的定义

过去完成进行时用于表示过去之前发生的动作持续到过去的时间并可能继续进行下去。

2. 过去完成进行时的结构

过去完成进行时的结构为"had been + 现在分词"。

3. 过去完成进行时的用法

(1) 表示动作在过去某一时间之前发生并延续到过去时间,这一动作可能还在进行,可能已经停止。例如:

They had been fighting before the teacher came in.

He had been looking for a job, but he still didn't find one.

(2) 过去完成时和过去完成进行时的区别:过去完成时表示动作已完成,而过去完成进行时表示动作仍在进行中。例如:

He had repaired the house. (动作已完成)

He had been repairing the house. (动作仍在进行)

He had called the police before the thief escaped.

The couple had been fighting over the whole day.

第二节　语态（Voice）

一、语态的定义

语态是动词的一种形式，用以说明主语和谓语动词之间的关系，分为主动语态（Active Voice）和被动语态（Passive Voice）。主动语态表示主语是动作的执行者，被动语态表示主语是动作的承受者。一般来讲，只有拥有动作对象的及物动词才有被动语态。

被动语态是英语语态学习的重点和难点。因此，语态部分着重讲解被动语态。

二、被动语态的结构

并不是所有时态都有被动语态，在十六种英语时态中，有被动语态的时态有10个。被动语态的通用结构为 be + 动词过去分词，如表 2-2 所示。

表 2-2　被动语态的 10 个时态

被动语态	一般时	进行时	完成时
现在时	am/are/is done	am/are/is being done	have/has been done
过去时	was/were done	was/were being done	had been done
将来时	Will/shall be done		will have been done
过去将来时	Would/should be done		Would have been done

（1）一般现在时的被动语态为"am/is/are + 过去分词"。例如：

The boy is called Johnny.

Potato is eaten by most people in Western countries.

（2）一般过去时的被动语态为"was/were + 过去分词"。例如：

The book was written by Margaret.

She was given a chance to perform on the stage.

（3）一般将来时的被动语态为"will/shall be + 过去分词"。例如：

The result of the exam will be shown on Tuesday.

When will the graduation ceremony be started?

（4）过去将来时的被动语态为"would be + 过去分词"。例如：

I was sure that he would be accepted by the college.

I thought she would be punished for her mistake.

（5）现在进行时的被动语态为"am/are/is + being + 过去分词"。例如：

She is being called by her boss.

The case is being investigated by the police.

（6）过去进行时的被动语态为"was/were + being + 过去分词"。例如：

The employees were being inspected by the leader.

The road was being constructed yesterday.

（7）现在完成时的被动语态为"have/has been + 过去分词"。例如：

The robber has been sent to the prison.

They have been warned for their improper behavior.

（8）过去完成时的被动语态为"had been + 过去分词"。例如：

I was told that he had been sent to the hospital.

I heard that the school had been renovated.

（9）将来完成时的被动语态为"will have been + 过去分词"。例如：

They will have been punished for their childish behavior.

The summer holiday will have been finished soon.

（10）过去将来完成时的被动语态为"would have been + 过去分词"。例如：

I thought the plan would have been completed in the next few days.

She said she would have finished training by the end of this year.

三、语态的用法

英语中，大多数句子都使用主动语态，只有在下列情况下使用被动语态。

（1）不知道动作的执行者或者没有必要提及动作的执行者时。例如：

The rent has to be paid this week.

Money has been sent to the less developed regions.

（2）动作的承受者是句子的中心。例如：

The children are taken good care of by her.

You are invited to visit our family at any time.

（3）表示礼貌或婉转的措辞时。例如：

It is generally considered rude to speak loud in public places.

It is hoped that such things should never happen again.

 Exercises

Ⅰ. Choose the best answer to complete each sentence.

1. I always _____ music when I _____ at home.
   A. listening to; study
   B. listen to; study
   C. listen to; was studying
   D. listened to; study

2. The water _____. Let's make coffee.
   A. is boiling   B. are boiling   C. boils   D. boil

3. What _____? You _____ such a dreamy expression.
   A. do you think about; have
   B. are you thinking about; have

C. are you thinking about; are having D. do you think about; are having

4. Professor Han _____ the same college for ten years.
   A. has taught   B. have taught   C. taught   D. teaches

5. I'm sorry I'm late. How long _____?
   A. are you waiting
   B. you waiting
   C. have you waiting
   D. have you been waiting

6. _____ ever _____ a panda?
   A. Have you; see   B. Has you; seen   C. Do you; see   D. Have you; seen

7. We _____ across the street when a car _____ out of nowhere and almost ran into us.
   A. walked; appeared
   B. are walking; appear
   C. were walking; appeared
   D. had walked; appeared

8. We _____ at the driver, but he _____ us.
   A. shouted; didn't hear
   B. were shouting; didn't hear
   C. shout; doesn't hear
   D. are shouting; aren't hear

9. He _____ on his mobile phone while he _____.
   A. talked; was driving
   B. was talking; was driving
   C. talked; drove
   D. was talking; drove

10. How long _____ the house?
    A. did you own
    B. do you own
    C. have you owned
    D. have you been owning

11. She _____ her car to school because she _____ the bus.
    A. drove; missed
    B. drove; had missed
    C. had driven; missed
    D. had driven; had missed

12. The foolish young people _____ each other only two weeks when they _____ to get married.
    A. have known; decided
    B. had known; had decided
    C. knew; decided
    D. had known; decided

13. What time _____ the concert begin?
    A. will   B. shall   C. does   D. would

14. Please hurry! By the time we _____ there, the concert _____.
    A. get; will already start
    B. go; would have already started
    C. get; will have already started
    D. got; will start

15. I'll _____ her name as soon as I _____ her face.
    A. remember; see
    B. be remembering; see
    C. remember; have seen
    D. have been remembering; will see

16. By the time his plane _____, he _____ for thirty hours.
    A. will land; will travel
    B. lands; will have been traveling
    C. lands; will travel
    D. will land; will have been traveling

17. When my alarm clock rang this morning, I _____ for ten hours.

A. had been sleeping   B. had slept
C. have been sleeping   D. slept

18. Wake up, Michael! You _____ since nine o'clock last night. It's time to get up.
    A. have slept   B. have been sleeping
    C. had slept   D. had been sleeping

19. I _____ this watch three years ago.
    A. have bought   B. had bought
    C. bought   D. have been buying

20. My daughter _____ on a road trip with her classmates tomorrow.
    A. is going   B. will be going   C. will go   D. will have gone

21. Damage _____ by a storm.
    A. has caused   B. had caused   C. has been caused   D. caused

22. The storm _____ across the town last weekend.
    A. swept   B. sweeps   C. was swept   D. was sweeping

23. We believe that human life _____ by the medicine.
    A. can heal   B. can be healed   C. healed   D. not be healed

24. Tom _____ when he tried to start a quarrel.
    A. get hurt   B. hurt   C. got hurt   D. gets hurt

25. We want _____ a high salary.
    A. to pay   B. to be paid
    C. to be paying   D. to have been paying

26. The hospital _____ by the end of next year.
    A. will have been finished   B. has finished
    C. will have finished   D. has been finished

27. I have got a few things _____.
    A. to do   B. done   C. do   D. to be done.

28. I'm worried about _____ the registration date.
    A. to miss   B. be missed
    C. being missed   D. missing

29. I don't want _____ late with it.
    A. being   B. be   C. to be   D. to

30. The letters are _____ today.
    A. being written   B. written   C. to be written   D. be written

Ⅱ. Identify the mistake in each sentence and then correct it.

1. I have been in Beijing since three weeks.
2. I am here since last week.
3. I won't do it until I will find out my schedule.
4. We will throw a party when the exam will be over.

5. By this time of next week, I will finish my degree.
6. My brother visit Nanning every month.
7. The party begins as soon as my friends come.
8. My math homework was due today. After I finish writing it last night, I would ask my roommate to check it.
9. I haven't slept well since he is gone.
10. I'm sure my son calls tonight because he always calls on Friday.

主谓一致

第一节 主谓一致的概念

一、主谓一致的定义

主谓一致（Subject-Verb Agreement）是指谓语动词在人称和数上要与主语保持一致。

二、主谓一致的原则

主谓一致一般要遵循三个原则，即语法一致原则、意义一致原则与就近原则。

（一）语法一致原则

语法一致原则是指谓语动词在语法形式上与主语必须保持一致，即主语是单数形式，谓语动词也要用单数形式；主语是复数形式，谓语动词也要用复数形式。如：
The little girl likes swimming very much.
小女孩非常喜欢游泳。
Everyone in the town is surprised at the news.
镇里的每个人听到这个消息都很惊讶。
We love our motherland.
我们热爱我们的祖国。
Both cities are beautiful.
两座城市都很美丽。

（二）意义一致原则

意义一致原则是指谓语动词的形式取决于主语所表达的内在含义，即当主语形式是单数，但在意义上表示的为复数时，谓语动词应该用复数形式；当主语形式是复数，但在意义

上被视为单数时,谓语动词应该用单数形式。如:

Ten years is a long time.

十年是很长一段时间。

My family are waiting for me.

我的家人在等我。

(三) 就近原则

就近原则是指谓语动词的人称和数的形式与靠它最近的那个主语(名词、代词或其他词)保持一致。如:

Either my wife or I am going to work there.

不是我妻子就是我将去那里工作。

There are five apples and a pear on the table.

桌子上有五个苹果和一个梨。

第二节　主谓一致的用法

1. 谓语动词用单数的情形

(1) 可数名词单数、不可数名词、单个动名词、不定式、从句作主语时,谓语动词用单数形式。例如:

Smoking is not good for your health.

吸烟对你的身体没有好处。

What I said is true.

我说的都是真的。

To learn English well is not easy.

学好英语不是一件容易的事。

(2) 以 ics 结尾的学科名称,如 politics, physics, mathematics, linguistics, phonetics 等形式上为复数而意义上为单数。这类名词作主语时,谓语动词用单数形式。例如:

Politics is an important subject.

政治是一门重要的科目。

Physics is difficult to learn.

物理很难学。

(3) 国名、地名、书名、组织机构等专有名词,作主语时,形式上即使是复数,如 the United Nations, the United States, the New York Times 等,谓语动词也要用单数形式。例如:

The United Nations was established in 1945.

联合国成立于 1945 年。

The Arabian Nights is a very interesting story-book.

《一千零一夜》是一本很有趣的故事书。

(4) 某些疾病的名称,如 AIDS, measles(麻疹), mumps(流行性腮腺炎)等,以及一些游戏的名称，如 bowls，billiards（台球），dominoes（多米诺骨牌）等作主语时，谓语动词用单数形式。例如：

Mumps is a children's disease.
流行性腮腺炎是一种儿童疾病。
Billiards is not only played by men.
台球并非只是男人可以打。

（5）表示时间、距离、金额、重量、长度、空间、体积等意义的复数名词作主语时，如果把主语当作整体，谓语动词用单数形式。例如：

Five million dollars is too much.
五百万美元太多了。
Eight hours of sleep is enough for me.
八个小时的睡眠对我来说足够了。
Ten years has passed since he left his hometown.
他离开家乡已经 10 年了。
Six hundred kilometers is too far for me to drive in one afternoon.
六百公里①太远，我开车一下午跑不完。

（6）"more than one/many a + 单数名词"作主语时，意义上虽是复数，但谓语动词常用单数（形单意复）。例如：

More than one student has read the story.
不止一个学生读过这个故事。
Many a child is playing in the playground.
许多孩子在操场上玩儿。

（7）"each/every/many a/no + 单数名词 and each/every/many a/no + 单数名词"作主语时，谓语动词用单数形式。例如：

Each boy and (each) girl has a right to be educated in our country.
在我们国家，每个男孩和每个女孩都有受教育的权利。
Every minute and (every) second is precious.
每分每秒都很宝贵。
Many a teacher and (many a) student wants to go there.
很多老师和学生都想去那里。

（8）由 some，any，no，every 构成的复合不定代词或者 either，neither，each 作主语时，谓语动词用单数形式。例如：

Someone is knocking at the door.
有人在敲门。
No one knows the answer.
没有人知道答案。
Something has gone wrong with my watch.

---

① 1 公里 = 1 000 米。

我的手表出毛病了。
Each one has his own hobby.
每个人有自己的爱好。
Neither of the films is interesting.
两部电影都很没趣。

（9）由 little, a little, a bit of, a great deal of, much, a large amount of 等修饰的不可数名词作主语时，谓语动词用单数形式。例如：
A great deal of work awaits us.
大量的工作等着我们去做。
A little patience is not enough for him.
对他来说一点耐心是不够的。
A large amount of money was wasted on the construction of the bridge.
建这座桥浪费了大量的钱。

（10）主语是单数，后跟 with, along with, together with, besides, as well as, but, except, no less than, rather than, more than, like, including, in addition to 时，谓语动词用单数形式。例如：
She, as well as you, is very honest.
她和你一样都很诚实。
Her brother, together with his wife and children, has gone abroad.
她哥哥和他的妻子儿女一起出国了。
The teacher, including his students, is preparing for the examination.
那位老师和他的学生们正在为考试做准备。

（11）算术式通常用单数。表示两数相加、相乘时，谓语动词用单、复数均可；表示两数相减、相除时，谓语动词只能用单数。例如：
Two plus five equals/equal seven.
二加五等于七。
Ten and ten is/are twenty.
十加十等于二十。
Twelve minus four is eight.
十二减四等于八。
Three times five equals/equal fifteen.
三乘五等于十五。
Ten divided by two is five.
十除以二等于五。

（12）"one and a half + 复数名词"作主语时，谓语动词用单数。例如：
One and a half hours is all I can spare.
一个半小时是我所能挤出的全部时间。

（13）由 who, why, how, whether 或 that 引导的从句作主语时，谓语动词用单数。由 how and why, when and where 引导的从句作主语时，谓语动词仍用单数。例如：

Why she left here is not known.

她为何离开这里不得而知。

When and where we will have the meeting has not been decided.

我们何时何地开会还没有决定。

Whether we will have our sports meeting on time depends on the weather.

我们能否准时开运动会取决于天气。

How and why that thing happened is not clear to anyone.

那件事是如何发生的，为什么会发生，谁也不清楚。

2. 谓语动词用复数的情形

(1) 可数名词复数，由 and 连接的两个动词不定式、动名词短语及从句，或者有表示数量的复数名词修饰的不可数名词作主语时，谓语动词用复数形式。例如：

Playing the piano and reading books are my favourite hobbies.

弹钢琴和阅读是我喜欢的爱好。

Nine million tons of steel were imported last year.

去年进口了九百万吨钢材。

(2) 由 both... and... 连接的并列主语，不管其是单数、复数还是不可数名词，谓语动词一律用复数形式。例如：

Both he and I are students.

我和他两个都是学生。

Both teaching and research work have made great progress.

教学和科研都取得了很大的进步。

(3) 有些集合名词如 police, cattle, people 作主语时，形式上虽是单数，但意义上是复数，因此谓语动词用复数形式。例如：

The police are chasing the thief.

警察正在追小偷。

The Chinese people are great.

中国人民很伟大。

(4) glasses, shoes, scissors, trousers, clothes, chopsticks 等作主语时，谓语动词用复数形式。例如：

My trousers are new.

我的裤子是新的。

His shoes are worn out.

他的鞋子穿破了。

Your glasses are on the desk.

你的眼镜在课桌上。

但是，当上述名词前有 A pair of, this sort of, that kind of, a type of 等修饰时，谓语动词用单数形式。例如：

A pair of new shoes is in the box.

盒子里有一双新鞋。

This sort of chopsticks is made of bamboo.
这种筷子是用竹子做的。
That kind of glasses is very expensive.
那种眼镜很贵。
A special kind of clothes is being made by the workers.
工人们正在生产一种特殊材质的衣服。
This pair of trousers was made by Master Li.
这条裤子是李师傅做的。

（5）由 both, both of, many, several, few, a few, few of, a few of, dozens of, a great many, a good many 等结构限定的某个名词或代词作主语时，谓语动词用复数形式。例如：
Many students have passed the exam.
很多学生通过了考试。
Few of us know this secret place.
我们很少有人知道这个秘密的地方。
Both of them were tired.
他俩都累了。
Dozens of buildings have been destroyed by the fire.
数十栋建筑被这次大火烧毁了。
A good many students took part in the English contest.
很多学生参加了英语竞赛。

3. 谓语动词的单、复数要视情况而定的情形

（1）当主语是 class, family, army, team, club, crowd, audience, government, public, group 等集合名词时，如果该集合名词表示一个组织或单位的概念，谓语动词就用单数形式；如果该集合名词表示组织或单位里的一些个体的概念，谓语动词就用复数形式。例如：
The committee is made up of 12 members.
这个委员会由12名成员组成。
The committee are divided in opinion.
委员们意见有分歧。
My family is a big one.
我家是个大家庭。
Her family are very proud of her.
她的家人为她感到十分骄傲。
Class 1 is a united class.
一班是一个团结的班级。
Class 1 are unable to agree on a monitor.
一班在班长的人选上不能取得一致意见。

（2）由 and 连接两个并列主语，如果表示同一个人、同一件事、同一个概念或一个不可分割的整体，谓语动词就用单数形式；如果表示不同的概念，则谓语动词用复数形式。例如：

The singer and the dancer are famous all over the world.
这位歌手和这位舞蹈演员在全世界都很出名。
The writer and editor of the magazine is my friend.
这本杂志的作者兼编辑是我的朋友。
To go to bed early and to rise early is a good habit.
早睡早起是个好习惯。
To learn a language well, listening and speaking are very important.
要学好一门语言,听和说非常重要。

(3) what, who, which, all, most, none of 等作主语时,谓语动词的单、复数形式由其所指代的名词的数来决定。如果名词是单数,谓语动词用单数形式;如果名词是复数,谓语动词用复数形式。例如:

Who are the people over there?
那边那些人是谁?
What are the names of the books?
这些书的书名是什么?
Which exercise is better——swimming or running?
游泳和跑步,哪种运动比较好?
Which are your rooms?
哪几间房间是你们的?
Most of the workers are local people.
大部分的工人是当地人。
All of her spare time was spent in writing.
她所有的空余时间都用来写作。
All of the teachers are having meeting now.
所有的老师现在正在开会。
None of my classmates are afraid of difficulties.
我的同学没有一个害怕困难。
None of the money is mine.
这钱都不是我的。

(4) 由"a lot of (lots of, plenty of, the rest of, half of, part of) +名词"构成的短语以及由"分数或百分数+名词"构成的短语作主语时,其谓语动词的数要根据短语中所接名词的数而定。例如:

Fifty percent of her money was spent on clothes.
她花了50%的钱去买衣服。
Two-thirds of the students in his class are men.
他的班中三分之二的学生是男生。
A lot of women work outside after they get married.
很多妇女婚后在外面工作。
Half of the peach is rotten.

这个桃子坏了一半。
Half of the peaches are rotten.
这些桃子有一半是坏的。
Part of the guests have arrived.
部分客人已经到了。
Three-fourths of the surface of the earth is covered by sea.
地球表面的四分之三被海洋覆盖。

(5) 在"one of+复数名词+定语从句"结构中，定语从句的谓语动词与复数名词的数保持一致，即用复数形式。当有 the（only）修饰 one 时，谓语动词用单数形式。例如：
She is one of the students who were awarded.
她是当时获奖的学生之一。
He is the only one of the persons who is from Canada.
他是那些人中唯一一个来自加拿大的人。

(6) "the + 形容词/过去分词"表示一类人时，谓语动词用复数；表示一个事物或抽象的概念时，谓语动词用单数。例如：
The injured were sent to the nearest hospital.
伤者被送到了最近的医院。
The old are more likely to catch cold than the young.
老年人比年轻人更容易感冒。
The unknown is always scary.
未知的事物总让人害怕。

(7) 表示数量的 number, quantity, variety, majority, population 等作主语时，有时用单数，有时用复数，主要根据意思来定。例如：
The number of the workers in this factory is 650.
这个工厂的工人人数是650人。
A number of people like playing basketball.
很多人喜欢打篮球。
A large quantity of beer was sold out last week.
上周大量的啤酒卖完了。
A quantity of books were collected by the volunteers.
志愿者们收集了大量的书。
Quantities of coffee were sold last month.
上个月销售了大量的咖啡。
The majority of teachers are in favour of her proposal.
大多数老师是赞成她的建议的。
The majority is for you.
过半数的人是赞成你的。
The population of China is very large and 40% of the population live in rural areas.
中国人口很多，其中40%的人住在农村。

注意：a number of 用于"a number of（许多）+复数名词+动词复数"结构中；the number of 用于"the number of（...的数目）+复数名词+动词单数"结构中；a quantity of 后如接复数名词，谓语动词用复数，如接单数名词，谓语动词用单数；quantities of 后接复数名词或不可数名词，谓语动词用复数。

（8）"this kind of + 单数名词或复数名词"结构作主语时，谓语动词用单数；"these kinds of + 复数名词"作主语时，谓语动词用复数；"all kinds of + 复数名词"结构作主语时，谓语动词用复数结构。例如：

This kind of book is worth reading.

这种书值得一读。

This kind of men is hard to believe.

这种人很难相信。

These kinds of men/Men of this kind are dangerous.

这种人很危险。

（9）当主语是 means, sheep, fish, Japanese, Chinese 等名词时，谓语动词的形式必须依照它们在句中的意义来确定。例如：

Every means has been tried but we can't save him.

每一种方法我们都试用过了，但是我们还是救不了他。

All the means have been tried but we can't save him.

所有的方法我们都试用过了，但是我们还是救不了他。

A sheep is grazing beside the river.

一只绵羊正在河边吃草。

Some sheep are grazing beside the river.

一些绵羊正在河边吃草。

（10）当主语是两个名词或代词并且由 not only... but（also）..., either... or..., neither... nor..., or 连接时，谓语动词应该与邻近的主语的人称和数一致。例如：

Not only his parents but（also）he likes traveling.

不但他父母喜欢旅游，就连他也喜欢旅游。

Either you or I am wrong.

不是你错了，就是我错了。

Neither he nor you are fit for the work.

他和你都不适合干这个工作。

（11）在 there be 句型或由 there, here 引起的句子中，当主语不止一个时，谓语动词通常与邻近的主语的数一致。例如：

Here is a pen, two envelops and some paper for you.

这儿有一支钢笔、两个信封和一些纸给你。

There are ten chairs and a table in the room.

房间里有十把椅子和一张桌子。

There is a pencil-box and five books in his bag.

他的书包里有一个铅笔盒和五本书。

(12) no... but... 结构中，谓语动词与 no 后面的主语保持一致；not... but... 结构中，谓语动词与 but 后面的主语保持一致；"名词或代词 + and not..." 结构中，谓语动词与前面的名词或代词保持一致。例如：

No one in our class but Jane and I knows this secret.
我们班除了我和简之外没有人知道这个秘密。
Not you but I am responsible for the accident.
不是你而是我应该为这次事故负责。
His parents, and not he, are going to buy the house.
他的父母打算买这个房子，而不是他想买这个房子。

 Exercises

Ⅰ. Choose the best answer to complete each sentence.

1. The number of people invited _____ eighty, but a number of them _____ absent for different reasons.
   A. were; was   B. was; was   C. was; were   D. were; were
2. There _____ a few students in the library after school every day.
   A. has been   B. have been   C. is   D. are
3. More than one child in this village _____ ever been to Beijing.
   A. has   B. have   C. had   D. having
4. Many a student and many a teacher _____ the film.
   A. see   B. has seen   C. have seen   D. sees
5. Every man and every woman _____ at work.
   A. be   B. are   C. is   D. am
6. Bread and butter _____ their daily food.
   A. is   B. are   C. be   D. am
7. The whole family _____ enjoying the beautiful music now.
   A. is all   B. all is   C. all are   D. are all
8. Three hundred dollars a month _____ not enough to live on.
   A. are   B. is   C. has   D. have
9. The shoes _____ mine. This pair of shoes _____ nice on me.
   A. are; looks   B. is; looks   C. are; look   D. is; look
10. He is one of the best doctors who _____ in our hospital.
    A. works   B. working   C. is working   D. work
11. In 1850, about a third of U. S. A _____ covered by forests.
    A. were   B. has been   C. /   D. was
12. These police often _____ the children across the street.
    A. help   B. helps   C. helping   D. is helping

13. Not only Tom but also Alice and Mary _____ busy.
    A. is   B. was   C. are   D. has
14. Both Lily and Lucy _____ to the party yesterday.
    A. invited   B. was invited   C. had invited   D. were invited
15. Everyone except Tom and John _____ there when the meeting began.
    A. are   B. is   C. were   D. was
16. Half of the class _____ most of the work. Some of the work _____ really difficult.
    A. have done; is   B. has done; are   C. has done; is   D. have done; are
17. In our class _____ of the students _____ girls.
    A. three-fifth; are B. three-fifths; are C. third-fifth; is D. three-fifths; is
18. We each _____ strong points and each of us, on the other hand, _____ weak points.
    A. have; have   B. have; has   C. has; has   D. has; have
19. They had water running all night, so large quantities of water _____ wasted.
    A. were   B. was   C. have   D. has
20. Fifty tons of coal _____ wasted in the factory last year.
    A. is   B. are   C. were   D. was
21. When and where to go for the picnic _____ yet.
    A. are not decided   B. has not been decided
    C. is not being decided   D. have not been decided
22. She is the only one of those who _____ invited to attend the conference.
    A. has been   B. have been   C. was   D. were
23. The population of this village _____ 680 and 30% of the population _____ in the factory.
    A. are; works   B. is; works   C. is; work   D. are; work
24. Neither Tony nor his parents _____ at home yesterday.
    A. is   B. are   C. was   D. were
25. The beautiful _____ not always useful.
    A. has   B. have   C. is   D. are
26. Collecting stamps and playing the piano _____ my favorite hobbies.
    A. are   B. is   C. has been   D. being
27. What I think and what I say _____ nothing to do with you.
    A. have   B. are   C. is   D. has
28. Both teaching and studying _____ important.
    A. is   B. being   C. are   D. is being
29. The eighth and the last chapters _____ difficult to understand.
    A. is   B. are   C. is being   D. are being
30. Politics _____ a compulsory course in the university.
    A. are   B. has   C. have   D. is
31. His father's factory used 70% of the raw materials, the rest of which _____ saved for other

purposes.

  A. is   B. are   C. was   D. were

32. Over twenty percent of the country _____ covered with trees and the majority of the citizens _____ living a happy life.

  A. is; are   B. is; is   C. are; are   D. are; is

33. As a result of the serious earthquake, three-fourths of the buildings in this city _____.

  A. need repairing   B. needs to repair   C. needs repairing   D. need to repair

34. Thirty minus fourteen _____ sixteen.

  A. was   B. were   C. is   D. are

35. Every possible means _____ to prevent the air pollution.

  A. have been used   B. are used   C. is used   D. has been used

36. Not Mary and I but Tom _____ going to leave the company.

  A. are   B. is   C. has been   D. have been

37. With more forests being destroyed, huge quantities of good earth _____ each year.

  A. is washing away   B. is being washed away

  C. are washing away   D. are being washed away

38. This kind of apples _____ well. I want to buy some, but they _____.

  A. sell; have sold out   B. sell; sell out

  C. sells; have been sold out   D. sells; was sold out

39. Neither Ann nor her cousins _____ to England, but _____ of them know English culture and customs very well.

  A. have been; all   B. has been; all   C. have been; both   D. has been; both

40. One and a half apples _____ on the table.

  A. are left   B. has left   C. is left   D. have been left

Ⅱ. Identify the mistake in each sentence and then correct it.

1. This pair of scissors belong to me.
2. Three pounds of tea cost 6 dollars.
3. Eighty percent of this area are covered by forests.
4. The majority of the staff in his company is against his plan.
5. The Browns is going to visit the Great Wall tomorrow.
6. Not only my parents but also my brother have been to Beijing twice.
7. The committee is divided into four groups.
8. No student and no teacher want to have classes on Saturdays.
9. Few of the villagers knows the importance of protecting environment.
10. Neither of Peter's parents are engineers.

第四章

情态动词

第一节 情态动词的概念

一、情态动词的定义

情态动词（Modal Verbs），表示说话人对某一动作或状态的态度。

二、情态动词的特征

情态动词具有以下四个特征：
（1）本身有一定的词义。
（2）不能单独作谓语，必须与谓语动词的原形一起构成谓语。
（3）没有人称和数的变化。
（4）情态动词的否定式直接在其后面加"not"，疑问式把情态动词提到主语之前。

三、情态动词的分类

情态动词可分为以下四类：
（1）只作情态动词：can（could），may（might），must，ought to。
（2）可作情态动词又可作助动词：shall（should），will（would）。
（3）可作情态动词又可作实义动词：need，dare。
（4）具有情态动词特征：have to，used to

第二节　情态动词的用法

一、can 和 could 的用法

（1）表示具有某种知识或技能。can 用于一般现在时，could 用于过去时。例如：
He can play the guitar.
他会弹吉他。
Can you speak English?
你会说英语吗？
I could take care of myself when I was nine.
我九岁时就能够照顾我自己了。
（2）表示客观可能性。can 表示确定的可能性，could 表示不确定的可能性。例如：
Human beings cannot live without air.
没有空气，人类是不可能生存的。
They could go for a picnic on Sunday.
星期日他们可能去野餐。
（3）在口语中，表示允许、请求、要求、建议等。此时，can 可以代替 may，might。与 can 相比，could 的语气更加婉转，且不表示过去。例如：
You can (may) smoke in the smoking area.
你可以在吸烟区吸烟。
Could you tell me the way to the nearest railway station?
请告诉我去最近的火车站怎么走，好吗？
Can (May) we park here?
我们可以把车停在这里吗？
You could have your hair cut.
你该理发了。
（4）在否定句、疑问句或感叹句中表示惊异、怀疑、不相信等态度。此时，can't 意思是"不可能"。例如：
That can't be my brother——he is in Shanghai now.
那不可能是我哥，他现在在上海。
How can he be so careless?
他怎么这么粗心？
He looks so young. He can't be over fifty.
他看上去很年轻，他不可能超过50岁。

二、may 和 might 的用法

（1）表示可能性，常用于肯定句和否定句，表示对现在或将来的猜测，暗含不确定。

通常，may 表示的可能性比 can 小，might 表示的可能性比 may 更小。

My friends may not know anything about it.

我的朋友们可能不知道这件事。

John may come, or he may not.

约翰也许会来，也许不会来。

Professor Li was afraid that they might not agree with him.

李教授担心他们可能不同意他的意见。

（2）表示允许，请求。例如：

A: May I smoke here?

我可以在这里吸烟吗？

B: Yes, you may. /Yes, please.

可以。

B: No, you mustn't. /No, you'd better not.

不行。

Might I have a word with you for a moment? （Might I...? 比 May I...? 更婉转客气）

我可以和您说一会儿话吗？

（3）May 用在祈使句中表示祝愿（表示祝愿时不用 might）。例如：

May happiness follow you wherever you go!

愿您幸福快乐，直到永远。

May joy and health be with you always.

祝您永远健康快乐。

三、must 的用法

（1）表示必须或应该承担在法律、法规、道德等方面规定的义务、责任。must 的否定式是 mustn't（禁止）；以 must 开头的疑问句中，否定回答应用 needn't 或 don't have to（不必要）。例如：

People must obey the traffic regulations.

人们必须遵守交通规则。

Drivers mustn't drive after drinking.

司机酒后禁止驾车。

A: Must we finish our task today?

我们必须今天完成任务吗？

B: Yes, you must.

是的。

B: No, you needn't. /No, you don't have to.

不必。

（2）表示一种揣测。must 可表示符合逻辑的猜测、推断，可对现在、过去和将来进行揣测，意思是"想必，准是，一定"。此时，must 只用于肯定句中，否定句中应用 can't。例如：

You look so pale. You must be ill.
你脸色苍白。你一定是生病了。
The lights in his room are on. He must be at home now.
他房间里的灯是亮着的。他现在准在家。
He must be having meeting now.
他现在一定是在开会。
The ground is wet. It must have rained last night.
地面是湿的。昨天晚上一定是下雨了。
You can't have seen him there, because he has gone abroad.
你不可能在那儿见到他，因为他已经出国了。
（3）表示必然性，意思是"注定要，必定会"。例如：
Summer must be followed by autumn.
夏天过后一定是秋天。
All living things must die.
一切生物都会死亡。

四、have to 的用法

（1）表示"必须""不得不"。在此意义上 have to 与 must 十分接近。但是，must 侧重表达说话者的主观看法，意为"必须做某事"；have to 则不带说话者的任何主观感情色彩，表示因客观条件或客观环境的迫使而"不得不做某事"。例如：
He said that he must work hard.
他说他必须努力工作。（主观要求）
I'm near-sighted. I have to wear glasses.
我眼睛近视。我不得不戴眼镜。（客观需要）
You have to work hard to make a living.
为了谋生你必须努力工作。（客观需要）
Boys, you must go to bed right now.
孩子们，你们必须马上上床睡觉。（主观要求）
（2）可用于过去时、将来时等时态。例如：
He had a high fever yesterday and he had to stay in bed.
昨天他发高烧，不得不躺在床上休息。
We will have to get up early tomorrow in order to catch the first bus.
为了赶第一班公共汽车，明天早上我们必须早起。

五、shall 的用法

（1）表示单纯的将来。在陈述句中通常只用于第一人称，在疑问句中只用于第二人称，意思是"会，将要"。例如：
I shall let you know as soon as he arrives.

他一到我就会告诉你。
Shall you go with me tomorrow?
明天你会跟我一起去吗?
(2) 在疑问句中,表示征求对方的意见或请求,通常用于第一人称和第三人称。例如:
Shall we meet at five o'clock?
我们五点钟见面,好吗?
Let's work hard together, shall we?
我们一起努力,好吗?
Shall the boy wait outside the office?
让那男孩子在办公室外面等吗?
(3) 表示允诺、警告、命令、决心、强制等,通常用于第二人称和第三人称。例如:
If you behave well, you shall get what you want.
如果你表现好的话,你就会得到你想要的东西。
The girl shall be sorry for it one day.
总有一天这个女孩会后悔的。
Nothing shall stop us from carrying out the plan.
什么也不能阻止我们执行这项计划。

六、should 的用法

(1) 表示劝告、建议、命令、推测等。例如:
You should be polite to other people.
你对其他人应该有礼貌。
He shouldn't do things like that.
他不应该做那样的事情。
It's 9 o'clock. My family should be there now.
九点钟了,我的家人现在应该到那里了。
(2) 表示惊奇、愤怒、失望、遗憾等情绪,意思是"竟然、居然"。例如:
I don't know why she should be so careless?
我不知道她竟然这么粗心。
It's strange that you should know my new address.
很奇怪,你竟然知道我的新地址。

七、ought to 的用法

(1) 表示应该承担相应的义务或责任。与 should 相比,语气较强。例如:
You ought to make apology to your parents.
你应该向你父母道歉。
Every citizen ought to abide by the law.
每一个公民都应该遵守法律。

(2) 表示劝告、建议等，意思是"应当，应该"。例如：

The film is great. You ought to go and see it.

这部电影很好看。你应该去看。

(3) 表示推测、猜测。例如：

The monitor ought to know his telephone number.

班长应该知道他的电话号码。

八、will 和 would 的用法

(1) 表示意愿、决定。例如：

I will help you no matter what happens.

不管发生什么事我都会帮助你。

He says that he will never do that again.

他说他再也不会做那样的事了。

My sister promised that she would try her best to learn English.

我妹妹答应过要尽力学习英语。

(2) 表示推测、可能、猜测等，意思是"可能，大概，也许"。例如：

That will be the person you are looking for.

那个也许就是你要找的人。

I would be about 14 when my grandma died.

我奶奶去世的时候我大概是 14 岁。

(3) 表示请求、建议、邀请等，一般用于第二人称的疑问句。例如：

Will you tell me when the examination begins?

告诉我考试什么时候开始，好吗？

Will you wait for me for a minute?

等我一下好吗？

Would you please show me the way to the department store?

请告诉我百货商店怎么走，好吗？

Would you help me with my English?

请你帮我学英语好吗？

(4) 表示经常性、习惯性的行为或动作，可用于各人称，意思是"总是，经常，老是"。例如：

When Tom is in trouble, he will ask his parents for help.

汤姆遇到困难时，总是向他父母求助。

She will study in the library for hours.

她总是连续几个小时在图书馆学习。

When we were young, we would go swimming in the river every summer.

我们年轻的时候，每年夏天我们常常去河里游泳。

九、need 的用法

(1) 表示"需要，必要"。作情态动词时，无时态、人称和语态的变化，一般用于否定句和疑问句中，在肯定句中，常用 must 和 have to。例如：

Need we go there now?
我们需要现在去那里吗？
You needn't be sorry, it is not your fault.
你不必难过，这不是你的错。

(2) 作实义动词时，有时态、人称和语态的变化。例如：

need to do sth.　　　（某人）需要做某事
sth. need doing　　　（某事）需要被做
sth. need to be done　（某事）需要被做

He needs to go to hospital immediately.
他需要马上去医院。
She doesn't need to hand in her assignment this morning.
她不需要今天早上交作业。
Students need to study hard.
学生必须努力学习。
The window needs cleaning.
窗户需要擦洗了。
The car needs to be washed.
车子需要洗了。

十、dare 的用法

(1) 表示"敢"。作情态动词时，无人称的变化，常用于否定句和疑问句。例如：

He dare not tell his parents what he thinks.
他不敢把他心里所想的告诉他父母。
Dare you go out alone at midnight?
半夜你敢独自外出吗？

(2) 作实义动词时，有人称和数的变化，可用于各种句式。例如：

He dares to admit his mistake.
他敢于承认他的错误。
Does he dare (to) admit his mistake?
他敢承认他的错误吗？
She doesn't dare (to) ask her question.
她不敢问老师问题。
He left the room without daring to say a word.
他一句话也不敢说地离开了房间。

注意：在否定句和疑问句中，to 可以省略，但当 dare 是动词 ing 形式时，后面的 to 不可以省略。

十一、used to 的用法

used to 后面接动词原形，表示"过去常常（做某事）"，无人称和数的变化。例如：

They used to go fishing together.

他们过去常常一起去钓鱼。

We usedn't to/usen't to/did not use to go to the cinema.

我们过去不常去看电影。

Used he to/Did he use to come home to see his mother?

过去他常常去看他母亲吗？

Yes, he used to./Yes, he did.

是的。

十二、情态动词 + have done 的用法

（1）must have done，表示对过去某事的肯定猜测，意思是"一定或肯定做过某事"。例如：

She must have heard the news, for she was so sad.

她肯定已经知道那个消息了，因为她很伤心。

（2）can't/couldn't have done，表示对过去某事的否定猜测，意思是"不可能做过某事"。例如：

Professor Wang can't have gone abroad, because I saw him 10 minutes ago.

王教授不可能出国去了，因为10分钟前我刚见过他。

（3）may/might have done，表示对过去某事的可能性猜测，意思是"可能已经或也许已经"。例如：

It may have rained last night.

昨晚可能下了雨。

Tom might have gone lost.

汤姆可能已经迷路了。

（4）should/ought to have done，表示过去应该做而实际上未做，含有责备、埋怨、遗憾之意，意思是"本应该……"。例如：

The manager should have arrived here at 9 for the meeting, but he didn't show up.

经理本应该9点钟到这里开会，但他并没有出现。

You should have come here twenty minutes earlier.

你本应该早20分钟到这儿。

（5）shouldn't/oughtn't to have done，表示过去不应该做而实际上做了，意思是"本不应该……"。例如：

You shouldn't have left the child alone at home.

你本不应该把孩子独自留在家里。

She shouldn't/oughtn't to have gone there alone.

她本不该一个人去那里的。

（6）needn't have done 表示本没有必要做的事实际上却做了，意思是"本不必……"。例如：

As you were tired yesterday, you needn't have seen us off at the airport.

昨天因为你很累，你本不必到机场给我们送行。

He needn't have bought such an expensive bag.

他本不必买一个那么贵的包。

（7）can/could have done 表示过去本来能够做（有能力做）的事实际上却未做到，意思是"本来可以……"。例如：

He could have passed the examination, but he didn't.

他本来可以通过考试的，但他没有。

He could have learned the language well if he worked hard.

如果努力学的话，他本来是能够把这门语言学好的。

 Exercises

Ⅰ. Choose the best answer to complete each sentence.

1. Mary's temperature has dropped, so she _____ take that medicine.
   A. must not　　　　B. should not have　　　C. do not　　　　D. needn't
2. The construction of the main building _____ by the end of the year.
   A. must complete　　　　　　　　　　B. must be completed
   C. must have completed　　　　　　　 D. must have been completed
3. The coffee tastes bitter, it _____ too long.
   A. must have been boiling　　　　　　B. ought to have been boiling
   C. should have boiled　　　　　　　　D. may not have boiled
4. —Could I borrow your dictionary?
   —Yes, of course you _____.
   A. will　　　　　B. can　　　　　C. might　　　　　D. should
5. My sister _____ come with us tonight, but she isn't sure yet.
   A. may　　　　　B. will　　　　　C. must　　　　　D. can
6. Children _____ play with the knife, they _____ hurt themselves.
   A. can't; shouldn't　B. won't; can't　C. mustn't; may　D. shouldn't; must
7. My parents are really worried about my brother, he _____ home without a word.
   A. mustn't leave　B. needn't leave　C. couldn't have left　D. shouldn't have left
8. You _____ the truth to your family. Why didn't you?
   A. should tell　　B. should have told　　C. must have told　　D. ought to tell

9. —Need we finish our task today?
   —Yes, you _____.
   A. need   B. should   C. must   D. can
10. —I want to know if I _____ smoke here.
    —No, you _____. Could you see the sign "NO SMOKING" there?
    A. must; can't   B. may; mustn't   C. can; needn't   D. shall; won't
11. —I wonder why John didn't come to school.
    —He _____ have been ill.
    A. needn't   B. should   C. might   D. can
12. Your composition _____ any more.
    A. needs not be corrected   B. need not to be corrected
    C. doesn't need to be corrected   D. doesn't need to correct
13. We had a good time yesterday. You _____ come.
    A. ought to have   B. must have   C. should   D. need have
14. Half of the students felt very disappointed at the party. They say that it _____ better.
    A. had been   B. must have been   C. had to be   D. could have been
15. He _____ be in the classroom now, because someone saw him playing basketball in the playground.
    A. mustn't   B. needn't   C. can't   D. shouldn't
16. _____ you _____ go to work by bus before you bought your car?
    A. Did; used to   B. Use; to   C. Did; use to   D. Does; use to
17. My little sister _____ there alone at night.
    A. not dare go   B. dares not go   C. dare not go   D. dare not to go
18. There was a lot of time. We _____.
    A. mustn't have hurried   B. couldn't have hurried
    C. must not hurry   D. needn't have hurried
19. Please shut the door, _____?
    A. can't you   B. aren't you   C. do you   D. will you
20. You _____ read when the car is moving. It is bad for your eyes.
    A. couldn't   B. mustn't   C. may not   D. needn't
21. —May the students leave the classroom?
    —No, they _____. They _____ to leave until the bell rings.
    A. mustn't; are allowed   B. needn't; aren't allowed
    C. can't; aren't supposed   D. don't have to; are supposed
22. If they had taken the other road, they _____ earlier.
    A. had arrived   B. arrived   C. might arrive   D. might have arrived
23. Mr. Jones, many workers want to see you. _____ they wait here or outside?
    A. Do   B. Will   C. Shall   D. Are
24. My friend _____ my letter, otherwise she would have replied before now.

A. couldn't have received B. must receive
C. has received D. shouldn't have received

25. She _____ away my computer, for I wanted to use it.
    A. mustn't have taken B. shouldn't have taken
    C. needn't have taken D. can't have taken

26. Your hands need _____.
    A. wash B. washed C. be washed D. washing

27. He _____ speak English before such a crowd.
    A. dare not to B. didn't dare to C. dare to D. didn't dares

28. — What does the sign over there read?
    — "No person _____ smoke or carry a lighted cigarette, cigar or pipe in this area."
    A. will B. may C. shall D. must

29. When she was there, she _____ go to that coffee shop at the corner after work every day.
    A. would B. should C. might D. had better

30. She is studying computer science now but she _____ a nurse.
    A. used to be B. would be C. were D. had been

31. What a pity! Considering his ability and experience, he _____ better.
    A. need have done B. must have done
    B. can have done D. might have done

32. —I'm sorry. I _____ at you the other day.
    —Forget it. I was a bit out of control myself.
    A. mustn't have shouted B. shouldn't have shouted
    C. shouldn't shout D. mustn't shout

33. He _____ have flown to Guangzhou last night, because I stayed with him all the time.
    A. mustn't B. may not C. shouldn't D. can't

34. John didn't do well in the exam. He _____ hard at his lessons.
    A. has worked B. ought to have worked
    C. would have worked D. must have worked

35. —She daren't climb the tree, dare she?
    —_____.
    A. Yes, she dare. B. No, she dare.
    C. Yes, she dares. D. Yes, she daren't.

36. I often see lights in that empty room. Do you think I _____ report it to the police?
    A. should B. may C. will D. can

37. Why did you just sit and watch? You _____ me.
    A. could help B. should help
    C. could have helped D. must have helped

38. —You _____ your English teacher for help. She is kind-hearted.
    —Yes. A whole day _____.

A. must have asked; has wasted B. can ask; will waste
C. could have asked; was wasted D. shouldn't have asked; would be wasted

39. One of our rules is that every student _____ wear school uniform while at school.

    A. might B. could C. shall D. will

40. You should bear in mind that he is not so strong as he _____.

    A. was used to be B. used to be C. was used to D. use to

Ⅱ. Identify the mistake in each sentence and then correct it.

1. Tom's score in the examination is the highest in his class; he should have studied very hard.
2. Oh, it works like this; but how would I know?
3. We can't imagine that he might be so rude to a lady.
4. You don't have to get close to the lion. It's too dangerous.
5. He shouldn't have worried before he came to the new school, for his classmates here are very friendly to him
6. Judging from his accent, he won't be from America.
7. With all the work on hand, Mary wouldn't have gone to the theatre last night.
8. I think Tom dares tell his parents the truth.
9. —Who do you think could have done such a foolish thing?

    —It can have been George, but I'm not sure.
10. Your room is in terrible mess; it wouldn't have been cleaned.

第五章

名　词

第一节　名词的定义与分类

一、名词的定义

名词（Noun）是指用以表示人名、地名、时间名称、事件名称及抽象概念的词。根据所表达事物的具体内涵及形式，名词可分为不同的类别。另外名词有单、复数形式的词形变化；有主格、宾格和属格等形式（其后有独特的后缀形式）。名词在句中能作许多成分，是句子话题的中心词。

二、名词的分类

名词分为专有名词（Proper Noun）和普通名词（Common Noun）。其中，普通名词又可分为个体名词（Individual Noun）、集体名词（Collective Noun）、物质名词（Material Noun）和抽象名词（Abstract Noun）四类。个体名词与集体名词一般为可数名词（Countable Noun），有单、复数形式；抽象名词与物质名词一般为不可数名词（Uncountable Noun），通常只有单数形式，在其前面不能加 a、an，或者 one。名词的具体分类如表 5-1 所示。

表 5-1　名词的分类

类别	说明	举例
专有名词	表示个人、地方、节日等特有的名称。专有名词中每个实词的首字母必须大写	Mary 玛丽，Beijing 北京，the United Nations 联合国

续表

类别		说明	举例
普通名词	可数名词 个体名词	表示以个体存在的某一类人或物的名称	student 学生，book 书，house 房子
	可数名词 集体名词	表示由若干个体组合成的一个整体的总称	class 班级，family 家庭，people 人民
	不可数名词 物质名词	表示无法分为个体，常无固定形状的物质	air 空气，water 水，steel 钢，gold 黄金
	不可数名词 抽象名词	表示动作、状态、品质、感情等抽象概念	work 工作，quiet 安静，honesty 诚实

名词的分类不是绝对的。有些名词兼属两类，在某些情况下是不可数名词，在另一些情况下又是可数名词，如表 5-2 所示。

表 5-2 兼属两类的名词

物质名词（不可数）	个体名词（可数）	抽象名词（不可数）	个体名词（可数）
glass 玻璃	a glass 玻璃杯	agreement 同意	an agreement 协议
iron 铁	an iron 熨斗	beauty 美	a beauty 美人
paper 纸	a paper 报纸	necessity 必要性	a necessity 必需品
wood 木头	a wood 树林	power 威力	a power 大国

第二节 名词的数与所有格

一、名词的数

英语中，可数名词具有单数（singular）、复数（plural）两种形式。大多数可数名词的复数形式是在单数形式后面加"s"或"es"，少数可数名词的复数形式为不规则变化。

（一）可数名词复数形式的规则变化

通常，可数名词复数形式的规则变化为在单数名词的词尾加"s"或"es"。不同类别名词的复数形式规则变化如表 5-3 所示。

表 5-3 词尾加"s"或"es"构成复数形式的规则变化

类型	构成	例词
一般情况下	加"s"	car—cars 汽车，book—books 书，school—schools 学校

续表

类型	构成	例词
以 s, x, z, ch, sh 结尾的词	加"es"	bus—buses 公共汽车，box—boxes 盒子，dish—dishes 盘子，buzz—buzzes 嗡嗡声，coach—coaches 教练
以 o 结尾的词	1. 加"es"	hero—heroes 英雄，tomato—tomatoes 番茄 potato—potatoes 土豆，echo—echoes 回声
	2. 加"s"	radio—radios 收音机，zoo—zoos 动物园 piano—pianos 钢琴，photo—photos 照片
	3. 两种形式都可	cargo—cargoes（s）货物，mango—mangoes（s）杧果 mosquito—mosquitoes（s）蚊子，volcano—volcanoes（s）火山
以"辅音字母+y"结尾的词	变 y 为 i，再加"es"	lady—ladies 女士，city—cities 城市，baby—babies 婴儿
以"元音字母+y"结尾的词	加"s"	way—ways 方法，key—keys 钥匙，toy—toys 玩具
以 f, fe 结尾的词	1. 变 f 或 fe 为 v，再加"es"	leaf—leaves 树叶，thief—thieves 小偷，knife—knives 小刀，life—lives 生命
	2. 加"s"	roof—roofs 房顶，proof—proofs 证据，chief—chiefs 首领，gulf—gulfs 海湾
	3. 两种形式都可	dwarf—dwarves（dwarfs）小矮人，scarf—scarves（scarfs）围巾

（二）可数名词复数形式的不规则变化

（1）有些名词沿用古英语的复数形式，其变化方式为变换元音或添加后缀。例如：
woman—women 妇女，man—men 男人，foot—feet 脚，tooth—teeth 牙齿，
goose—geese 鹅，mouse—mice 老鼠，ox—oxen 牛，child—children 孩子。
（2）有些名词的单复数同形。例如：
cattle 牛，sheep 羊，deer 鹿，Chinese 中国人，aircraft 飞机，
means 手段，series 系列，species 种类，headquarters 司令部。
（3）有些外来词的复数形式的构成较为特殊。例如：
alumnus—alumni 校友，analysis—analyses 分析，crisis—crises 危机，
datum—data 数据，thesis—theses 论文，phenomenon—phenomena 现象。

（三）不可数名词的数

物质名词和抽象名词都属于不可数名词，通常没有复数形式，但可以借助单位词来表示一定的数量。例如：

a piece of paper 一张纸，a cup of coffee 一杯咖啡，
a glass of water 一杯水，a loaf of bread 一条面包，
a piece of advice 一条建议，a burst of applause 一阵掌声，
a ray of hope 一线希望，a shower of criticism 一阵批评。

二、名词所有格

名词和代词都有"格"的形式，即通过一种格式来表示其在句中与其他词的关系。英语中，名词有三种格式：主格（作主语的格式）、宾格（作宾语的格式）和所有格（表示所属关系的格式）。名词的主格和宾格形式相同。因此，本节只讲述名词的所有格——表示名词的所属关系的格式。名词所有格的具体构成方式有以下三种形式。

（一）用"'s"所有格表示所属关系

（1）单数名词词尾加"'s"，复数名词词尾没有 s 的，也要加"'s"。例如：
the boy's bag 男孩的书包
men's room 男厕所

（2）若名词已有复数词尾"s"，则只加"'"。例如：
the boxes' weight 这些盒子的重量

（3）表示店铺或教堂的名字或某人的家的名词，其所有格的后面通常不出现其所修饰的名词。例如：
the barber's 理发店

（4）如果两个名词并列，并且分别带有"'s"，则表示两者"分别有"；如果只有一个"'s"，则表示两者"共有"。例如：
John's and Mary's room（两间）
John and Mary's room（一间）

（5）复合名词或短语的所有格为在最后一个词的词尾加"'s"。例如：
an hour and a half's talk 一个半小时的谈话

（二）用 of 所有格表示所属关系

（1）"'s"形式的所有格主要用于表示有生命的东西的名词；表示无生命的东西的名词的所属关系多用 of 短语来表示。例如：
the title of the article 这篇文章的题目
the object of the sentence 句子的宾语

（2）有些表示无生命的东西的名词（时间、国家、城镇等），也可添加"'s"或"'"构成所有格。例如：
today's news 今天的新闻
China's capital 中国的首都
twenty minutes' break 20 分钟的休息

（三）双重所有格："'s"形式的所有格与 of 短语结合在一起使用

（1）所有格修饰的名词前有表示数量的词（a, two, some, few, no 等）。例如：
He is a classmate of Tom's.
他是汤姆的一个同学。
I know three friends of my mother's.
我认识我母亲的三个朋友。
（2）在某些场合下，of 所有格与双重所有格表示的意义完全不同。例如：
a bone of the dog's 一根狗吃的骨头
a bone of the dog 一根狗骨头
a portrait of Mr. Li's 一张由李先生画的（或收藏的）肖像
a portrait of Mr. Li 一张李先生画像

第三节 名词的功能

名词可在句子中作主语、宾语、表语、定语、补语、状语和同位语等多种句子成分。
（1）名词作主语。例如：
Mark Twain wrote many novels.
马克·吐温写过许多小说。
（2）名词作宾语。例如：
He did not catch the train.
他没有赶上火车。
（3）名词作表语。例如：
Susan is a musician.
苏珊是一位音乐家。
（4）名词作定语。例如：
She is my English teacher.
她是我的英语老师。
（5）名词作补语。例如：
They elected Xiao Li captain.
他们选小李当队长。
（6）名词作状语。例如：
The meeting lasted three hours.
会议持续了三个小时。
（7）名词作同位语。例如：
We students should work hard.
我们学生应该努力学习。

Exercises

I. Choose the best answer to complete each sentence.

1. The commander said that two _____ would be sent to the Iraqi front the next day.
   A. women's doctor   B. women doctors
   C. women's doctors   D. women doctor
2. "Look! The police _____ here to keep order! Go away quickly!" one of them shouted.
   A. is coming   B. comes   C. are coming   D. has come
3. She could not speak English, but made her wishes known by means of _____.
   A. signs   B. sighs   C. movements   D. words
4. In my opinion, what he told us just now about the affair simply doesn't make any _____.
   A. idea   B. meaning   C. sense   D. point
5. Shelly had prepared carefully for her English examination so that she could be sure of passing it on her first _____.
   A. intention   B. attempt   C. purpose   D. desire
6. _____ food is kept in his new cave, but at last Saddam was still arrested.
   A. Large quantities of   B. A great deal of   C. A large number of   D. Quite a few
7. —Let's try operating the machine right now.
   —Wait. Better read the _____ first.
   A. instructions   B. explanations   C. information   D. introduction
8. The rest of the magazines _____ within half an hour.
   A. is sold out   B. was sold out   C. were sold out   D. are sold out
9. You'd have more _____ of catching the train if you took a bus to the station instead of walking.
   A. opportunity   B. chance   C. time   D. energy
10. The number of deer, mountain lions and wild roses _____ much if people leave things _____ they are.
    A. doesn't change; as   B. aren't changed; like
    C. don't change; like   D. don't change; as
11. I knew I shouldn't accept anything from such a person, but I found it difficult to turn down his _____.
    A. offer   B. suggestion   C. request   D. plan
12. _____ it is to gather with President Bush at such a special Thanksgiving Day in Iraq!
    A. What a fun   B. What fun   C. How fun   D. What joy
13. Oh, John, _____ you gave us!
    A. how a great surprise   B. how pleasant surprise
    C. what a pleasant surprise   D. what pleasant surprise
14. He is _____ as a leader but he hasn't _____ in teaching.

A. success; many experiences	B. a success; much experience
C. great success; an experience	D. a great success; a lot of experiences

15. —Who did you spend last weekend with?
    —_____.
    A. Palmer's	B. The Palmers'	C. The Palmers	D. The Palmer's

16. The idea sounds good in theory, but it is useless if not put into _____.
    A. fact	B. event	C. deed	D. practice

17. I'm very grateful to you because you have taken _____ to show me how to do the work.
    A. efforts	B. pains	C. attempts	D. difficulties

18. You are in no _____ to work. What has happened?
    A. mood	B. idea	C. attitude	D. feeling

19. — I haven't seen you for ages. Let's have a get-together next week.
    —OK, it's a _____.
    A. charge	B. price	C. reward	D. deal

20. I suggest we go to the Qingdao Restaurant for lunch, which is famous for its wide _____ of foods that suit all tastes.
    A. division	B. area	C. range	D. circle

21. We can see the blue sky and the shining sun. There is no _____ that it will rain today.
    A. doubt	B. avenue	C. chance	D. point

22. The Imperial Palace, also known as the Forbidden City, is a tourist _____ in Beijing, drawing millions of visitors every year.
    A. interest	B. attraction	C. scene	D. view

23. —Would you like to go out for dinner with me, Ann?
    —Of course, but the only _____ is that you'll be my guest.
    A. position	B. instruction	C. condition	D. invitation

24. Mr. Zhang has taught for thirty years. Everybody sings high praise for his _____ to the cause of education.
    A. application	B. impression	C. reception	D. devotion

25. There are twenty-four _____ students in our class and we have three _____ teachers.
    A. girl; woman	B. girls; women	C. girl; women	D. girls; woman

26. I don't see the _____ in discussing the matter any further—we're just wasting our time.
    A. theme	B. reason	C. point	D. aim

27. —Do you think Mary is competent to be an interpreter?
    —Sure. She once studied in Australia and has a good _____ of English.
    A. need	B. command	C. recognition	D. standard

28. As an excellent translator, he reached a high level of _____ in his English.
    A. competence	B. independence	C. intelligence	D. experience

29. I refuse to lie about it; it's against my _____.
    A. ambitions	B. principles	C. regulations	D. opinions

30. There's a _____ in our class that we have a party on New Year's Eve.
    A. tradition   B. balance   C. concern   D. relationship

Ⅱ. Identify the mistake in each sentence and then correct it.

1. I saw a lot of peoples in the meeting-room.
2. My younger sister always wears beautiful cloth.
3. I went to my uncle's on Sunday and had good time there.
4. The boy's face is like his father.
5. My mother is a good cooker.
6. He had a little white hairs.
7. It's about half an hour drive from here.
8. The Summer Palace is one of Beijing's finest park.
9. Some friends of my brother will come to join us.
10. Mr. Zhang looks very happy today. He has got many good news from here.
11. Will you please make a room for the lady outside?
12. The number of the students in our school are increasing.
13. She has made some progresses in English.
14. His work is better than anyone else.
15. We've missed the last bus. I'm afraid we have no way but to take a taxi.
16. He dropped the coffee's cup and broke it.
17. He gained his wealth by printing works of famous writers.
18. I spent last weekend with the Smith
19. My brother has had one of his tooth taken out.
20. You'll find this map of great valuable in helping you to get round London.

第六章

冠　词

第一节　冠词的定义与分类

一、冠词的定义

冠词（Article），是指放在名词前用以帮助说明名词所表示的人或事物的一类词。冠词是一种虚词，是名词的一种标志，不能脱离名词而独立存在，因此不能单独作句子成分。

二、冠词的分类

冠词分为不定冠词"a/an"、定冠词"the"和零冠词"(/)"三种。不定冠词表示其后面的名词为某一类特定事物中的一个，但具体是哪一个并不重要。其中，不定冠词 a 用在以辅音（辅音并不等同于辅音字母）开头的名词前，an 用在以元音开头的名词前。例如，a university 一所大学，an apple 一个苹果。定冠词表示特指，用来限定其后面的名词为某个特定的事物，意思是"这个"或"那个"。

第二节　冠词的用法

零冠词指名词前不用冠词的情况。

一、不定冠词的基本用法

（1）表示"一"时，相当于 one。例如：
I saw a lion and a tiger in the zoo yesterday.
昨天我在动物园里看见一头狮子和一只老虎。
（2）表示"任何一个"时，相当于 any。例如：

Give me a book.

给我一本书。

（3）表示"每"时，相当于 each。例如：

We work eight hours a day.

我们每天工作八小时。

（4）表示"同样的"时，相当于 the same。例如：

They are of a size.

它们大小都是一样的。

（5）表示"某一个"时，相当于 a certain。例如：

A Mr. Smith is waiting for you downstairs.

有位史密斯先生在楼下等你。

（6）表示"一个像……的人"时，相当于 one like。例如：

He thinks he is an Einstein(= a man like Einstein)。

他认为他是个像爱因斯坦那样的人。

（7）表示某类人或物，相当于 someone or something。例如：

Even a child can answer this question.

即使小孩也能回答这个问题。

二、定冠词的基本用法

（1）表示第二次提到的上文中的人或物。例如：

I saw a film yesterday. The film is very interesting.

昨天我看了一部电影，这部电影非常有趣。

（2）用于一个名词虽然第一次出现，但其所表示的人或物为对话的双方所知道的句子。例如：

Where is the visitor?

来客在哪里？

（3）用于单数可数名词前，表示某一种类的人或物。例如：

The lion is the king of beasts.

狮子为兽中之王。

（4）用于世界上独一无二的东西前。例如：

The moon moves round the earth, and the earth moves round the sun.

月亮绕着地球转，地球则绕着太阳转。

（5）用于某些形容词前，代表一类人或物。例如：

The Chinese(= The Chinese people) are hard-working.

中国人是勤劳的。

（6）用于名词后面有介词短语、分词短语或定语从句修饰的句子中。例如：

I like the view from the window.

我喜欢从窗口看出去的景色。

（7）用于名词前面有序数词、形容词的最高级或 only 之类的词时修饰的句子中，例如：

The third boy in the third row is her brother.

第三排的第三个男孩是她的弟弟。

（8）用于姓氏的复数形式前，表示一家人。例如：

The Lius live upstairs.

刘家住楼上。

（9）用于下列专有名词前。

①用于表示江河、海洋、海湾、海峡、山脉群岛、沙漠等专有名词前。例如：

the Yangtze River　长江

the Yellow River　黄河

②用于表示某些国名、组织机构、建筑物、报纸、条约等名称的专有名词前。例如：

the People's Republic of China　中华人民共和国

the United Nations　联合国

（10）与 radio，telephone，piano，violin 等词连用。例如：

Do you play the piano?

你会弹钢琴吗？

三、零冠词的使用场合

（1）在节日名称前。例如：

Christmas Day　圣诞节

May Day　五一节

Children's Day　儿童节

但是，在下列中国节日名称前通常用定冠词。

the Spring Festival　春节

the Dragon Boat Festival　端午节

the Lantern Festival　元宵节

（2）在固定的短语中。例如：

go to school（bed，hospital，work，class，college）

去上学（去睡觉，去住医院，去上班，去上课，上大学）

go by train（bus，plane，boat，car）

坐火车（公共汽车，飞机，船，小汽车）去

（3）在球类运动、棋类游戏等名词前。例如：

play basketball（football，table tennis）　打篮球（踢足球，打乒乓球）

play chess　下棋

（4）在表示身份、头衔、职务（只有一人担任时）的名词前。例如：

Lincoln was elected President in 1860.

林肯于1860年被选为总统。

（5）在表示对比或并列的两个名词前。例如：

Father and son attended the meeting together.

父子两人一起出席了这次会议。

（6）在人名、地名、街名、城镇名、学校名、广场名、公园名、国名及语言名称前。例如：

Newton 牛顿，Shanghai 上海，French 法语。

（7）在季节、月份、星期前。例如：

In spring the weather gets warmer.

春天天气更暖和。

 Exercises

Ⅰ. Choose the best answer to complete each sentence.

1. Tom owns _____ larger collection of _____ books than any other student in our class.
   A. the；/   B. a；/   C. a；the   D. /；the

2. For a long time they walked without saying _____ word. Jim was the first to break _____ silence.
   A. the；a   B. a；the   C. a；/   D. the；/

3. When he left _____ college, he got a job as _____ reporter in a newspaper office.
   A. /；a   B. /；the   C. a；the   D. the；the

4. If you buy more than ten, they will knock 20 pence off _____.
   A. a price   B. price   C. the price   D. prices

5. _____ on-going division between English-speaking Canadians and French-speaking Canadians is _____ major concern of the country.
   A. The；/   B. The；a   C. An；the   D. An；/

6. The Wilsons live in _____ A-shaped house near the coast. It is _____ 17th century cottage.
   A. the；/   B. an；the   C. /；the   D. an；a

7. When you come here for your holiday next time, don't go to _____ hotel; I can find you _____ bed in my flat.
   A. the；a   B. the；/   C. a；the   D. a；/

8. When you finish reading this book, you will have _____ better understanding of _____ life.
   A. a；the   B. the；a   C. /；the   D. a；/

9. It is _____ world of wonders, _____ world where anything can happen.
   A. a；the   B. a；a   C. the；a   D. /；/

10. The most important thing about cotton in history is _____ part that it played in _____ Industrial Revolution.
    A. /；/   B. the；/   C. the；the   D. a；the

11. While he was investigating ways to improve the telescope, Newton made _____ discover which completely changed _____ man's understanding of colour.

A. a；/   B. a；the   C. /；the   D. the；a

12. —I'd like _____ information about the management of your hotel, please.
    —Well, you could have _____ word with the manager. He might be helpful.
    A. some；a   B. an；some   C. some；some   D. an；a

13. Many people agree that _____ knowledge of English is a must in _____ international trade today.
    A. a；/   B. the；an   C. the；the   D. /；the

14. —Have you seen _____ pen? I left it here this morning.
    —Is it _____ black one? I think I saw it somewhere.
    A. a；the   B. the；the   C. the；a   D. a；a

15. Paper money was in _____ use in China when Marco Polo visited the country in _____ thirteenth century.
    A. the；/   B. the；the   C. /；the   D. /；/

16. Most animals have little connection with _____ animals of _____ different kind unless they kill them for food.
    A. the；a   B. /；a   C. the；the   D. /；the

17. Jumping out of _____ airplane at ten thousand feet is quite _____ exciting experience.
    A. /；the   B. /；an   C. an；an   D. the；the

18. The sign reads "In case of _____ fire, break the glass and press _____ red button."
    A. /；a   B. /；the   C. the；the   D. a；a

19. On _____ news today, there were _____ reports of heavy snow in that area.
    A. the；the   B. the；/   C. /；/   D. /；the

20. _____ is used by one-fourth of all human beings on earth.
    A. The Chinese   B. The Chinese Language
    C. Chinese Language   D. A Chinese

21. —I hear _____ hostess was murdered last year.
    —Where was _____ hostess killed?
    A. a；the   B. an；the   C. a；a   D. the；the

22. I took _____ pickpocket by _____ hand.
    A. a；his   B. an；a   C. the；the   D. the；his

23. That was _____ most happy occasion.
    A. an   B. the   C. /   D. a

24. _____ went to Class 3.
    A. First prize   B. The first prize   C. A first prize   D. The prize first

25. In the sentence "might" refers to _____.
    A. the present   B. a present   C. an present   D. present

26. I own a dog and a cat. _____ former is black, and _____ latter is white.
    A. a；a   B. an；an   C. the；the   D. a；an

27. Students should study _____ greater part of their time.

A. a B. the C. an D. /

28. It is _____ hour's walk from here to the bus-stop.

A. a B. the C. one D. an

29. There is _____ "m" in the word "meet."

A. the B. one C. an D. a

30. There is _____ "u" and _____ "s" in the word "use."

A. a; an B. an; an C. an; a D. a; a

II. Identify the mistake in each sentence and then correct it.

1. The Chinese are the industrious people.
2. Do you like music of the film "Titanic"?
3. He goes to a hospital every Sunday for treatment.
4. He was taken to hospital and treated by the doctor.
5. The boy walks to a school every day.
6. The foreigners visited school yesterday.
7. Some people go to a church and some don't.
8. Church is open every day and all day.
9. The Kings came to us at the noon.
10. The scientists from the United States live in Ninth Street.
11. Mr. Black arrived here on the Tuesday morning.
12. There are four seasons in the year. The first season is spring.
13. Some people have been to the moon in the spaceship.
14. China is a old country with a long history.
15. They are living happy life now.
16. There is the empty box on the table.
17. Don't make any noise in a class.
18. This is such the interesting story that you must listen to it.
19. Next week they will go to Australia by the air.
20. Which is bigger, a sun or a moon?

第七章

代　词

第一节　代词的概念

代词（Pronoun），是指代替名词或起名词作用的短语、分句以及句子的一类词。代词是一种功能词，在句子中起指代、修饰、限定的作用。

代词的种类繁多，各种代词的形式、性质和功能都不尽相同。英语中，代词使用得十分广泛，其旨在减少用词的重复。

第二节　代词的分类及用法

英语中，代词按其意义、特征及在句中的作用可分为九类：人称代词、物主代词、反身代词、相互代词、指示代词、疑问代词、关系代词、连接代词和不定代词。

一、人称代词（Personal Pronoun）

人称代词是指表示"我""我们""你""你们""他""她""他们"等的一类词。人称代词有人称、数与格之分，如表 7-1 所示。

表 7-1　人称代词的人称、数和格

单、复数及人称　　格	单数					复数		
	第一人称	第二人称	第三人称			第一人称	第二人称	第三人称
主格	I	you	he	she	it	we	you	they
宾格	me	you	him	her	it	us	you	them

人称代词在句中可用作主语、宾语、表语以及介词宾语。

（1）作主语时，人称代词用主格。例如：

It is a tape recorder.

这是部收录机。

（2）作宾语时，人称代词用宾格。例如：

She likes him.

她喜欢他。

（3）作表语时，用宾格较多。例如：

If I were her, I would go.

如果我是她，我就去。

（4）作介词宾语时，一般用宾格。例如：

Our teacher is very strict with us.

我们老师对我们很严格。

二、物主代词（Possessive Pronoun）

物主代词，是指表示所有关系的代词。英语中，每个人称代词都有其对应的物主代词，如表 7-2 所示。

表 7-2　物主代词

人称代词	物主代词	
	形容词性	名词性
I	my	mine
you	your	yours
he	his	his
she	her	hers
it	its	its
we	our	ours
you	your	yours
they	their	theirs

形容词性的物主代词只能够在句中作定语。例如：

This is my video deck.

这是我的录像机。

名词性的物主代词在句中可用作主语、宾语、表语，以及与 of 连用作定语。

（1）作主语。例如：

Theirs(=Their room) is a big room.

他们的房间是个大房间。

（2）作宾语。例如：

My dictionary is not here. Please give me yours.
我的词典没有在这儿。请把你的给我。

（3）作表语。例如：

Whose dictionary is this? It is his(= his dictionary).
这是谁的词典？是他的。

（4）与 of 连用作定语。例如：

He is a friend of mine. (= He is one of my friends.)
他是我的一个朋友。

三、反身代词（Reflexive Pronoun）

反身代词，是指表示"我自己""我们自己""你自己""你们自己""他自己""他们自己"等的代词。反身代词的具体形式如表 7 - 3 所示。

表 7 - 3　反身代词

单数	myself	yourself	himself	herself	itself
复数	ourselves	yourselves	themselves		

反身代词在句中可用作宾语、表语以及主语或宾语的同位语。

（1）作宾语。例如：

I can express myself in English.
我能用英语来表达自己的思想。

（2）作表语。例如：

I am not quite myself these days.
我近来身体不大舒服。

（3）作主语或宾语的同位语。例如：

The thing itself is not valuable, but I want it as a keepsake.
这东西本身并无价值，但是我要它留作纪念。

四、相互代词（Reciprocal Pronoun）

相互代词，是指表示相互关系的代词，有 each other 和 one another 两组。一般来讲，each other 表示两个人或事物之间的关系；one another 表示两个以上的人或事物之间的关系。例如：

We learn from each other.
我们互相学习。

For years the sisters looked after one another.
多年来姐妹们都互相照顾。

五、指示代词（Demonstrative Pronoun）

指示代词，是指表示这个（this）、那个（that）、这些（these）、那些（those）等的代词。指示代词在句中可用作主语、宾语、表语以及定语。

（1）作主语。例如：

This is a map, and that is a picture.

这是一张地图，那是一幅画。

（2）作宾语。例如：

She wants that (those).

她要那个（那些）。

（3）作表语。例如：

My idea is this.

我的意见是这样。

（4）作定语。例如：

This coat is mine, and that one is yours.

这件外衣是我的，那件是你的。

六、疑问代词（Interrogative Pronoun）

疑问代词，是指表示谁（who）、谁（whom）、谁的（whose）、什么（what）、哪个或哪些（which）等的代词。疑问代词用于特殊疑问句中，其一般放在句子的最前面，在句中可用作主语、宾语、定语以及表语。

（1）作主语。例如：

Who is speaking?

你是谁？（打电话用语）

What has happened to him?

他出了什么事？

（2）作宾语。例如：

Whom do you wish to speak to?

你想找谁接电话？

Which do you prefer?

你比较喜欢哪一个？

（3）作定语。例如：

Which train will you take?

你赶哪一班火车？

Whose dictionary is this?

这是谁的词典？

（4）作表语。例如：

What are the results of the examination?

考试成绩怎样？

Whose is it?

这是谁的？

七、关系代词（Relative Pronoun）

关系代词，是指用来引导定语从句的代词。关系代词有 who，whom，whose，that，which 等，可用来引导定语从句。例如：

It is very hard to find a person who is almost perfect.
很难找到一个几乎是十全十美的人。

八、连接代词（Conjunctive Pronoun）

连接代词包括 who，whom，whose，what，which，whoever，whoseever，whatever，whichever 等。连接代词可用来引导主语从句、宾语从句和表语从句。

（1）引导主语从句。例如：
What has been said must be kept secret.
说的话必须保密。

（2）引导宾语从句。例如：
Please carry out what has been decided.
请执行决定。

（3）引导表语从句。例如：
The question is who（m）we should trust.
问题是我们该相信谁。

九、不定代词（Indefinite Pronoun）

不定代词，是指没有明确指定代替任何特定名词或形容词的代词。常用的不定代词包括 one，some，any，each，every，either，neither，much，many，little，few，none，other，another，both，all 以及由 some，any，no，every 与 body，one，thing 构成的合成词。不定代词的具体用法如下。

1. some 和 any

（1）some 和 any 有"某个""某些""任何""一些"等意思，具体为哪个意思视上下文而定。some 一般用于肯定句，any 用于否定句和疑问句。另外，any 也可用于肯定句，意思是"任何一个"。例如：

I want some interesting books.
我要几本有趣的书。

Have you got any French books? No, I haven't got any.
你有法语书吗？没有，一本也没有。

Come any day you like. 你哪天来都行。

（2）在表示建议、请求，并希望得到肯定答复时，疑问句中应用 some 而不用 any。例如：

Would you like some beer?
来点啤酒好吗？

Will you give me some paper?

请给我一点纸好吗?

(3) 条件句中，some 和 any 都可以用。例如：

If you want any/some of this tea, please let me know.

如果你想要点这种茶的话，请告诉我。

2. no 和 none

(1) no 的意思是"没有"，常用作定语构成否定句。例如：

No man is born wise.

没有人生来就聪明。

There is no short cut in the study of English.

学英语无捷径。

(2) none 的意思是"没有一个人（东西）"，其后面的动词可以用复数或单数。例如：

None of us has ever been to Paris.

我们中没有一个人去过巴黎。

None of my friends have been to Beijing.

我的朋友中没有一个人去过北京。

3. much, many, little, few

much 表示"很多"，little 表示"很少"，二者用于修饰不可数名词；many 表示"很多"，few 表示"很少"，二者用于修饰可数名词。little 和 few 表示否定意思，而 a little（有一点）和 a few（有几个）表示肯定意思。例如：

He has much time.　　他有许多时间。

He has many friends.　　他有许多朋友。

I have little time for reading.　　我很少有时间读书。

I have few friends.　　我有很少几个朋友。

He knows a little French.　　他懂一点法语。

A few of us know French.　　我们当中有几个人懂法语。

4. either 和 neither

either 表示两个人或事物中的任何一个；neither 表示两者中的任何一个都不。例如：

I like neither. (= I don't like either.)

两个我一个都不喜欢。

5. both 和 all

both 用于两个人或事物；all 用于两个以上的人或事物。例如：

Both of you are right.　　你们两人都对。

All of them enjoyed themselves.　　他们所有的人都过得愉快。

6. each 和 every

each 和 every 都表示"每一个"，但在用法上稍有不同。each 强调个别，every 强调整体，此时，every 的含义与 all 相似。例如：

Every boy in the class(= All the boys in the class) passed the examination.

班上所有的男生考试都及格了。

Each boy may have three tries.

每个孩子可以试三次。

7. other 和 another

other 与 another 分别表示"另外"与"另外一个"。其中 other 有单、复数之分。the other 表示二者之中的"另外一个"；the others 表示"其余的"，有特指之意；others"其他的"，有泛指之意。例如：

His brothers are both abroad：One is in the U. S. A. , and the other in the U. K.

他的两个兄弟都在国外：一个在美国，另一个在英国。

Some went by train, the others went by plane.

有些人坐火车去，其余的人坐飞机。

The glass is broken, get me another.

这个玻璃杯坏了，另外给我拿一个来。

8. one

one 表示"某一"，可以指代人或物。one's 是 one 的所有格形式。例如：

One day last week I met him.

上周的某天，我遇见了他。

One can't work all the time.

人不能老是工作。

One must do one's duty.

人必须尽责。

ones 是 one 的复数形式，one 可用于代替上文出现的单数可数名词，ones 可用于代替复数可数名词。例如：

I haven't got a car. I must buy one(= a car).

我没有小汽车，我必须买一辆。

She likes reading books, especially interesting ones(= books).

她喜欢读书，特别是有趣的书。

 Exercises

Ⅰ. Choose the best answer to complete each sentence.

1. I agree with most of what you said, but I don't agree with _____.
   A. everything   B. anything   C. something   D. nothing
2. "What do you think of them?" "I don't know _____ is better, so I've taken _____ of them."
   A. what; both   B. what; none   C. which; both   D. which; none
3. "Would you like a cup of coffee or a glass of beer?" "_____ will do, but milk is _____ popular with me."
   A. Neither; not   B. Both; more   C. Either; the most   D. All; the most

4. I read about it in some book or other, does it matter _____ it was?
   A. where　　　　　B. what　　　　　C. how　　　　　D. which
5. "Who told you?" "Oh, somebody or other, I've forgotten _____."
   A. what　　　　　B. when　　　　　C. which　　　　D. who
6. Some of the students were late for the meeting, but I can't remember _____.
   A. what　　　　　B. when　　　　　C. which　　　　D. whom
7. These trousers are dirty and wet — I'll change into my _____.
   A. another　　　B. trousers　　　C. others　　　　D. other
8. Her lecture was hard to follow because she kept jumping from one subject to _____.
   A. other　　　　B. the other　　　C. the others　　D. another
9. There are four bedrooms, _____ with its own bathroom.
   A. all　　　　　B. each　　　　　C. every　　　　　D. either
10. "It's said that he is a wise leader." "Oh, no, he is _____ but a wise leader."
    A. anything　　B. anyone　　　　C. anybody　　　　D. anywhere
11. I didn't make _____ clear when and where the sports meet would be held.
    A. this　　　　B. that　　　　　C. it　　　　　　D. one
12. To tell you the truth, I really don't like _____ when people talk with you with their eyes staring into the sky.
    A. which　　　B. that　　　　　C. it　　　　　　D. what
13. —Which one can I take?
    —You can take _____ of them; I'll keep none.
    A. both　　　　B. any　　　　　C. either　　　　D. all
14. —Which coat would you prefer, sir?
    —I'll take _____, to have a change sometimes.
    A. all them　　B. them all　　　C. both them　　　D. them both
15. The movie is _____ boring; it is, in fact, rather exciting and interesting.
    A. anything but　B. nothing but　C. no more　　　D. all but
16. Alan sold most of his belongings. He has hardly _____ left in the house.
    A. everything　B. anything　　　C. nothing　　　D. something
17. I have lived in Shanghai for two years, but I haven't covered _____ of the city.
    A. anything　　B. much　　　　　C. many　　　　　D. plenty
18. She kept looking _____ behind to see if she was being followed.
    A. her　　　　B. herself　　　C. her own　　　D. she
19. All of us want very much to see these recommended movies, especially _____ you referred to just now.
    A. as　　　　　B. which　　　　C. the one　　　D. that
20. If a student can make what has been learned _____ whether in class or from social practice, he will make steady progress.
    A. he　　　　　B. him　　　　　C. himself　　　D. his

21. — Do you want tea or coffee?
    —_____. I really don't mind.
    A. None   B. Neither   C. Either   D. All
22. The manager believes prices will not rise by more than _____ four percent.
    A. any other   B. the other   C. another   D. other
23. The manager was very angry, for he had sent his business partner two thousand machines yesterday, half of _____ unqualified.
    A. whom   B. what   C. them   D. which
24. — Did you visit many places while you were in Canada?
    — Yes, _____.
    A. a few quite   B. only few   C. only a few   D. quite few
25. In some countries, _____ is called equality does not really mean equal rights for all people.
    A. that   B. what   C. which   D. how
26. —May I have a glass of beer, please?
    —Beer? Sorry, there is _____ left, but would you mind having some juice instead?
    A. none   B. no one   C. nothing   D. few
27. —When can we go to visit you?
    —Anytime you feel like _____.
    A. one   B. it   C. so   D. that
28. We need a more capable leader, _____ with strong will as well as good humour.
    A. who   B. that   C. one   D. which
29. The number 2008 is a special number, _____ I think will be remembered by the Chinese forever.
    A. which   B. what   C. one   D. it
30. —How do you like his wife?
    —She is _____ like a good housekeeper, for the children's room is always in a terrible mess.
    A. somebody   B. nobody   C. something   D. nothing

Ⅱ. Identify the mistake in each sentence and then correct it.

1. He was wounded in his leg.
2. —Who is that man?
   — He is a teacher.
3. He covered his eyes with hands.
4. We should point out each other shortcomings.
5. The students went out of the classroom one after the another.
6. — Do you like the pen I bought for you?
   — Yes, very much. It's just one I wanted.
7. They were both very tired, but none of them would stop to take a rest.

73

8. It is impossible for so few worker to do so much work in a single day.
9. I ask him for some oil, but he hadn't some.
10. Four of them are in the workshop. What about others?
11. It is me who am going to help her.
12. He thinks more of others than of oneself.
13. He is too young to look after he.
14. I haven't brought the dictionary with me. Will you lend me your?
15. Kate and her sister went on holiday with a cousin of hers.
16. The weather in summer in Guangzhou is hotter than it in Beijing.
17. He runs faster than anyone in our class.
18. I don't think that possible to master a foreign language in a short time.
19. Each of them knew about the plan because it was kept a secret.
20. That took him three hours to finish the homework.

第八章

数　　词

第一节　数词的定义及表示

一、数词的定义

数词（Numeral），是指表示数量或顺序的一类词。数词分为两大类，即基数词与序数词。基数词表示数目，即数量的多少。例如，one，two，three，four，……序数词表示顺序，例如，first，second，third，fourth，……序数词前一般要加"the"。英语中，数词可以作句子的主语、宾语、表语和定语。另外，数词与不定代词、冠词、指示代词、形容词性物主代词等共同被称作限定词。

二、数词的表示

（一）基数词的表示方法

1. 表示基数词的基础词汇

英语中的基本基数词是表示任何其他基数词的基础，需要逐个记忆。这些基础的基数词主要包括以下部分。

（1）0～12为独立单词，分别读作：

zero 零　　　one 一　　　two 二　　　three 三　　　four 四
five 五　　　six 六　　　seven 七　　　eight 八　　　nine 九
ten 十　　　eleven 十一　　　twelve 十二

（2）13～19的表示方法为在个位数词的词干后加-teen。其中，thirteen，fifteen，eighteen 变化不规则。具体的表示方法如下：

thirteen 十三　　　fourteen 十四　　　fifteen 十五　　　sixteen 十六
seventeen 十七　　　eighteen 十八　　　nineteen 十九

(3) 20~90十位数词的表示方法为在个位数词后面加-ty。其中，twenty，thirty，forty，fifty，eighty 变化不规则。具体的表示方法如下：

twenty 二十　　　thirty 三十　　　forty 四十　　　fifty 五十
sixty 六十　　　seventy 七十　　　eighty 八十　　　ninety 九十

(4) 百位、千位、百万位、十亿的表示方法分别为：

hundred 百　　thousand 千　　million 百万　　billion 十亿

2. 两位数 21~99 的表示方法

基数词 21~99 的表示由十位数词后面加上个位数词合成，中间用连字符"-"连接。如，"62"可表示为 sixty-two，"23"可表示为 twenty-three。

3. 三位数的表示方法

三位数的表示方法为"百位数词 + and + 两位数/个位数"。例如，"253"可表示为 two hundred and fifty-three。

4. 四至六位数的表示方法

四至六位数的表示方法为"千位数词 + 百位数词 + and + 两位数/个位数"。例如，"7179"可表示为 seven thousand one hundred and seventy-nine。

5. 七至九位数的表示方法

七至九位数的表示方法为"百万数词 + 千位数词 + 百位数词 + and + 两位数/个位数"。用阿拉伯数字书写千以上的数目时，要由右向左每三位数间留一个空格或写一个逗号。例如，"87 651 234"（一般用在汉语中）或"87,651,234"（一般用在英语中）可表示为 eighty seven million six hundred and fifty-one thousand two hundred and thirty-four。

（二）序数词的表示方法

1. 表示序数词的基础词汇

与基数词的基础词汇相对应的序数词的表示方法为：

first 第一　　　second 第二　　　third 第三　　　fourth 第四
fifth 第五　　　sixth 第六　　　seventh 第七　　　eighth 第八
ninth 第九　　　tenth 第十　　　eleventh 第十一　　twelfth 第十二
thirteenth 第十三　　fourteenth 第十四　　fifteenth 第十五
sixteenth 第十六　　seventeenth 第十七　　eighteenth 第十八
nineteenth 第十九　　twentieth 第二十　　thirtieth 第三十
fortieth 第四十　　fiftieth 第五十　　sixtieth 第六十
seventieth 第七十　　eightieth 第八十　　ninetieth 第九十
hundredth 第一百　　thousandth 第一千　　millionth 第一百万
billionth 第十亿

2. 序数词的构成规则

英语中的序数词可以由基数词变化而来，具体的变化方法为：

(1) 第1至第19一般是在基数词后加"th"，但变化特殊的有 one—first，two—second，three—third, eight—eighth, nine—ninth, five—fifth, twelve—twelfth。

(2) 十位数词 twenty, thirty...ninety 变化规则为分别改 y 为 ieth。例如，twenty—

twentieth，ninety-ninetieth。

（3）非整十的多位序数词的构成方法为：将相应基数词的个位变为序数词，即表示第几十几或第几百几十几，只需将其个位数改为序数词。例如，第 56：fifty-sixth；第 635：six hundred and thirty-fifth。

（4）序数词的缩写形式为阿拉伯数字加序数词的最后两个字母。例如，first——1st；second——2nd；third-3rd；thirty-first——31st。

（5）需要注意的是，某些情形既可以用基数词也可以用序数词来表示其顺序。例如：

the second part = Part two（第二部分）

the first chapter = Chapter one（第一章）

the fourth section = Section four（第四节）

（三）其他数词的表示方法

1. 倍数的表示方法

（1）倍数 + 形容词/副词比较级 + than，倍数用基数词加 times 表示。例如：

The girl is ten times braver than her brother.

（2）如果表示"是……的两倍"，一般用 twice。例如：

Your room is twice as large as your brother's.

（3）倍数 + as + 形容词/副词/名词 + as。例如：

His room is three times as large as mine.

（4）倍数 + 名词。例如：

The volume of the sun is about 1,300,000 times that of the earth.

太阳的体积约为地球的 1 300 000 倍。

（5）动词 + 倍数，用-fold 或基数词加 times 表示。例如：

Productivity is increased three-fold. 生产效率提高了三倍。

The shirt has shortened two thirds since it was bought.

（6）用 double（翻一番），triple（三倍于），again（再次）等词表示倍数。例如：

My cousin is as old again as I am.

我表姐年龄比我大一倍。

The output has doubled.

产量增加了一倍。

2. 小数的表示方法

小数点左边的数通常按基数词表示，若为三位以上的数，也可按编码式读法读出，即将数字单个表示出来；小数点右边的数通常按编码式读法单个读出。例如：

13.14　thirteen point one four

456.321　four five six point three two one/four hundred and fifty-six point three two one

注意：小数中"0"的读法。

"0"在小数中通常读作 nought（英）或 zero（美），也可读作字母 o。例如：

0.06　(nought) point nought six/(zero) point zero six

9.07　nine point o seven

3. 百分数的表示方法

百分数中的百分号"%"读作 percent。例如：

6%　　six percent

0.6%　　(nought) point six percent

500%　　five hundred percent

12.34%　　twelve point three four percent

4. 加、减、乘、除的读法

$7+4=11$　　Seven plus four is eleven./Seven and four is eleven.

$11-2=9$　　Eleven minus two is nine./two from eleven is nine.

$8\times5=40$　　eight multiplied by five is forty./eight times five is forty.

$60\div4=15$　　sixty divided by four is fifteen./Four into sixty goes fifteen.

$20:5=4$　　The ratio of twenty to five is four.

$2^2=4$　　Two squared is four.

$2^3=8$　　Two cubed is eight.

$2^4=16$　　The fourth power of two is sixteen.

$\sqrt[2]{X}=Y$　　The square root of X is Y.

$\sqrt[3]{X}=Y$　　The cubic root of X is Y.

$a>b$　　a is more than b.

$a<b$　　a is less than b.

$a\approx b$　　a approximately equals to b.

$a\neq b$　　a is not equal to b.

5. 分数的表示方法

（1）较小分数的一般表示方法为"基数词 + 连字符'-' + 序数词"。例如：

1/3 one-third　　2/3 two-thirds　　4/5 four-fifths

（2）较复杂分数的简明表示方法"...over..."或"...divided by..."。例如：

a/b　　a over b/a divided by b

22/97　　twenty-two over ninety-seven/twenty-two divided by ninety-seven

（3）整数与分数之间须用 and 连接。例如：

four and a half　　nine and two fifths

（4）分数用作前置定语时，分母要用单数形式。例如：

a one-third mile　　1/3 英里

a three-quarter majority　　3/4 的多数

6. 年代的表示方法

年代用年份的阿拉伯数字加's/s 表示。例如：

17 世纪 20 年代　　1620's/1620s

初期、中期、末期分别用 early，mid-和 late 表示。例如：

50 年代初期　　the early fifties

50 年代中期　　the mid-fifties

50 年代末期　　the late fifties

20 世纪 30 年代初期　the early 1930's
20 世纪 30 年代中期　the mid-1930's
20 世纪 30 年代末期　the late 1930's

7. 时刻的表示方法

（1）二十四小时计时法

二十四小时计时法通常采用"小时数：分钟数""小时数．分钟数"或"小时数分钟数"的形式。例如：

01：00　　（o）one hour/one o'clock
12．00　　twelve hours/midday/noon
21：15　　twenty one fifteen
23：45　　twenty-three forty-five
00：00　　midnight/zero hour

（2）十二小时计时法

十二小时计时法通常采用"小时数：分钟数"或"小时数．分钟数"的形式，例如，8：12 或 8.12。为了避免误解，通常加上 in the morning/a. m.（上午）或 in the afternoon p. m.（下午）以示区别。a. m. 是拉丁语 ante meridiem 的缩写形式，读作/'ei'em/，意思是"上午"；p. m. 是拉丁语 post meridiem 的缩写形式，读作/'piː'em/，意思是"下午；晚上"。若表示整点钟，可加 o'clock，也可不加。例如：

8．00 a. m./8：00 a. m.　　eight a. m./eight in the morning.

另外，大于 30 分钟时，可将小时加 1，再用 60 减去分钟数后用 to 连接；小于或等于 30 分钟时，直接在小时和分钟间加上 past。例如：

01：20　　（o）one twenty 或 twenty past one
3：05　　（o）three (o) five 或 five past three
09：45　　（o）nine forty-five 或 a quarter to ten
10：15　　ten fifteen 或 a quarter past ten
12：45　　twelve forty-five 或 a quarter to thirteen
15：30　　fifteen thirty 或 half past fifteen
8.45 a. m./8：45 a. m.　　eight forty-five a. m./a quarter to nine in the morning
3.30 p. m./3：30 p. m.　　three thirty p. m./half past three in the afternoon
5.15 p. m./5：15 p. m.　　five fifteen p. m./a quarter past five in the afternoon
8：55 p. m.　　eight fifty-five at night/five to nine at night（at night 指日落后到半夜零时。）

8. 年、月、日的表示方法

（1）年份通常用阿拉伯数字表示，用基数词读出。公元前用 B. C. 表示，公元用 A. D. 表示。例如：

公元前 802 年　802 B. C.
公元 732 年　732 A. D.
1000 年　year one thousand

（2）"日"用基数词或序数词表示。例如：

1949 年 6 月 8 日　June 8, 1949 或 June eighth, 1949

（3）表示月、日既可以先写"月"再写"日"（英式），也可先写"日"再写"月"（美式）。例如：

7月1日写作July 1，读作July the first；或1 July，读作the first of July。

（4）表示"年"和"月"时，在"年"和"月"前用介词in；表示具体日期时，在"日"前用介词on。例如：

in 2003　　in July　　on June 24, 1983

9. 货币单位的表示方法

（1）英镑的符号"£"放在数字前面，但单位词"pound（s）"放在数字后面。例如：

£60　　sixty pounds

（2）便士可用"P"表示，单数为penny，复数为pence，放在数字后面。例如：

1P　one penny

9P　nine pence

£94.56　ninety-four pounds fifty-six pence

They imported two thousand pounds worth（or value）of tea.

他们进口了价值两千英镑的茶叶。

（3）美元的符号"$"放在数字前面，但单词"dollars"放在数字后面。例如：

$1.24　one dollar twenty-four cents

$453　four hundred and fifty-three dollars

I got the coat for 70 cents.

我花了70美分买了这件衣服。

在借据、文书、账单等重要文件中，钱数多以英语和阿拉伯数字两种形式写出。例如：

I owe you（IOU）two thousand dollars（$2,000）.

今借到2 000美元（$2 000）。

10. 编码式读法

编码式读法是指将数字逐一按基数词读出的方法。通常，门牌号码、房间号码、电话号码、邮政编码、车牌号码及其他专用编码均采用编码式读法。凡采用编码式读法的数字都应在三位以上，两位数字通常按基数词读。例如：

Room 34　　room thirty-four

extension 2238　　extension double two three eight

page 218　　page two one eight

11. 不定数目的表示方法

（1）"大约"的表示方法。

①about, approximately, around, more or less, roughly, some 等加数词，或数词加more or less, or so, or thereabouts 等。例如：

about/some 100 books

3,000 seats more or less

approximately 67 miles

sixty or so pages/sixty pages or so/sixty pages or thereabouts

somewhere 也可表示"大约"，如somewhere 300 people。

②基数词或阿拉伯数字末尾加 ish。例如：
I'll come (at) tenish tomorrow.（十点左右）
She is 40ish.（四十岁左右）
③十位数加 s。例如：
He is in his teens.
She is in her forties.
（2）"多于"的表示方法。
①above, more than, over 等加数词。例如：
above 50 Yuan
students over 89
②数词加-odd。例如：
70-odd chairs
（3）"少于……""不到……"的表示方法。
almost, below, less than, under 等加数词。例如：
almost ten years old
less than a minute
under two hours

第二节 数词的语法功能

一、基数词的语法功能

（1）作定语。例如：
There are only three teachers in this school.
这所学校只有 3 名老师。
Six guests will come to the party.
六位来宾要来参加聚会。
（2）作主语。例如：
Thirteen is said to be an unlucky number.
据说 13 是个不吉利的数字。
Four of them will play volleyball.
他们中有四人要去打排球。
（3）作宾语。例如：
It is worth five thousand Yuan.
这件东西值 5 000 元。
The town has a population of eighty thousand.
这个镇有八万人口。
（4）作表语。例如：

I am ten.

我 10 岁。

Two and two is four.

二加二等于四。

(5) 作同位语。例如：

Are you four coming?

你们四人来吗？

They two will go abroad.

他们俩将出国。

二、序数词的语法功能

(1) 作主语。例如：

The first was better.

第一个好些。

(2) 作表语。作表语时，序数词前面的定冠词往往省去。例如：

He was third last year.

他去年是第三。

(3) 作宾语。例如：

He was among the first to hand in the report.

他是首批交报告的人员之一。

(4) 作定语。例如：

March is the third month of the year.

三月是一年中的第三个月。

(5) 作同位语。例如：

Who is the man, the first in the second line?

位于第二列第一个的男子是谁？

第三节　数词学习要点

一、序数词的冠词使用方法

(1) 序数词前一般要加定冠词 the。例如：

It's the second time mom has been to his home.

这是我妈妈第二次到他家去。

(2) 表示在原有的基础上增加，即意为"又一，再一"时，用不定冠词。例如：

A second student asked the question.

又一个（第二个）学生问了这个问题。

Shall I call her a third time?

我还要再打电话给她一次吗?

（3）序数词前用定冠词和不定冠词的区别在于：定冠词表示特指，不定冠词表示泛指，其意思类似于 another，但比 another 更为明确。例如：

I like the third book.

我喜欢第三本书。（至少有三本书可供选择，表示特指）

I read a third book。

我又读了第三本书。（原来已读两本，这是第三本）

（4）序数词在下列情况下不用冠词。

①序数词前已有物主代词或名词所有格时，不能再用冠词。例如：

This is my second visit to Singapore.

这是我第二次访问新加坡。

②表示比赛或考试的名次时，通常省略定冠词。例如：

My sister was(the) second in the contest.

我姐姐在竞赛中得了第二名。

③序数词被用作副词时不用冠词。例如：

I have to finish my paper first.

我得先把论文写完。

④在某些习语中不用冠词。例如：

at first　开始

at first sight　乍看起来

first of all　首先

二、基数词使用复数形式的情形

基数词一般为单数形式，但下列情况中常用复数。

（1）表示某基数词有多个。此时，基数词转化为名词，可用复数形式。例如：

Four twos are eight.

四乘二等于八。

The students queued up in tens.

学生们10人一列排队。

（2）表示一群一群的人或一批一批的事物。例如：

The girls came in ones and twos.

女孩们三三两两地来了。

Invitations are sent in(by) twos and threes.

邀请函三三两两地发出了。

（3）用于某些习语。例如：

I heard a strange news from my hometown so I'm all at sixes and sevens.

我听到了家乡一则奇怪的消息，因此心里七上八下的。

（4）表示整十的基数词用复数形式可以表示岁数或年代，其结构为"in + the/物主代词 + 数词复数"。例如：

The war broke out in the thirties.

这次战争爆发于30年代。

My grandpa began to learn English in his fifties.

我爷爷五十多岁开始学英语。

三、dozen，score，hundred，thousand，million 用法要点

（1）dozen，score，hundred，thousand，million 作数词时，不用复数，前面可以加 one，two…等其他数词或某些表示数量的形容词。例如：

I want three dozen apples.

我要三打苹果。

The lady is of three score years.

那位女士六十岁。

A few hundred (thousand) students took part in the sports meeting.

有几百（千）学生参加了运动会。

About two million workers were on strike.

大约有两百万工人参加了罢工。

（2）dozen，score，hundred，thousand，million 用作名词时，复数形式表示"成……上……"，且后面必须接 of。当表示"几百""几千""几百万"等笼统的数目时，前面可以加 some，many，several 等词。例如：

I've read the book dozens (scores) of times.

我读过这本书好几十次。

Several thousands of women entered the contest.

数千名女子参加了这次比赛。

注意：数词后若不出现名词，则不用介词 of。例如：

Millions (of people) are homeless.

千千万万的人无家可归。

（3）当 dozen，score，hundred，thousand，million 后面的名词有 the，these，those 等特指限定词修饰，或其后接的是 us，them 等宾格人称代词时，后面必须接介词 of。例如：

two dozen of them

它们中的两打

Three hundred of the workers

这些工人中的三百人

（4）注意下列与介词 by 连用的实例：

The fruits are sold by the dozen.

水果按打出售。

The ants swarmed by the hundred(s).

蚂蚁成群结队地移动。

比较：Pack them in dozens.

把它们成打地包起来（即每12个一包）。

四、数词用法的几个易错点

1. "一两天""一两年"之类的表达方法

"一两天"可表示为 a day or two 或 one or two days，但不能表示为 one day or two 或 a or two days。例如：

a year or two/one or two years 一两年

a month or two/one or two months 一两个月

2. "一个半"之类的表达方法

表示"一个半"可用 a... and a half 或 one and a half...。例如：

We waited for an hour and a half. ／We waited for one and a half hours.

我们等了一个半小时。

3. "每隔几……"的表达方法

例如，"每隔一天"可表示为 every two days，every second day，every other day；"每隔三天"可表示为 every three days 或 every third day。

4. "另外几……"的表达方法

例如，"另加两个星期"可表示为 another/a further two weeks 或 two other/more weeks。

 Exercises

Ⅰ. Choose the best answer to complete each sentence.

1. There are _____ days in a year.
   A. three hundreds sixty-five B. three hundreds and sixty-five
   C. three hundred and sixty-five D. three hundred and sixty five
2. My sister is in _____.
   A. Three Class, One Grade B. Class Three, Grade One
   C. Grade One, Class Three D. class three, grade one
3. We are going to learn _____ this term.
   A. book two B. two book C. the book two D. Book Two
4. We can say the number 87,654 in English like this _____.
   A. eighty-seven thousand and six hundred and fifty-four
   B. eighty-seven thousand six hundred and fifty-fourth
   C. eighty-seven thousand six hundred and fifty-four
   D. eighty-seven thousand six hundred and fifty-fourths
5. "The year 1988" should be read "The year _____."
   A. nineteen and eighty-eight
   B. nineteen eighty-eight
   C. one thousand nine hundred and eighty-eight
   D. nineteen hundred and eighty-eight

6. Every day she begins to have breakfast _____.
   A. at ten past seven   B. at seven pass ten   C. on ten past seventh   D. until ten

7. They moved to Hangzhou _____.
   A. in 1960s   B. in 1960's   C. in the 1960s   D. on the 1960's

8. We admired the brave girl _____.
   A. of ten years old   B. ten-year-old   C. at ten old   D. of age of ten

9. There are _____ months in a year. December is the _____ month of the year.
   A. twelve; twelve   B. twelve; twelfth   C. twelfth; twelve   D. twelve; twelveth

10. Ms Lee was _____ to get to school and Mr. Wu was _____.
    A. first; ninth
    B. the first; the ninth
    C. a first; a ninth
    D. the second; the nineth

11. —What's the date today?
    —It's _____.
    A. Sunday   B. time to go   C. cloudy   D. June 6th

12. My best friend is _____ in the row.
    A. a second   B. the second   C. two   D. second

13. Now let's have _____.
    A. the third try   B. a third try   C. third try   D. this third try

14. I sent invitations to 100 people, _____ have replied.
    A. of whom only 30 of them
    B. of whom only 30
    C. only 30 of those who
    D. only 30 who

15. When the bell rang announcing the end of the lecture, the students came out _____.
    A. by twos and threes
    B. by two and three
    C. by two or three
    D. by twos or threes

16. My youngest sister was born _____.
    A. in the year 1984, at 10 a.m. on June 18th
    B. on June 18th at 10 a.m. in the year 1984
    C. at 10 a.m. in the year 1984 on June 18th
    D. at 10 a.m. on June 18th in the year 1984

17. Li Lei helps his mother with the housework every Saturday for about _____.
    A. one and half hours
    B. a half and an hour
    C. an hour and half
    D. one and a half hours

18. This is a _____ building, which is about _____ high.
    A. six-storey; 18 metre
    B. six-storeys; 18-metre
    C. six-storeyed; 18 metres
    D. six-storey; 18-metres

19. The coal production has increased by _____ percent this year compared with last year.
    A. five point six eight
    B. five point sixty-eight
    C. fifth point and six eight
    D. five point and six eight

20. The airport is _____ from my school.

A. two hour's ride B. two hours' ride
C. two hour ride D. two hours ride.
21. _____ people take up English courses of one kind or another, for they have come to realize the importance of learning English.
A. Hundred and thousand B. One hundred and thousand of
C. A large amount of D. Hundreds of thousands of
22. She was so ill that she had to leave her work half-done to ask for _____.
A. a three day sick leave B. three-days sick leaves
C. a sick leave of three days D. three-day sick leaves
23. Shortly after the chaos, two _____ police were sent to the spot to keep order.
A. dozen of B. dozens C. dozen D. dozens of
24. About _____ the people of the patients are male workers.
A. sixty percent B. sixty percent of
C. percent sixty D. sixty percents of
25. He came to Florida in _____.
A. forty B. forties C. late forties D. his early forties
26. — When is your birthday?
 — It's on Sunday, _____.
A. fifth October B. five October
C. the fifth of October D. the five of October
27. I _____ met him in Guangzhou in 1997.
A. the first B. the firstly C. first D. first time
28. Mark and I went to the cinema but we weren't able to get tickets for _____.
A. two of us B. the two of us C. the second of us D. second of us
29. _____ people have visited the _____ pyramid.
A. Two millions of; 500-foot-high B. Several millions of; 500-feet-high
C. Two million; 500-feet-high D. Millions of; 500-foot-high
30. Staying in a hotel for a day is _____ renting a house in the country for a week.
A. twice more than B. twice as much as
C. as much as twice D. as much twice as
31. The Yangtze River is _____ the Pearl River.
A. three times long as B. three times as long as
C. as three times longer as D. as long three times as
32. —What time is it now?
A. —Seven and thirty. B. —Seven thirty. C. —Thirty seven. D. —Seven-thirty.
33. We have to write a _____ composition every other week.
A. six-hundred-words B. six-hundreds-words
C. six-hundreds-word D. six-hundred-word
34. 1880s is read in English as _____.

A. nineteen eightys   B. eighteen eighth

C. eighteen eighties   D. eighteen eighty

35. —How can I get to the zoo?

 —_____ will take you there.

 A. 803 No. Bus   B. No. 803 Bus   C. Bus No. 803   D. Bus 803 No.

36. _____ birthday I got a new schoolbag.

 A. In my ten   B. On my ten   C. In my tenth   D. On my tenth

37. _____ of the people in this village is about three hundred. _____ of them are working outside.

 A. A number; Three-fourth   B. The number; Three quarters

 C. A number; Three-fourths   D. The number; Three-fours

38. I work in a tall building and I work _____ floor.

 A. in twelfth   B. on the twelfth   C. in twelve   D. on the twelve

39. Those pears are for _____.

 A. we three   B. three us   C. three we   D. us three

40. Great changes have taken place in this region in the past _____.

 A. twenties years or so   B. twenty year or so

 C. or so twenty years   D. twenty years or so

41. Be nice to her. She is only _____.

 A. a twelve years old girl   B. a twelve year's old girl

 C. a girl of twelfth   D. a girl of twelve

42. It is believed that man can reach Mars by _____.

 A. the year 2030   B. years 2030

 C. 2030 year   D. 2030 the year

43. _____ finished writing almost at the same time.

 A. The four   B. The fours   C. Four   D. Fours

44. Anne is _____ girl in her family.

 A. the second shortest   B. a second shortest

 C. second shortest   D. two shortest

45. Professor Wang visits Thailand almost _____.

 A. twice a year   B. a twice year   C. a year twice   D. a year two times

46. We met _____ schoolmate of yours in Kunming.

 A. any one   B. a certain   C. a some   D. certain

47. Both of them think _____ is quite interesting.

 A. the fortieth part   B. the part fortieth

 C. forty part   D. part fourty

48. Light travels at about _____.

 A. 300,000 kilometres a second   B. a second 300,000 kilometres

 C. every second 300,000 kilometres   D. 300,000 kilometre every second

49. _____ of the earth _____ made up of oceans.
   A. Two-third; is   B. Two-thirds; is
   C. Two-third; are   D. Two-thirds; are

50. _____ of the population in this city _____ minority nationalities.
   A. Three fifth; are   B. Three fifths; are
   C. Third fifth; are   D. Third fives; is

Ⅱ. Identify the mistake in each sentence and then correct it.

1. About three-fifth of the workers in that factory are young people.
2. When he was in his fifty, he moved to Finland.
3. 469 is four hundreds and sixty-nine.
4. The sun is 93 millions miles away from the earth.
5. This big plant has a thousand of workers.
6. Hundred of people attended the lecture yesterday evening.
7. They said they lived a hard life in forties.
8. 555 is five hundred fifty-five.
9. He wrote a two-thousand-words essay.
10. There are about three hundreds people in the parade on National Day.

第九章

形 容 词

第一节 形容词的定义与分类

一、形容词的定义

形容词（Adjective），是指用来描述或修饰名词或代词，表示人或事物的性质、状态、特征或属性的一类词。形容词是许多语言中均有的一种主要词类，常用作定语，也可用作表语、补语或状语。形容词通常置于其修饰的名词之前，且多数形容词具有比较等级。

二、形容词的分类

1. 前置形容词

前置形容词是指位于所修饰名词之前的形容词，用以描述或限定名词。例如：

a pretty woman　　　a handsome man

2. 后置形容词

后置形容词是指位于所修饰名词之后的形容词，通常为主语补足语或宾语补足语。

（1）常用的后置形容词有：

afraid → be afraid　　alone → be alone　　　asleep → fall asleep
awake → be awake　　likely → be likely

（2）修饰词尾为-body，-one，-thing 等不定代词时，采用后位修饰。例如：

anyone happy　　　anything suitable　　　everybody absent　　everything edible
nothing much　　　someone important　　　something special

（3）当 else 作为形容词，表示"别的，其他的"时，位于疑问词以及 no-，any-．some- 等词后面。例如：

Who else has been to the commodity fair?

Jack has to prepare for something else.

（4）说明数词的度量衡性质时，采用后位修饰。例如：
Bingo is a dog. He is two years old and fifty centimeters tall, but his dog house is five feet long, three feet wide and six feet high.

注意：大多数形容词兼具前置形容词与后置形容词性质。例如：
This is a big house.
This house is big.

第二节 形容词的构成与用法

一、形容词的构成

（1）许多形容词是规则动词的现在分词（-ing）或过去分词（-ed）形式。例如：

satisfy	满意 → satisfying	令人满意的	satisfied	感到满意的
relax	放松 →relaxing	令人放松的	relaxed	感到放松的
excite	激动 → exciting	令人激动的	excited	感到激动的
tire	疲倦 → tiring	令人疲倦的	tired	感到疲倦的

I've had a tiring day, so I'm very tired now.
我度过了疲劳的一天，所以我现在很累。
The film I saw last night was very exciting.
我昨晚看的那场电影太好看了。
I was so excited that I couldn't speak.
我激动得说不出话了。

注意：-ing 表示主动意义，-ed 表示被动意义。

（2）一部分形容词由表示身体部位或其他物品组成部分的名词加后缀-ed 构成。例如：
a red-haired woman 一个红发女人
a big-nosed man 一个大鼻子男人
black-eyed peas 一堆豇豆
leather-jacketed teenagers 一群穿皮夹克的少年

注意：名词用作形容词时，复数形式不用加-s。
a 12-year-old boy（not：a 12-years-old boy） 一个12岁的男孩
a ten-dollar bill（not：a ten-dollars bill） 一份十美元的账单

（3）当两个名词并列（名词＋名词或者复合名词）时，第一个名词作为形容词修饰第二个名词。例如：
the city walls 城墙
the computer keyboard 电脑键盘
a business partner 一位生意伙伴

通常第一个名词修饰第二个名词的这一结构可用于下列情形中。
①构建事物与事物之间或者事物与一座城市之间的关联（与所有格无关，因此不用

"'s"形式）。例如：

  the kitchen table 餐桌   the church choir 教堂唱诗班
  London Transport 伦敦公交系统 York Minster 约克大教堂

②表达时间或节日。例如：

  the winter holiday 寒假   a weekend trip 一次周末旅行
  Christmas carols 圣诞颂歌   a birthday car 一张生日贺卡

③表达衣物、设备、交通工具等的用途。例如：

  football boots 足球鞋   a tennis racket 一只网球拍
  a pencil sharpener 一只转笔刀 the school bus 校车

④物品的用途经常用动词的-ing形式来表示

  a frying pan 一个煎锅   a washing machine 一台洗衣机
  a shopping bag 一个购物袋   a swimming pool 一个游泳池

⑤表示文学、电影、音乐、绘画等艺术题材。例如：

  crime stories 犯罪故事   action film 动作片
  disco music 迪斯科音乐   performance art 行为艺术

⑥三个或三个以上名词组合在一起时，也可应用此种结构。例如：

  the World Football Champion 世界足球锦标赛
  the UK Energy Center(UKERC) 英国能源研究中心

二、形容词的用法

（1）作定语。例如：

The company is in a difficult situation.

（2）作表语。例如：

The shop assistant is very responsible.

（3）作主语或宾语。此时，形容词处于"定冠词+形容词"的结构中，已被名词化。

①the+形容词，表示具有同一特征的人，含复数语意。例如：

  the rich = rich people
  the poor = poor people
  the blind = blind people

②the+国名形容词，表示具有相同国籍的人。例如：

  the English = English people
  the Chinese = Chinese people

③the+分词，当指示人时，单、复数按语意而定。例如：

The injured will be sent to hospital.
The accused was fined twenty thousand dollars.

（4）作宾语补足语。例如：

Some people find the transportation in this district not so convenient.

（5）作主语补足语。例如：

He spent seven days in the wind and snow, cold and hungry.

（6）作感叹词。例如：

Sorry！Fantastic！Wonderful！

三、形容词的比较级

1. 同级比较

（1）升级比较，表示形容词的程度一样，其结构为：

A 如同 B 一样的……→ A + be 动词 + as + 形容词原级 + as + B

例如：Marry is as tall as Jane.

（2）降级比较，表示形容词的程度较少，其结构为：

A 不如 B……→ A + be 动词 + not as + 形容词原级 + as + B

例如：Tom is not as tall as William.

2. 比较级

（1）升级比较，表示形容词的程度较多，其结构为：

A 比 B……→ A + be 动词 + 形容词比较级 + than + B

例如：Shirley is taller than Emily.

当描述 A 在 A 与 B 中较……，即表示形容词在两者中程度较多时，结构为：

A 比 B……→ A + be 动词 + the + 形容词比较级 + 介词短语

例如：Shirley is the taller of the two girls.

（2）降级比较，表示形容词的程度较少，其结构为：

A 不比 B……→ A + be 动词 + less + 形容词原级 + than + B

例如：Fred is less tall than Milo.

= Fred is not as tall as Milo.

= Fred is shorter than Milo.

当描述 A 在 A 与 B 中比较不……，即表示形容词在两者中程度较少时，结构为：

A 不比 B……→ A + be 动词 + less + 形容词比较级 + 介词短语

例如：Fred is the less taller of the two.

3. 最高级

（1）升级比较，表示形容词的程度最多，其结构为：

A 在范围中最……→ A + be 动词 + the + 形容词最高级 + 介词短语

例如：Jackson is the tallest boy in his class.

= Jackson is taller than all other boys in his class.

= Jackson is taller than any other boy in his class.

= No other boys are taller than Jackson in his class.

= No other boys are as tall as Jackson in his class.

（2）降级比较，表示形容词的程度最少，其结构为：

A 在范围中最不……→ A + be 动词 + the least + 形容词原级 + 介词短语

例如：Jackie is the least tall in his class.

= Jackie is shorter than all other boys in his class.

= Jackie is shorter than any other boy in his class.

= No other boys are shorter than Jackie in his class.
= No other boys are as short as Jackie in his class.

4. 形容词比较级的变化规则

（1）一般单音节词和少数以 -er，-ow 结尾的双音节词，比较级在后面加 -er。

单音节词，例如：

small→smaller   short→shorter   tall→taller   great→greater

双音节词，例如：

clever→cleverer   narrow→narrower

（2）以不发音 e 结尾的单音节词，比较级在原级后加 -r。例如：

large→larger   nice→nicer   true→truer

（3）在重读闭音节（即：辅音+元音+辅音）中，先双写末尾的辅音字母，再加 er。例如：

big→bigger   hot→hotter   fat→fatter

（4）以"辅音字母+y"结尾的双音节词，把 y 改为 i，再加 er。例如：

easy→easier   heavy→heavier   busy→busier   happy→happier

（5）其他双音节词和多音节词，在前面加 more。例如：

beautiful→more beautiful   different→more different   easily→more easily

 Exercises

Ⅰ. Choose the best answer to complete each sentence.

1. Jack didn't do _____ in the exam, but his exam results are _____ than last year's.
   A. bad; worse   B. good; better   C. well; better   D. well; worse

2. Which animal do you like _____, cat or dog?
   A. very much   B. best   C. better   D. well

3. We can jump _____ on the moon than on the earth.
   A. more high   B. much   C. high   D. much higher

4. When she heard the good news, she felt _____.
   A. happier   B. happiest   C. happy   D. happily

5. The _____ she is, the _____ she feels.
   A. busy; happy   B. busiest; happiest   C. busier; happier   D. busy; happily

6. I don't feel very _____ today.
   A. good   B. well   C. nice   D. fine

7. I think English is as _____ as maths.
   A. important   B. more important   C. most important   D. importanter

8. That building is about 150 meters _____.
   A. tall   B. high   C. taller   D. higher

9. China has a larger population than _____ in the world.
   A. all the countries   B. every country   C. any country   D. any other country

10. The sick boy is getting _____ day by day.
    A. worse   B. bad   C. badly   D. worst
11. The smile on my father's face showed that he was _____ with me.
    A. sad   B. pleased   C. angry   D. sorry
12. —What animals do you like _____?
    —I like pandas.
    A. better   B. best   C. very   D. well
13. We are going to do our work better with _____ money and _____ people.
    A. less; fewer   B. less; less   C. fewer; fewer   D. fewer; less
14. The boy is _____ than his brother.
    A. two years older   B. two years elder   C. two-year older   D. two-year elder
15. On the moon, things aren't _____ they are on the earth.
    A. so heavy as   B. as heavier as C. as heavy than D. heavy than
16. The Changjiang River is one of the _____ in China.
    A. longer river   B. longest river C. longest rivers D. long rivers
17. It's _____ today than yesterday.
    A. cold   B. colder   C. more colder   D. many colder
18. Please be _____ next time.
    A. carefulest   B. more careful   C. carefuler   D. the most careful
19. Which do you like _____, pork, beef or chicken?
    A. good   B. well   C. better   D. best
20. What is _____ food in the U.S.A?
    A. very popular   B. more popular   C. the most popular D. most popular
21. My brother is _____ to lift the heavy box.
    A. enough strong B. strong enough C. too strong   D. strong
22. The little girl was afraid of staying _____ in the _____ house.
    A. alone; alone   B. alone; lonely C. lonely; lonely D. lonely; alone
23. —Do you like Beijing Opera?
    —Yes. It sounds nice. But it is _____ for me to learn.
    A. hardly   B. hard   C. good   D. best
24. The cheese cake tasted so _____ that the kids asked for more.
    A. delicious   B. well   C. bad   D. badly
25. —Is chemistry more difficult than physics?
    —No, chemistry isn't as _____ as physics.
    A. easy   B. difficult   C. easier   D. more difficult
26. It takes _____ time to go there by plane than by train.
    A. less   B. little   C. more   D. fewer
27. Of the four seasons, the _____ time to come to Hangzhou is in spring.
    A. good   B. well   C. better   D. best

28. My brother doesn't like studying. He watches TV for _____ two hours every day.
    A. less than   B. more than   C. little than   D. much than
29. The question is _____ than the last one.
    A. very easy   B. much easy   C. very easier   D. much easier
30. Our classroom is _____ in the whole school.
    A. cleanest   B. the cleanest   C. cleaner   D. the cleaner

II. Identify the mistake in each sentence and then correct it.

1. Last Sunday, police cars hurried to the taller building in New York.
2. She is very taller than Anna.
3. After an hour or so we began to feel very frightening.
4. I'm sure we will have a wonderfully time together.
5. I used to play ping-pang a lot in my spare time, but now I am interesting in football.
6. After learning the basics of the subject, nothing else seemed very practically to me.
7. Finding information on the net is easily.
8. Yes, a concert can be very excited.
9. However, we seldom felt lonely or helplessly.
10. People in industrial countries can expect to live for twice so long as people who lived a few hundred years ago.

第十章

副　　词

第一节　副词的定义与作用

一、副词的定义

副词（Adverb），是指在句子中表示行为或状态特征的一类词。通常用以修饰动词、形容词、其他副词或全句，表示时间、地点、程度、方式等概念。

二、副词的作用

（1）修饰动词。例如：
Alice enjoyed a romantic candle-lit dinner with her boyfriend leisurely
爱丽丝悠闲地和她男朋友享受了一顿完美的烛光晚餐。
（2）修饰形容词。例如：
The evening gown looks pretty nice on Marry.
那件晚礼服玛丽穿起来相当漂亮。
（3）修饰名词。例如：
The family next door came from Paris long time ago.
隔壁那户人家很久以前来自巴黎。
（4）修饰全句。例如：
Theoretically, polar bears won't mate with brown bears.
理论上来说，北极熊不会和棕熊交配。
常用于修饰全句的副词有：
basically 基本上，certainly 当然地，frankly 坦白地，ideally 理想地，undoubtedly 无疑地，briefly 简要地，fortunately 幸运地，generally 一般地，obviously 明显地，unfortunately 不幸地，hopefully 希望地。

※修饰全句的副词可与 speaking 搭配：
generally speaking   一般来说
briefly speaking   简单地说
frankly speaking   坦白地说

第二节　副词的分类与构成

一、副词的分类

（一）疑问副词

疑问副词通常置于句首用以提出疑问，表示"何时""何地""为何"以及"如何"等。常见的疑问副词有 When（什么时候）、Where（在哪里）、Why（为什么）、How（如何）。

（1）When 表示询问时间。例如：

——When will the bus come?

——The bus comes every 15 minutes.

（2）Where 表示询问地点。例如：

——Where does she learn to play the guitar?

——She learns to play the guitar here at the Cultural Center.

（3）Why 表示询问原因。例如：

——Why did you come to school late this morning?

——I went to school late this morning because I did not sleep well last night.

（4）How 表示对频率、程度、状况及方法的询问。例如：

①表示询问多久。例如：

——How often do you see each other?

——We meet each other once a month.

②表示询问程度。例如：

——How much does he love her?

——He loves her through and through.

③表示询问状况。例如：

——How's everything going?

——Everything is going well.

④表示询问方法。例如：

——How do you lose so much weight within two weeks?

——I lost the weight by long running every morning.

（二）一般副词

从意义上看，一般副词可分为时间副词、频率副词、地点副词、程度副词、方式副词、表示原因和理由的副词以及表示肯定或否定的副词。同学们需重点掌握的一般副词如下所示。

时间副词：then，now，soon，yesterday，today，tomorrow。
频率副词：always，usually，often，sometimes，seldom，once。
地点副词：here，there，everywhere，far，near，up，across。
程度副词：very，enough，almost，hardly。
方式副词：well，lovely，pretty。
表示原因和理由的副词：consequently，therefore，hence。
表示肯定或否定的副词：yes，absolutely，exactly，surely，certainly，never。

（三）连接副词

连接副词虽然具有连接功能，但在语法上仍是副词。常见的连接副词有：
- however，meanwhile，furthermore，as a result；
- in addition，besides，on top of that，表示除此以外（包括在内）；
- except for，apart from，aside from，表示除此以外（排除在外）。

（四）关系副词

关系副词具有连词与副词的功能，常见的关系副词有 when（指时间）、where（指地点）、why（指原因）、how（指方法），分别用来修饰表示时间、地点、原因与方法的先行词。

1. 限定性定语从句中关系副词的用法

关系副词引导定语从句时，用以修饰先行词所指的时间、地点、原因与方法。限定性定语从句对被修饰的先行词起限定制约作用，不能被省略。关系副词之前的先行词可以省略。例如：

This is the day when they met each other.
这是他们相遇的日子。
It is the building where the conflict occurred.
这是冲突发生的地方。
The response to a stimulus explains the reason why the dog barks.
对刺激的反应说明了狗为什么吠叫的原因。
An expert shows us the method how we can turn leftover food waste into fertilizer for organic gardens.
一位专家告诉我们如何将厨房垃圾变成有机庭园用的肥料。

上述例句可省略先行词，变为：
省略 the day：This is when they met each other.
省略 the building：It is where the conflict occurred.

省略 the reason：The response to a stimulus explains why the dog barks.

省略 the method：An expert shows us how we can turn leftover food waste into fertilizer for organic gardens.

2. 非限定性定语从句中关系副词的用法

关系副词的非限定用法，目的在于补述，需要在关系副词前面加上逗号。此时，关系副词所引导的不是定语从句，而是独立分句，用以补述主句的不足之处。例如：

At eight o'clock on every Monday night, when she has her math class.（补述时间）

Hangzhou, where West Lake is located, impresses its visitors with beautiful scenery.（补述地点）

His claim of sunflowers as bananas, the reason why he was harshly criticized, was known to the world as a joke.（补述原因）

This is the method, how I open the door, without other's help.（补述方法）

二、副词的构成规则

1. 规则变化

（1）形容词词尾加 ly。例如：

abrupt→abruptly：The car turned abruptly on the street.

careful→carefully：We carefully assessed the report.

quick→quickly：She runs quickly.

（2）词尾去 y 加 ily。例如：

easy→easily：They can work with computers easily.

happy→happily：I can get along with colleagues easily and happily.

heavy→heavily：The problem weighed heavily on her mind.

（3）词尾 le 变成 ly。例如：

possible→possibly：This disease can possibly be cured.

simple→simply：Simply put, it is very simple to be happy, but it is very difficult to be simple.

comfortable→comfortably：They live comfortably.

（4）词尾 ue 去 e 加 ly。例如：

true→truly：They love each other truly.

（5）词尾 ll 加 y。例如：

dull→dully：This knife cuts dully.

full→fully：We reported the event fully.

（6）词尾 ic 加 ally。例如：

automatic→automatically：The robot arm operates automatically.

historic→historically：The exchange rate to convert Euros into Dollars hit historically high in February.

（7）现在分词或过去分词形式的形容词加 ly。例如：

surprising→surprisingly：The hotel room in Tokyo was surprisingly small.

unexpected→unexpectedly：When I tried to connect my computer with the Internet, an error occurred unexpectedly.

2. 不规则变化

（1）形容词变成副词的不规则变化。例如：

good→well：He writes well.

（2）形容词与副词相同。例如：

early：She was early to the meeting.（形容词）
　　　She came to the meeting early.（副词）

enough：We don't have enough time to finish the project.（形容词）
　　　　They did not work hard enough to finish the project.（副词）

fast：It is a fast train.（形容词）
　　　The high speed train runs very fast.（副词）

far：It is far between two cities.（形容词）
　　　We don't need to walk far to the lake.（副词）

hard：Math is hard to me.（形容词）
　　　We have to study hard to pass the math exam.（副词）

high：Their emotions are high.（形容词）
　　　Their emotions ran high.（副词）

late：It is late now.（形容词）
　　　She arrived late.（副词）

little：We only have little water left.（形容词）
　　　　I little think of him.（副词）

low：The price is low for a tablet computer.（形容词）
　　　The stock price of that company went low due to poor financial statements.（副词）

much：I have much work to do today.（形容词）
　　　　She loves him very much.（副词）

only：He is the only son of Mr. Smith.（形容词）
　　　I only want to be with you.（副词）

Well：We are well.（形容词）
　　　We have been doing well.（副词）

第三节　副词的用法

（1）绝大多数副词可用来修饰动词。例如：

She died *here*.（地点）

She died *yesterday*.（时间）

She died *suddenly*.（方式）

She *nearly* died.（程度）

She has *probably* died. （肯定性）

（2）程度副词可用来修饰形容词、另一副词、动词。例如：

i. She is *rather* silly.

　The room is *very* dark.

　She has an *extremely* difficult problem.

ii. She ran *much* faster than I.

　She speaks English fluently *enough*.

　She works *too* hard.

iii. He loves her wife very *much*.

　I *little* know that he is his brother.

（3）表示程度、时间、地点的副词可用来修饰介词。例如：

i. He is *much* against her proposal.

　He arrived *exactly* at six o'clock.

　He sat *just* behind her.

ii. He came *soon* after noon.

　He left *long* before the war.

iii. He stood *close* beside her.

　It is *near* by the building.

（4）表示程度、时间的副词可用来修饰连词。例如：

i. He fell ill partly because he worked too hard.

　He met her exactly when she was angry.

ii. He got married long before he was graduated.

　He died soon after he got sick.

（5）表示肯定程度、方式的副词可用来修饰整个句子。例如：

i. He will *surely* succeed.

　He will *probably* come.

　We must *positively* get the license.

　Yes, I can. /*No*, I can't.

ii. *Happily*, he was pardoned.

　Luckily, he has tried his best and succeeded.

第四节　副词的比较等级

1. 单音节副词的比较等级

单音节副词的原级、比较级和最高级形式如下例：

hard→harder→hardest

—You worked hard.

—You worked harder than me.

= I didn't work as hard as you.

—You worked hardest in our office.

fast→faster→fastest

—He ran fast.

—He ran faster than me.

—Among us, he ran fastest.

soon→sooner→soonest

late→later→latest

early→earlier→earliest

2. 两个以上音节的副词的比较等级

两个以上音节的副词原级、比较级和最高级形式如下例：

often→more often→most often

kindly→more kindly→most kindly

carefully→more carefully→most carefully

—He drives carefully.

—He drives more carefully than she.

—He drives most carefully among his classmates.

quickly→more quickly→most quickly

3. 副词比较级与最高级的不规则变化

副词比较级与最高级的不规则变化如下例：

well→better→best

—She writes well.

—She writes better than her brother.

= Her brother does not write so well as she.

—She wrote best in the contest.

badly→worse→worst

much→more→most

 **Exercises**

Ⅰ. Choose the best answer to complete each sentence.

1. After a long walk, little Jim was hungry and tired. He could _____ walk any father.
   A. suddenly   B. hardly   C. luckily   D. mostly
2. Write _____ and try not to make any mistakes.
   A. as careful as possible   B. as carefully as you can
   C. most careful   D. more careful
3. What _____ wind! It's blowing _____.
   A. a strong; strongly   B. strong; strongly   C. a strong; big   D. strong; strong

4. — "_____ and _____ are we going to have the meeting?"
   — "At half past eight in our school."
   A. What; where   B. When; how   C. Who; where   D. When; where

5. She walked so _____ that she missed the last bus.
   A. fast   B. quietly   C. brightly   D. slowly

6. Last time Mary's exam results were the best in our class. This time Alice took first place _____.
   A. carefully   B. nearly   C. clearly   D. instead

7. Which do you like _____, apples, oranges or pears?
   A. good   B. well   C. better   D. best

8. It was _____ cold yesterday. William caught a bad cold. He can't go to school today.
   A. much too   B. too much   C. very much   D. much

9. His school is in the northeast, thousands of kilometers _____.
   A. away   B. long   C. out   D. far

10. Her bike is not new, and mine is not new _____.
    A. too   B. also   C. either   D. so

11. The Internet is very useful for us. We can find information _____.
    A. easy   B. easily   C. hard   D. hardly

12. As we all know, smoking is bad for us, _____ for children.
    A. especially   B. recently   C. probably   D. nearly

13. I heard that the airplane has _____ landed at the airport.
    A. success   B. successful   C. successfully   D. succeed

14. Because of having parents' love, I can grow up _____.
    A. happy   B. happily   C. happier   D. more happily

15. —Does Alice often work until 2 a.m?
    —No, she _____ does.
    A. nearly   B. certainly   C. seldom   D. always

16. — I didn't know you take a bus to school.
    — Oh, I _____ take a bus, but it is snowing today.
    A. hardly   B. never   C. sometimes   D. usually

17. — Were you often late for school last term, Tom?
    —No, _____. I got to school early every day.
    A. always   B. usually   C. sometimes   D. never

18. The woman looked at the man _____.
    A. pleasant   B. scary   C. friendly   D. angry

19. —How _____ do you weigh?
    —About 50 kilograms.
    A. tall   B. large   C. many   D. much

20. He spoke _____ quickly for me to follow.

A. so　　　　　　B. too　　　　　　C. such　　　　　D. very

21. We can't praise her _____ much.

    A. too　　　　　B. very　　　　　C. so　　　　　D. only

22. _____, John passed the test.

    A. Luckier　　　B. Lucky　　　　C. Luck　　　　D. Luckily

23. I want to go _____ to study fashion design next year.

    A. board　　　　B. abroad　　　　C. aboard　　　D. broad

24. — How _____ will Tom come here?

    — In five minutes.

    A. long　　　　　B. often　　　　　C. soon　　　　D. fast

25. The old woman lived in the house _____.

    A. aloud　　　　B. along　　　　　C. alone　　　　D. lonely

26. He has worked on his homepage _____.

    A. late　　　　　B. lately　　　　　C. last　　　　　D. latest

27. Tim worked _____ in his youth.

    A. hard　　　　　B. hardly　　　　　C. tired　　　　D. busy

28. Tom was away from home for quite a bit and _____ saw his family.

    A. frequently　　B. seldom　　　　C. always　　　D. usually

29. Thank you for your directions to the market; we wouldn't have found it _____.

    A. nowhere　　　B. however　　　　C. otherwise　　D. instead

30. The aim of education is to teach young people to think for themselves and not follow others _____.

    A. blindly　　　　B. unwillingly　　　C. closely　　　D. carefully

Ⅱ. Identify the mistake in each sentence and then correct it.

1. I think I liked those classes because I felt that they helped me understand what the world works.

2. Unfortunate, there are too many questions for me to answer.

3. She called 119 immediate.

4. Therefore, there are still some countries where people have shorter lives.

5. I told mother, father, sister and all my friends here that a great time I had.

6. Whenever I see them I will often think of my English teacher.

7. But one of the best players in our team told me just then that he wouldn't play basketball anymore.

8. I promise to return back before 10.

9. It was real very dangerous. You might have injured yourself.

10. The workers warm welcomed us at their offices.

第十一章

介　词

第一节　介词的定义及用法

一、介词的定义

介词（Preposition），又称作前置词，是英语中使用最活跃的词类之一，表示名词、代词等与句中其他词的关系，在句中不能单独作句子成分。介词后面一般跟有名词、代词或相当于名词的其他词类、短语或从句作为其宾语，表示与其他成分的关系。介词可与其宾语构成介词词组，在句中作状语、表语、补语或介词宾语。例如：in front of, out of, instead of, far from, apart from 等。

通常介词可以分为时间介词、地点介词、方式介词、原因介词、数量介词和其他介词。例如：before, after, in, on, under, about, to, for, of 等。

二、常见介词的用法

介词在英语词汇中所占比例很小，但其用法非常灵活、复杂。下列为英语中十分常见的介词及其用法。

(1) About，表示关于、附近、大约、周围、随身。例如：
There are about nine horses in the picture.
图片里大约有九匹马。

(2) Above，表示在……上、高出、以上、超过、在……上游。例如：
The plane is flying above the clouds.
飞机在云上飞行。
I think the man is above forty years old.
我想那人有四十多岁了。

(3) Across，表示横过、对面、交叉、在……的对面。例如：

We used to live across the street.

我们曾经住在这条街的对面。

（4）After，表示在……后面、依照。例如：

He went home after school.

他放学后就回家了。

Read after me, please.

请跟我朗读。

（5）Against，表示撞到、靠着、反对、违背。例如：

The car hit against the tree.

汽车撞了树。

He is standing against the wall.

他靠墙站着。

（6）Along，表示沿着、顺着。例如：

They are walking along the avenue.

他们沿着林荫路散步。

（7）Among，表示在……当中（三者或三者以上）。例如：

He is the oldest among them.

他是他们当中年纪最大的。

（8）Around，表示在……的周围、在……那边。例如：

They sat around the table enjoying the feast.

他们绕桌而坐享受大餐。

There is a laundry around the corner.

拐角处有一家洗衣店。

（9）As，表示作为。例如：

He doesn't like people to treat him as a patient.

他不喜欢人们把他当病人对待。

（10）At，表示在……时刻、在……点钟、在……岁时、向、在……之中、按……速度、值（卖）……钱、在……（强调地点）。例如：

He always gets up at five in the morning.

他时常早上五点钟起床。

He shot at the bird but missed it.

他朝鸟开枪，但是没射中。

The car goes at eighty km an hour.

汽车以每小时八十公里的速度行驶。

（11）Before，表示在……的前面（位置）、在……之前（时间）。例如：

He took a picture before the church.

他在教堂前照了张照片。

He can't finish his work before weekend.

周末前他完不成工作。

（12）Behind，表示在……的后面（位置）、落后于、不如、迟于、晚于（时间）。例如：

What is behind the door?

门后有什么？

All of us are behind him in science subjects.

我们理科都不如他。

（13）Below，表示在……之下、低于。例如：

There are several lamps below the ceiling.

天花板下面有几盏灯。

（14）Beside，表示在……的旁边、在……之外、与……相比。例如：

He found the footprints beside the river.

他在河边发现了脚印。

Beside yours, my cellphone is too old.

与你的手机相比，我的手机旧多了。

（15）Besides，表示除……之外，还有……。例如：

We are all here besides Lily.

除莉莉外，我们也都来了。

（16）Between，表示在……两者之间。例如：

The relation between the two countries has improved as expected.

两国的关系正如预料的那样得到了改善。

（17）Beyond，表示在……那边。例如：

The restaurant you are looking for is beyond the street, you can't miss it.

你要找的餐馆在街的那边，你不会找不到的。

（18）But，表示除去。例如：

He left nothing but a letter.

他除了一封信，什么也没留下。

（19）By，表示被……、在……的近旁、在……之前、不迟于、以……为手段。例如：

The classroom was cleaned by the student on duty.

教室由值日生打扫干净了。

Linda came to China by air.

琳达是乘飞机来中国的。

（20）Down，表示沿着……往下。例如：

She walked down the street.

她沿着街道走。

（21）Except，表示除……之外。例如：

He remembered nothing except the accident.

他除了那场事故以外什么都记不起来了。

（22）For，表示为……。例如：

He works for his country.

他为祖国工作。

（23）From，表示从……、来自……、因为……。例如：

Where are you from?

你是哪里人？

He suffered from a serious illness.

他因生大病而受苦。

（24）In，表示在……、在……之内、从事于……、按照……、穿着……。例如：

I was born in 1992.

我生于1992年。

I try to finish the program in two weeks.

我尽量用两周时间完成这个项目。

He spent little time in reading.

他读书时间很少。

The man in black jacket is my uncle.

穿黑夹克的那个人是我的叔叔。

（25）Like，表示像……、如同……。例如：

The twins are like each other.

这对双胞胎长得很像。

（26）Near，表示靠近……。例如：

There are some trees near the house.

房子附近有一些树。

（27）Of，表示……的、属于……。例如：

This is a map of the world.

这是一张世界地图。

（28）Off，表示离开……、在……之外。例如：

Remember to get off the bus at the fifth stop.

记得在第五个站下车。

I lived in a village a little way off the town.

我以前住在离镇不远的一个村庄里。

（29）On，表示在……之上、在……之时。例如：

My pen is on the table.

我的笔在桌子上。

（30）Out of，表示从……出来、在……之外。例如：

The dog ran out of the kitchen.

狗从厨房里跑出来。

（31）Outside，表示在……外边。例如：

Please wait outside the gate.

请在门外等着。

（32）Over，表示在……之上、遍于……之上、越过……。例如：

109

There is a light over the desk.

桌子上方有盏灯。

He is over fifty years old.

他有五十多岁。

（33）Past，表示越过……、过……、超越……。例如：

The students walked past the office building.

学生们走过了办公大楼。

It is ten past four.

现在是四点十分。

（34）Round，表示围着……、绕过……、在……周围。例如：

The earth goes round the sun.

地球绕着太阳转。

（35）Since，表示自……以后、自……以来。例如：

I haven't written home since christmas.

自圣诞节以来，我未曾写信回家。

（36）Through，表示经过……、穿过……（立体层面）。例如：

They went through the forest.

他们穿过了森林。

（37）Throughout，表示遍及……、在各处。例如：

The news spread throughout the country.

这个消息在全国四处传播。

（38）Till，表示直到……、在……以前。例如：

He won't come back till next week.

他直到下周才回来。

We'll be home till six.

六点以前我们都会在家。

（39）To，表示到……、向……、趋于。例如：

How long is it from birth to death?

生死之间的距离有多远？

（40）Under，表示在……之下、低于。例如：

There are some boxes under the bed.

床底下有一些箱子。

These students are under twenty years old.

这些学生们不到二十岁。

（41）Until，表示直到……、在……以前。例如：

It was not until last week that I got a reply.

直到上周，我才得到回复。

（42）Up，表示在……上面、在……上。例如：

He went up the stairs.

他上了楼。

（43）Upon，表示在……之上、迫近……。例如：
It's not polite to look down upon others.
蔑视别人是不礼貌的。

（44）Within，表示在……之内。例如：
You must finish the work within two weeks.
你必须两周内完成这项工作。

（45）Without，表示没有、不、在…之外。例如：
We can't manage it without your help.
没有你的帮助，我们就做不成这事。
We couldn't live without air and water.
没有空气和水，我们就不可能生存。

第二节　介词的区分与辨别

（一）表示地点的介词

1. at，in，on，to

At，表示：①在小地方；②在……附近、旁边。例如：
We had dinner at a restaurant in Attle Borough.
我们在阿特尔·伯勒的一家餐厅里吃饭。

In，表示：①在大地方；②在……范围之内。例如：
in the north of China　在中国的北部

On，表示毗邻、接壤、在……上面。例如：
He was able to spend only a few dags at a time on the island.
他每次去岛上都只能待几天。

To，表示在……范围外、不接壤、到……。例如：
to the north of China　在中国以北

2. above，over，on

Above，表示一个物体高过另一个物体，不强调是否垂直，与 below 相对。例如：
The butterfly is flying above my head.
这只蝴蝶在我头顶上空飞舞着。

Over，一个物体在另一个物体的垂直上方，与 under 相对。另外，over 与物体有一定的空间，不直接接触。例如：
The bridge is over the river.
河上有一座桥。

On，表示一个物体在另一个物体表面上，并且两个物体互相接触，与 beneath 相对。例如：

He puts his notebook on the desk.

他把他的笔记本放在书桌上。

3. below, under

Under，表示在……正下方。例如：

There is a dog under the table.

桌子底下有一只狗。

Below，表示在……下，不一定在正下方。例如：

Please sign your name below the line.

请在这条线下签上你的名字。

4. in front of, in the front of

In front of，意思是"在……前面"，指甲物在乙物之前，两者互不包括。其反义词为 behind（在……的后面）。例如：

There are some trees in front of the house.

房子前面有些树。

In the front of，意思是"在……的前部"，指甲物在乙物的内部的前部。其反义词为 at/in the back of（在……范围内的后部）。例如：

There is a clock in the front of our classroom.

我们的教室前边有一个钟（钟在教室里）。

Our headmaster stands in the front of the classroom.

我们的校长站在教室前（校长在教室里）。

5. beside, behind, between

Beside，表示在……旁边。例如：

On the table beside an empty plate was a pile of books.

桌上空盘子的旁边是一堆书。

Behind，表示在……后面。例如：

Keith wandered along behind him.

基思跟在他后面闲逛。

Between，表示在两者之间。例如：

He had to decide between the two.

他必须在两者之间作出抉择。

6. on the tree, in the tree

On the tree，表示长在树上（如果实）

In the tree，表示外来的落在树上（如小鸟）

（二）表示时间的介词

1. in, on, at

In，表示较长时间，如世纪、朝代、时代、年、季节、月及一般（非特指）的早、中、晚等。例如：

in the 21th century, in the 1950s, in 1989, in summer, in January;

in the morning, in one's life, in one's thirties。

On，表示具体某一天及其早、中、晚。例如：

on May 1st, on Monday, on New Year's Day, on a cold night in January;
on a fine morning, on Sunday afternoon。

At，表示某一时刻或较短暂的时间，或泛指节日等。例如：

at 3∶15, at this time of year, at the beginning of, at the end of…;
at the age of…, at Christmas, at night, at noon, at this moment。

注意：在 last，next，this，that，some，every 等词之前一律不用介词，也不用冠词。例如：

What are you going to do this afternoon?

今天下午你要做什么?

He visits his parents every weekend.

他每周末都去看望父母。

She is going to Beijing next Monday.

她下个星期一去北京。

2. in，after

"in + 一段时间"，表示将来的一段时间以后，由"How soon"对其提问。("for + 一段时间"，表示某动作或情况持续的时间，动词用延续性动词，由"How long"对其提问。)例如：

He'll finish the boat in ten days.

十天后他将造完船。

"after + 一段时间"，表示过去的一段时间以后。例如：

After a month, they went back home to America.

一个月之后，他们返回了美国。

"after + 将来的时间点"，表示将来的某一时刻以后。

The day after christmas is generally a busy one for retailers.

圣诞节后的那一天零售商一般都比较忙。

3. from，since，for

From，仅说明什么时候开始，仅说明动作开始的时间，不说明某动作或情况持续多久。句子的谓语可用过去、现在、将来的某种时态。例如：

from now on　从现在开始

Since，表示从某时一直延续至说话时刻，意思是"自（某具体时间）以来"。后接时间点，常用作完成时态谓语的时间状语。例如：

since liberation　自从解放以来

For，指动作延续贯穿整个过程；后接时间段，主句一般用完成时态。例如：

They have been close friends for years.

他们多年来一直是好朋友。

注意：

（1）since the war 指"自从战争结束以来"；若指"自从战争开始以来"，须用"since

the beginning of the war"。

（2）不要将 since 与 after 混淆。

请比较下面两句话。

He has lived here since 1949.

自从 1949 年以来，他一直住在这儿（指一段时间，强调时间段）。

He began to live here after 1949.

从 1949 年以后，他开始住在这儿（指一点时间，强调时间点）。

4. after，behind

After，主要用于表示时间。例如：after tomorrow（明天之后）。

Behind，主要用于表示位置。例如：behind the door（在门后）。

（三）表示运动的介词

1. across，through，past

Across，表示横穿，即从物体表面通过（二维平面）。例如：

walk across the road   过马路

Through，表示穿过，即从物体内部穿过（三维立体）。例如：

walk through the forest   穿过森林

Past，表示从物体的旁边通过。例如：

Walk past the store   从商店旁边经过

2. from...to...

From...to...，表示从……到……。例如：

from my home to my school   从我家到学校

3. to，towards，onto，into，out of

To，表示到某处去。例如，go to school（到学校去）。

Towards，表示朝着某个方向去。例如，towards the door（朝门口）。

Onto，表示放到某物上面。例如，onto the field（入场）。

Into，表示进入物体内部。例如，go into a room（进入一个房间）。

Out of，表示从物体内部出来。例如，get out of the room（从房间里出来）。

4. up，down

Up，表示向上。例如，stand up（起立）；turn up（将音量调高）。

Down，表示向下。例如，sit down（坐下）；turn down（将音量调低）。

5. over，around，along

Over，表示从上方跃过。例如，over the southern tip of Florida（越过佛罗里达州南端）。

Around，表示环绕一圈。例如，around the corner（绕过拐角）。

Along，表示沿着。例如，along the river（沿着河流）。

（四）表示方位的介词

表示方位的介词有 in front of，behind，on，in，near，under，up，between，among 等。其中，between 指在两个人或两个事物之间；among 指在三个或三个以上的人或事物之间。

例如：

between 1793 and 1797　　　　　among young people
1793—1797 年　　　　　　　　　在年轻人当中

（五）表示进行的介词

作表语时，某些介词可以表示"正在进行""正在发生"。例如：
He is at work.
他正在工作。
The house is on fire!
房子着火了！

（六）表示其他意思的介词

1. on，about

On 表示书、文章或演说的内容较为严肃，或为学术性的，多用于正式行文；about 表示内容较为普通，一般不用于正式行文中。例如：
on paper writing and editing about the problem
关于这个问题的论文撰写和编辑

2. by，with，in

By，表示以……方法、手段或泛指某种交通工具。例如，by car（开车）。
With，表示用……工具、手段，一般接具体的工具和手段。例如，with the help of（在……的帮助下）。
In，表示用……方式，用……语言（语调、笔墨、颜色）等。例如，in English（用英语）。

3. except，besides

Except，表示除……之外（不包括在内）；besides 表示除……之外（包括在内）。例如：
Except for Dr. Sun, we went to see the film.（孙医生没去）
Besides Dr. Sun, we also went to see the film.（孙医生也去了）

第三节　常用介词短语

1. at 的常用介词短语

at a stretch 一连，连续地　　　　　at a time 一次，每次
at ease 稍息，安心　　　　　　　　at first sight 一见（钟情）
at first 最初，开始时　　　　　　　at heart 在内心
at home 在家，随便　　　　　　　　at last 最后
at least 至少　　　　　　　　　　　at length 最后，详细地
at most 至多　　　　　　　　　　　at once 立即，同时
at peace（war）处于和平（战争）状态　at play（work）在玩耍（工作）

at present 现在，目前
at the risk of 冒……的风险
at the start 一开头
at times 有时候

at random 随意地，胡乱地
at the same time （与此）同时
at the time 此刻，这时
at will 任意地

2. by 的常用介词短语

by accident 偶然
by all means 想一切办法
by chance 偶然
by choice 出于自愿
by day (night) 白天（夜间）
by mistake 错误地，误把……
by surprise 突然，出其不意

by air 航空
by bus (plane, etc) 坐巴士（飞机等）
by cheque 用支票
by daylight 在大白天
by force 靠武力
by turns 轮流
by the way 顺便说一句

3. in 的常用介词短语

in a sense 从某种意义上说
in advance 事前
in any case (event) 不管怎样，反正
in case 要是，如果
in comparison 比较起来
in debt 负债
in detail 详细地
in general 一般说来
in order to (that) 以便，为了
in part (s) 部分地
in practice 实际上
in regard to 关于
in the end 最后
in time 及时地

in addition (to) 此外（除……之外）
in all 总共
in brief 简而言之
in case of 在……情况下
in danger 处于危险中
in demand 有需求
in fact 实际上
in one's opinion 在（某人）看来
in other words 换句话说
in person 亲自
in public (private) 公开（私下）地
in short 总之
in the middle of 在……中间
in vain 白白地，没有结果

4. on 的常用介词短语

on account of 由于
on board 在船（飞机）上
on duty 值班
on foot 步行
on hand 在身边
on purpose 故意地
on strike 罢工
on the way 在路上
on the top of 在……上面

on behalf of 代表（某人）
on condition 在……条件下
on fire 着火
on guard 警惕地值班
on holiday 在休假
on sale 在出售
on the contrary 相反
on time 准时
on the run 正在逃窜

5. out of 的常用介词短语

out of action 失灵

out of breath 气喘吁吁

out of control 失去控制
out of doors 在户外
out of hand 失去控制
out of reach 无法得到（拿到）
out of temper 发脾气
out of touch（with）和……失去联系
out of use 不再使用

out of danger 脱离危险
out of fashion 过时
out of order 坏了
out of sight 看不见
out of the question 不可能
out of tune 走调
out of work 失业

第四节 省略介词的几种情况

（1）表示时间的短语中如果有 next, last, one, this, every, each, some, any, all 等单词，则不用介词。例如：

Can you come to see me next weekend?
下周末你能来看我吗？
We got married last month.
我们上个月结的婚。
You are welcomed any day.
你哪一天来都欢迎。

（2）在口语中，星期名称前的 on 常被省略。例如：

Why don't you come and play（on）Saturday morning?
星期六早上来玩不好吗？

（3）在不定冠词 a 或 an（a 或 an 的意思是"每一……"）的短语中不用介词。例如：

three meals a day　一日三餐
100 km an hour　每小时 100 公里

（4）what time 前的 at 经常被省略，尤其在口语中。例如：

（At）what time did she say she was arriving?
她说她几点钟到？

（5）含有 height（高度），length（长度），size（尺码），shape（现状），age（年龄），colour（颜色），weight（重量）等的短语在句子中做表语时，短语前不用介词。例如：

She is just the right height to be a model.
她的身高正合适当模特。
What size are your shoes?
你的鞋是多大号的？
Her bag is the same color as mine.
她的包和我的包颜色一样。

（6）在 in the same way, in this way, in another way 等短语中，in 常常被省略。例如：

Please try it again（in）the same way.
请用同样的方法再试一次。

（7）在表示持续一段时间的短语中，for 常被省略。例如：
They stayed there (for) six months.
他们在那里待了6个月。

Exercises

Ⅰ. Choose the best answer to complete each sentence.

1. In many countries, children get gifts _____ Christmas and _____ their birthdays.
   A. on; on　　　　B. at; on　　　　C. in; in　　　　D. in; on

2. —There is nothing _____ tomorrow afternoon, is there?
   —No. We can have a ball game.
   A. on　　　　B. in　　　　C. out　　　　D. up

3. Several friends of mine were born _____ May, 1999.
   A. in　　　　B. at　　　　C. on　　　　D. since

4. He suddenly returned _____ a sunny morning.
   A. on　　　　B. at　　　　C. in　　　　D. during

5. My grandfather was born _____ Sept. 10, 1938.
   A. on　　　　B. in　　　　C. at　　　　D. of

6. The plane is taking off _____ 20 minutes.
   A. in　　　　B. at　　　　C. for　　　　D. still

7. He does his exercises _____ five _____ the afternoon.
   A. on; to　　　　B. at; in　　　　C. by; of　　　　D. at; on

8. The population of the country has grown very fast _____ two hundred years.
   A. for past the　　B. in the pass　　C. in the past　　D. for past

9. They returned to their hometown _____.
   A. next week　　B. in the last week　　C. last week　　D. for a week

10. Great changes in my hometown have taken place _____.
    A. in the last few year　　　　B. in the last few years
    C. last year　　　　　　　　　D. on the last year

11. The kids wake up very early _____ the morning of Christmas Day.
    A. in　　　　B. on　　　　C. for　　　　D. at

12. I wonder why you got up so early _____ this morning.
    A. on　　　　B. /　　　　C. at　　　　D. in

13. He went abroad _____ September 15, 2001 and came back _____ a cold morning this month.
    A. in; on　　　　B. on; in　　　　C. on; on　　　　D. in; in

14. She was born _____ the night of May 11, 1995.
    A. on　　　　B. in　　　　C. at　　　　D. to

15. The Browns came to China _____ 2006.

A. on　　　　　　B. of　　　　　　C. to　　　　　　D. in
16. _____ the morning of November 12, 1975, people came to Beijing to show their mourning _____ the great man.
　　A. On; of　　　B. In; of　　　C. On; for　　　D. At; for
17. The family moved _____ Yangzhou _____ September, 1998.
　　A. /; in　　　B. to; in　　　C. to; on　　　D. in; in
18. I often go _____ school _____ six thirty _____ the morning.
　　A. for; to; in　　　B. to; at; in　　　C. to; for; at　　　D. for; at; to
19. He arrived _____ Wuhan _____ 11:30 _____ March 9.
　　A. at; in; at　　　B. to; on; at　　　C. in; on; at　　　D. in; at; on
20. The doctor worked _____ seven hours _____ a rest.
　　A. for; with　　　B. on; without　　　C. about; having　　　D. for; without
21. He worked on the problem _____ a long time and worked it out _____ himself _____ last.
　　A. for; by; at　　　B. in; with; on　　　C. on; by; in　　　D. for; for; at the
22. A new school will be set up _____ a year.
　　A. for　　　B. in　　　C. after　　　D. on
23. The woman workers had been _____ strike _____ almost a week.
　　A. on; in　　　B. at; in　　　C. on; for　　　D. on; during
24. The old man had lain _____ the ground _____ four hours before they finally found him.
　　A. on; for　　　B. at; in　　　C. on; after　　　D. in; during
25. Mom is coming back _____ an hour.
　　A. after　　　B. for　　　C. in　　　D. before
26. She lived in a remote village _____ the years 1970 – 1980.
　　A. between　　　B. during　　　C. in　　　D. since
27. The Civil War lasted four years and finally the North won _____ the end.
　　A. by　　　B. at　　　C. in　　　D. on
28. The son had finished his homework _____ the time his mother got home.
　　A. until　　　B. by　　　C. at　　　D. when
29. We stayed at the classroom _____ our monitor returned.
　　A. till　　　B. by　　　C. during　　　D. while
30. They didn't leave the bus stop _____ they got on the bus.
　　A. until　　　B. by　　　C. after　　　D. at
31. Don't worry. Mom will return _____.
　　A. before long　　　B. long before　　　C. long long ago　　　D. long ago
32. There lived an old man, fishing at sea _____.
　　A. long before　　　B. before long　　　C. long time ago　　　D. soon
33. It was not _____ she came back.
　　A. long before　　　B. before long　　　C. long time before　　　D. long after

34. I was told that his wife had gone to France _____.
    A. long before   B. shortly after   C. before long   D. long ago
35. I don't like to sit _____ Mike's right. I would like to sit _____ the back row.
    A. on; in   B. in; on   C. on; at   D. at; on
36. There flows a brook _____ red flowers and green grass _____ both sides.
    A. of; with   B. with; on   C. of; at   D. with; in
37. The bird is flying _____.
    A. in the sky   B. in the air   C. in space   D. in sky
38. There is an odd smell _____.
    A. in the air   B. in the open air   C. in the sky   D. in the space
39. They held an interesting ceremony _____.
    A. in the air   B. in the sky   C. in the open air   D. in space
40. The white students sat _____ the classroom while the black _____ the room.
    A. in front of; at back of   B. in the front of; at the back of
    C. in front of; at the back of   D. in the front of; at back of
41. Linda sits _____ the second row, _____ Nancy's left.
    A. on; on   B. in; at   C. at; in   D. in; on
42. Shanghai is _____ the east of China, but Japan is _____ the east of China.
    A. to; in   B. in; to   C. on; to   D. to; on
43. —Can I look up a word _____ your dictionary?
    —I haven't got _____ me.
    A. into; about   B. in; with   C. at; in   D. on; on
44. I don't like cakes _____ meat _____ them.
    A. in; on   B. with; on   C. in; the   D. with; in
45. When you are _____ trouble, you can ask help _____ us.
    A. in; from   B. in; for   C. on; from   D. on; of
46. The shop assistant said they had sold out the shoes _____ your size.
    A. about   B. in   C. to   D. of
47. I saw him leave _____ hurry at the moment.
    A. in a   B. in   C. on   D. on a
48. He put up a painting _____ the wall because there was a hole _____ it.
    A. on; on   B. at; in   C. on; in   D. on; at
49. There is a window _____ the wall.
    A. on   B. to   C. of   D. in
50. This kind of train is made _____ China.
    A. in   B. from   C. at   D. on
51. Any man _____ eyes _____ his head can see that he's exactly absent.
    A. with; on   B. with; in   C. on; with   D. in; with
52. There are some birds singing _____ the trees.

A. in　　　　　　B. on　　　　　　C. at　　　　　　D. from
53. Don't read _____ the sun. It's bad _____ your eyes.
　　A. in; to　　　B. under; for　　C. with; to　　　D. in; on
54. The man _____ a white shirt is my teacher.
　　A. in　　　　　B. on　　　　　　C. of　　　　　　D. at
55. There are so many oranges _____ that tree.
　　A. in　　　　　B. on　　　　　　C. at　　　　　　D. from
56. The boat is passing _____ the bridge.
　　A. through　　　B. below　　　　C. under　　　　D. across
57. Planes are often seen flying _____ the city.
　　A. through　　　B. over　　　　　C. on　　　　　　D. below
58. There is a river running to the east _____ the hill.
　　A. under　　　　B. below　　　　C. over　　　　　D. on
59. Do you see the kite _____ the house?
　　A. over　　　　B. cross　　　　C. on　　　　　　D. above
60. I live _____ the city. _____ I often go to the city by bike.
　　A. 20 miles in the east; However　　　B. to the east 30 miles of; But
　　C. in the east 35 miles from; But　　　D. 40 miles east of; However
61. The man stood _____ the window, watching his kids playing outside.
　　A. in　　　　　B. by　　　　　　C. with　　　　　D. to
62. It seems that the street is too narrow for the bus to go _____.
　　A. through　　　B. across　　　　C. on　　　　　　D. in
63. A mother camel was walking _____ her baby _____ the desert.
　　A. without; along　　B. with; through　　C. next to; pass　　D. beside; through
64. The river runs _____ my hometown.
　　A. across　　　　B. through　　　C. over　　　　　D. from
65. The writer arrived _____ No. 4 Middle School an hour ago.
　　A. at　　　　　B. in　　　　　　C. to　　　　　　D. /
66. Did your mother send you something _____ the end of last week?
　　A. at　　　　　B. by　　　　　　C. in　　　　　　D. to
67. The monument _____ those heroes stands _____ the foot of the mountain.
　　A. of; at　　　B. to; on　　　　C. for; by　　　　D. to; at
68. My aunt lives _____ 68 Chaoyang Street.
　　A. to　　　　　B. of　　　　　　C. at　　　　　　D. on
69. Many people are waiting _____ a bus _____ the bus stop.
　　A. for; in　　　B. on; at　　　　C. with; at　　　　D. for; at
70. Wood can be made _____ paper.
　　A. by　　　　　B. from　　　　　C. of　　　　　　D. into
71. _____ research _____ the ancient culture scientists have put a lot of information

_____ computers.

 A. With; over; at   B. On; at; to
 C. In; about; into   D. For; with; through

72. When you take a piece of ice _____ a warm room, you can see it get smaller and smaller until _____ the end it disappears completely.

 A. in; in   B. out of; at   C. into; in   D. to; by

73. A boy fell accidentally _____ the boat _____ the water.

 A. off; into   B. at; below   C. down; under   D. away; in

74. The desks in the classroom are so close together that it's hard to move _____ them.

 A. among   B. between
 C. in the middle of   D. at the centre of

75. Is there any difference _____ these two idioms?

 A. between   B. to   C. for   D. on

76. The police station is _____ the bank _____ the cinema.

 A. between; and   B. among; and
 C. near; of   D. on; right

77. He is _____ the greatest leaders in the world.

 A. among   B. between   C. in   D. of

78. There is a restaurant _____ our house.

 A. at   B. through   C. across   D. near

79. Our headmaster showed the visitors _____ our campus.

 A. to   B. for   C. around   D. near

80. Nobody knew the secret _____ me.

 A. but   B. beside   C. besides   D. without

81. What do you spend your money on _____ food and clothing?

 A. except   B. besides   C. but   D. without

82. No one knew where the old man lived _____ the girl.

 A. besides   B. and   C. only   D. except

83. _____ the help of the teacher, the boy has made great progress _____ his studies.

 A. For; at   B. Of; for   C. By; on   D. With; in

84. The children are interested _____ this game.

 A. to   B. with   C. in   D. at

85. His mother often helps him _____ maths so he does better _____ maths than others.

 A. with; in   B. on; in   C. in; with   D. with; at

86. I've lost my interest _____ chemistry.

 A. in   B. on   C. at   D. for

87. He drove away _____ the direction of the airport.

 A. in   B. at   C. to   D. for

88. The letter was written _____ ink.

  A. with   B. in   C. by   D. at

89. She tried to get on well _____ her classmates.

  A. with   B. in   C. to   D. at

90. There is something wrong _____ my computer.

  A. at   B. in   C. on   D. with

91. They are filling their bags _____ bread and fruits.

  A. in   B. with   C. of   D. by

92. They usually cover the Christmas trees _____ colour lights.

  A. in   B. use   C. for   D. with

93. His wife was surprised _____ his sudden death.

  A. by   B. with   C. at   D. on

94. The boy cried out _____ the top of his voice.

  A. at   B. in   C. on   D. to

95. We Chinese people are all _____ our motherland.

  A. famous for   B. proud of   C. busy with   D. good at

96. The fine bottle was made _____ glass.

  A. from   B. in   C. of   D. by

97. This is a map _____ London.

  A. in   B. at   C. of   D. on

98. What did you have _____ dinner?

  A. at   B. as   C. for   D. about

99. They were invited to an important banquet _____ the first time _____ their lives.

  A. for; in   B. at; in

  C. on; for   D. in; with

100. My grandpa caught hold _____ me and said, "This is a good lesson _____ you."

  A. of; for   B. for; of

  C. of; of   D. for; for

Ⅱ. Identify the mistake in each sentence and then correct it.

1. His uncle has been ill on bed for two years.
2. During the summer vacation, the boy worked in the farm.
3. Don't read under the strong light.
4. He is very angry to his naughty son for his failing in the exam.
5. He hit me on the face suddenly.
6. My boss is strict to me in my work.
7. The jar is filled of wine.
8. London stands to the Thames.
9. His wife took pride of his great achievements.
10. On my way home, I found I had lost the key of the door.

11. We are discussing to find the answer of the problem.
12. You are required to write your article with your own words.
13. He is the cleverest in all the children in the family.
14. At a clear night, he went out in search of the fortune.
15. Women should be equal with men.
16. She is blind on both her eyes.
17. My uncle is famous as his skill in cooking.
18. I called on my aunt's last night.
19. It is very clever for a dog to save its owner.
20. You should beware to dangers.

第十二章

非谓语动词

第一节 非谓语动词的定义与句法作用

非谓语动词（The Non-Finite Verb），又称非限定动词，是指并非用作句子的谓语、不受主语的人称和数的限制，而是担任其他语法功能的动词。非限定动词有三种形式：不定式（The Infinitive）、分词（The Participle）和动名词（The Gerund）。非谓语动词除了不能独立作谓语外，可承担句子的其他成分。非谓语动词具体的句法作用如表12-1所示。

表12-1 非限定动词的句法作用

句子成分 非限定动词	主语	宾语	主语补语	宾语补语	表语	定语	状语
不定式	√	√	√	√	√	√	√
现在分词			√	√	√	√	√
过去分词			√	√	√	√	√
动名词	√	√	√		√	√	

第二节 非谓语动词的分类及用法

一、不定式

不定式由不定式符号"to"加动词原形构成（有时 to 可省略），其结构为"（to）+ do"。不定式不能单独作谓语，不随主语的人称和数的变化而变化，具有名词、形容词和副词的特征。但不定式仍保留着动词的特征，可以与半助动词或情态动词连用构成复合谓语；可以被状语修饰；如果动词是及物动词，可以带宾语。动词不定式可连同其宾语、状语等一起构成短语，称为不定式短语（The Infinitive Phrase）。不定式短语可在句子中作主语、表语、宾语、定语、状语、宾语补足语和主语补足语。

（一）动词不定式的句法作用

1. 动词不定式作主语

动词不定式作主语时，一般表示具体、个别的、一次性的或具有将来意味的动作。在表示一般抽象概念时多用动名词，有时也可用不定式，二者均可互换使用。例如：

To read/Reading good books makes you happy.

读好书使你快乐。

动词不定式作主语时，谓语动词通常用单数。例如：

To combine theory with practice is a good way of learning.

理论联系实际是学习的一种好方法。

It was his duty *to attend to the matter*.

处理这个问题是他的责任。

It is important for a scientist *to look at matter from the viewpoint of movement*.

科学家以运动的观点看待事物是很重要的。

It was kind of Harry *to give up his seat in the bus to the old woman*.

哈利在公交车上让座给那位老妇人真是太体贴了。

It pays *to read this novel*.

这本小说值得一读。

When to start remains undecided.

出发时间未定。

It's essential *for there to be more houses built next year*.

明年这里建更多的房子是必要的。

2. 动词不定式作表语

动词不定式作表语时，一般表示的是与主语一样的东西，或是主语所产生的结果。例如：

To see is *to believe*.

眼见为实。

To teach is *to learn twice*.

教就是再学习。

3. 动词不定式作宾语

动词不定式作宾语时，一般表示特殊的、具体的、一次性的行为。常见的句型如下：

（1）直接作及物动词的宾语。常见的动词有 afford, agree, aim, apply, arrange, ask, attempt, begin, care, choose（宁愿，偏要）, claim, consent, continue, dare, decide, decline, demand, desire, determine, elect, endeavor, expect, fail, forget, guarantee, hate, help, hope, intend, learn, like, manage, mean, need, offer, plan, pledge, prepare, prefer, pretend, profess, promise, refuse, remember, require, resolve, seek, start, swear, threaten, try, undertake, venture, volunteer, vow, want, wish 等。其句型分为以下两种：

① "*subj.* +*vt.* +to do sth."结构。例如：
Harry aims to become a computer expert.
哈里的目标是成为一名计算机专家。
② "*subj.* +*vt.* +for sb. to do sth."结构。例如：
I shouldn't care for that man to be my doctor.
我不应介意让那人当我的医生。

注意：need, want, require, deserve 等词后面所接的动名词或不定式表示被动意义时，动名词作宾语用主动形式，动词不定式用被动形式。例如：
The furniture won't need polishing tomorrow.
明天这些家具不需要擦了。
The house needs to be painted both inside and outside.
这栋房子里外都需要粉刷。

（2）以 it 作形式宾语，动词不定式作真正的宾语。动词不定式作宾语时，如果宾语后面带有宾语补足语，要用 it 作形式宾语，将作真正宾语的不定式移到宾语补足语后面。例如：
I don't think it necessary *to go on with the experiment*.
我认为没有必要继续这项实验。
TV makes it possible for us *to see a distance scene*.
电视使我们有可能看到远方的景色。

（3）作介词的宾语。英语中只有少数几个介词，如 about, besides, but, except, save, than 等可以后接不定式作为其宾语。这些介词除 about 外，都表示"除……之外"。例如：
He thinks nothing *except* to be a doctor.
他一心想当医生。

（4）"疑问代词/疑问副词/连接词+不定式"结构。例如：
Tell me *whether* to trust him or not.
告诉我是否可以相信他。

（5）"there to be +*n.*/*pron.*"结构。例如：
I expect *there to be* no argument about this.
我预料人们对这件事情不会有争议。

4. 动词不定式作定语

动词不定式作定语时，一律位于其所修饰的名词或代词之后，不定式修饰的名词多为抽象名词，如 ability, means, order, thing, way, work 等。同时，不定式与其修饰的中心词之间有多种不同的关系，常见的关系分为以下五方面。

（1）中心词为由动词派生出来的抽象名词，原动词可用不定式作宾语，该中心词与修饰它的不定式之间存在同位关系。此时，不定式对中心词起解释作用。常见的这类名词中心词有 arrangement, attempt, claim, decision, desire, determination, failure, hope, intention, need, order, plan, promise, refusal, resolution, tendency, threat, wish 等。例如：
He expressed his wish to visit the Great Wall.
他希望游览长城。

（2）中心词为由形容词派生出来的抽象名词，其后接不定式作原因状语，或与不定式连用作复合谓语。常见的这类名词中心词有 ability, ambition, anxiety, curiosity, eagerness, impatience, patience, reluctance, willingness 等。例如：

He was filled with ambition to become an engineer.

他渴望成为一名工程师。

（3）不定式与其所修饰的名词中心词之间存在同位关系。此时，不定式用以说明被修饰名词的内容。常见的这类名词中心词有 campaign, chance, courage, efforts, evidence, means, measures, method, move, movement, opportunity, position, power, project, reason, right, skill, strength, struggle, way 等。例如：

We're starting a movement to clean up the city.

我们正在发起一项整顿城市的运动。

（4）中心词与作定语的不定式之间存在逻辑上的主谓关系，即中心词为定语不定式动作的执行者，是不定式的逻辑主语。此时，不定式作定语的句法作用相当于关系代词作主语的定语从句。在这种句型中，被修饰的中心词可以是名词、代词或数词。例如：

We are in need of nurses to take care of children. （=...nurses who can take care of...）

我们需要护理儿童的护士。

He is always the first to come and the last to leave.

他总是第一个来到，最后一个离开。

（5）中心词与作定语的不定式之间存在逻辑上的动宾关系，即中心词为定语不定式动作的接受者，是不定式的逻辑宾语。此时，不定式作定语，相当于关系代词作宾语的定语从句。因此，作定语的不定式后面不能接宾语。在这种句型中，作定语的不定式经常是以主动形式表示被动意义，其修饰的中心词可以是名词、代词或数词。例如：

There is no time to lose.

我们没有时间可浪费了。

I have a letter to send.

我有封信要寄。

Can you get me something to eat?

你能给我找点东西吃吗？

The thing to do now is to carry out an experiment.

现在要做的事是做实验。

如果中心词是表示定语的动词不定式动作的地点、方式、工具等，不定式后面一般要用介词来表示中心词与不定式之间的动宾关系。此时，带介词的不定式可以转换成由"介词+关系代词"引导的定语从句。例如：

He is looking for a room *to live in*. （=He is looking for a room in which to live.）

他正在找个房间住。

There is a tree over there *to sit under*.

那边有棵树可以坐在树下面。

另外，被 only, the first, the second, the last, the next, 或其他序数词与最高级形容词修饰的名词，通常用不定式作定语。例如：

Practice is the *only* way to learn a language.

练习/实践是学习语言的唯一方法。

I don't think he is *the best* man to do the job.

我想他不是做这项工作的最佳人选。

5. 动词不定式作状语

动词不定式作状语时，具有副词的特征，常被用作状语，在句中表示目的、原因、结果和程度等。

（1）不定式作目的状语。例如：

To learn a language well, you must make painstaking efforts.

要学好一种语言，必须下苦功夫。

In order to make better use of these materials, we have to study their properties.

为了更好地利用这些材料，我们必须研究其特性。

They worked hard *so as to* end the task success fully.

他们努力工作以便圆满完成任务。

A man must *so* train his habits *as to* rely upon his own courage in moments of emergency.

一个人必须养成这样的习惯，以便在紧急关头能够依靠自己的魄力。

For *there to be* no mistake, you must recheck the results got from the experiment.

为了不出错误，我们必须重新检查实验的结果。

（2）不定式作原因状语。动词不定式作原因状语的句型主要分为两种：一是位于表示感情的不及物动词之后，说明动词动作的原因；一是位于作表语的形容词和过去分词之后，说明形容词和过去分词。

①位于表示感情的不及物动词之后，说明其前面动词动作的原因。例如：

She trembled *to think of it*.

一想到此事她就不寒而栗。

②位于作表语的形容词和过去分词之后。例如：

I'm glad *to see* her in good health.

见她身体健康我很高兴。

You were careless *to leave* your bike unlocked.

丢下自行车不锁，你真粗心。

（3）不定式作结果状语。不定式作结果状语时，位于被修饰的动词之后。例如：

He was *too* excited *to* fall asleep.

他激动得睡不着。

She left home *only to* find life more difficult.

她离家出走，结果发现生活更困难。

She sang *so* well *as to* bring down the house.

她精彩的演唱博得满堂喝彩。

His remarks *were such as to* annoy everyone at the meeting.

他的话使会场上的人反感。

There is *such* a rapid increase in population *as to* cause a food shortage.

人口增长如此快，以至于粮食短缺。
It's too late *for there to be* any buses.
天太晚了，不会有公交车了。

（4）不定式作程度状语。不定式作程度状语时，多用于"enough to do something"句型中。例如：

They are old enough *to decide* what is good for them.
他们已经长大，足以判断什么对他们好。

I'm not scholar enough *to name* this plant.
我才疏学浅，讲不出这种植物的名字。

6. 动词不定式作宾语补足语

动词不定式作宾语补足语时，宾语为不定式的逻辑主语。此时，不定式作宾语补足语的句型分为可变为被动语态的句型与不能变为被动语态的句型。

可变为被动语态的句型：

（1）用于表示命令、教导、要求、允许、意向、起因、使、禁止、劝告、警告等意义的动词之后。常见的这类动词有：advise, allow, ask, beg, bribe, cause, challenge, command, compel, dare, direct, empower, enable, encourage, entitle, expect, forbid, force, get, give, impel, implore, induce, instruct, intend, invite, know, lead, mean, oblige, order, permit, persuade, press, remind, request, require, teach, tell, tempt, urge, warn 等。例如：

The doctor *warned* the patient not to smoke.
医生警告病人不要吸烟。

He *gave* me to understand that he could help me.
他使我明白他能帮助我。

（2）用于表示意见、判断、信念、料想、声明、认可或心理感觉等意义的词之后。此句型是比较正式的文体，多用于书面语。另外，作宾语补足语的不定式"to be"可以省略，但其完成式"to have been"不能省略。常见的这类动词有：acknowledge, announce, appoint, assure, believe, choose, claim, consider, declare, elect, feel, find, guess, hold, imagine, judge, know, name, proclaim, prove, realize, report, suppose, take, think, understand 等。例如：

Everyone *reported* him to be the best man for the job.
大家都说他是这项工作的最佳人选。

（3）表示生理感觉的动词，如 behold, feel, hear, look at, listen to, mark（注意）, notice, observe, perceive, see, watch 等，后跟不定式作宾语补足语时，不定式前省去 to。例如：

We *observe* tears come into her eyes.
我们看到她满眼含泪。

（4）用于表示"致使、让"等意义的动词，如 bid, have, let, make 等之后。这类动词后跟不定式作为其宾语补足语时，不定式前省去 to。例如：

The teacher made the students retell the text.

老师让学生们复述课文。

（5）句中的谓语动词为表示喜爱、厌恶、偏爱的词，如 bear, get, hate, help, leave, like, prefer, want, wish 等，后跟不定式（短语）作为其宾语补足语时，该句通常不能变为被动句。例如：

She can't bear me to be happy.

她不能容忍我快乐。

（6）动词短语后跟不定式作宾语补足语。常见的这类短语有：care for, call on, count on, depend on, long for, rely on, vote for 等。例如：

We cannot *count on* another country to help us.

我们不能指望别的国家会帮助我们。

7. 动词不定式作主语补足语

动词不定式作主语补足语时，主语为不定式的逻辑主语。例如：

Mathematics is known *to be the base of all other sciences.*

He is thought *to be the best player of basketball.*

8. 动词不定式作插入语

动词不定式作插入语的结构多为一些固定短语，如 so as to say, to be exact, to be frank, to begin with, to be honest, to be just, to be sure, to cut the matter short, to tell the truth 等。通常，这些短语在句中作评注性状语或连接性状语。

To begin with, there must be close co-operation between them.

9. 动词不定式作同位语

动词不定式可作名词的同位语，用以说明所修饰名词的具体内容，一般用逗号或破折号隔开。例如：

We all have a common desire—*to* realize communism.

10. 动词不定式的复合结构

由于不定式是非谓语动词，不能独立作谓语。因此，不定式没有自己的主语。通常，句子的主语为不定式的逻辑主语。当不定式的逻辑主语不是句子的主语而需要有自己的逻辑主语时，要用不定式复合结构。不定式复合结构在句中可作主语、表语、定语、状语。例如：

It will be good *for* you *to* spend the holidays in the country.（主语）

The answer to that question is *for* you *to* find.（表语）

I regard it as important *for* you *to* finish.（宾语）

English is one of the basic subjects *for* us *to* learn in the university.（定语）

For a lesson *to* be well taught, the teacher must make careful preparations.（状语）

（二）动词不定式的时态和语态

1. 动词不定式的时态和语态形式

动词不定式的时态和语态的具体形式如表 12-2 所示。

表 12-2　动词不定式的时态和语态形式

时态	主动态	被动态
一般式	to do	to be done
进行式	to be doing	
完成式	to have done	to have been done
完成进行式	to have been doing	

2. 动词不定式进行式

不定式进行式所表示的动作通常与句中谓语动词的动作同时发生。其在句中的作用等同于不定式一般式。例如：

He didn't expect her to be working so hard.

他没有料到她工作如此努力。

另外，不定式进行式可与情态动词连用，构成复合谓语，表示对正在进行或将要进行的动作或情况的猜测，也可表示义务与责任。例如：

You must be dreaming.

She may be coming next morning.

3. 动词不定式完成式

动词不定式一般式所表示的动作，一般和句中谓语动词所表示的动作同时发生或在其后发生。如果不定式动作在句中谓语动词所表示的动作之前发生，要用不定式完成式。不定式完成式在句中可以作主语、宾语、定语、宾语补足语、主语补足语和复合谓语。例如：

It would have been amusing to have gone to the exhibition.

She felt it an honor to have taken part in the work.

He was the first professor *to have been invited* to give a lecture on the laser technique.

I am sorry *not to have done the work well*.

The doctor found her heart *to have stopped beating*.

They are said *to have found out a simpler method for producing plastics*.

4. 动词不定式完成进行式

动词不定式完成进行式与不定式完成式相同，其动作发生在句中谓语动词之前，只是强调动作的连续性。例如：

I'm sorry to *have been troubling* you all the time.

He may *have been waiting* for his friend.

5. 动词不定式的被动态

当不定式的逻辑主语是不定式所表示动作的承受者时，不定式一般要采用被动形式。例如：

It is an honor for me *to be awarded* the first prize.

He asked *to be sent* to Tibet.

Please tell me the subjects *to be discussed* at the next session.

I am glad to be allowed *to* look around your research center.

The machine seems *to have been damaged*.

6. 动词不定式省略 to 的习惯用法

如前所述，动词不定式由不定式符号"to"加动词原形构成。但在某些情形下，to 可用可不用；在另外一些情形下，则一定不能用。不定式省略 to 的习惯用法分为以下三种情形。

（1）基本助动词、情态动词后面的不定式省略 to。例如：

Do ask, if you have any question.

We needn't return the book today, need we?

（2）用于知觉动词 behold, fell, hear, listen to, look at, notice, observe, perceive, see, watch 等后面作为其宾语补足语的不定式省略 to。例如：

I feel my health improve.

We watched the sun set behind the trees.

（3）用于致使动词 have, let, make 后作为其宾语补足语的不定式省略 to。例如：

Let him come as soon as possible.

二、分词

分词是另外一种非谓语动词。同动词不定式一样，分词不能独立作谓语动词，但又保留动词的若干特征。分词可以带有宾语并能被状语修饰，有时态和语态的变化。分词分为现在分词（v. -ing）与过去分词（v. -ed）。现在分词表示主动意义及正在进行的动作；过去分词表示被动意义及已被完成的动作。另外，分词具有形容词和副词的特征，在句中可作定语、表语、状语、主语补足语和宾语补足语。

（一）分词的句法作用

1. 分词短语作定语

分词短语作定语时，与其所修饰的词之间存在逻辑上的主谓关系，表示其所修饰的词发出或承受的动作，即从动作方面说明事物的特征。分词作定语的形式分为两种：前置定语和后置定语。单个分词作定语时，一般位于其所修饰的名词之前，称为前置定语；分词短语作定语时，一般位于其所修饰的名词之后，称为后置定语。

（1）现在分词作定语。现在分词作定语时，表示被修饰名词所发出的动作，即被修饰的名词是分词行为的实际发出者。因此，分词与其所修饰的名词存在逻辑上的主谓关系，表示名词的动作、行为的特征。

①现在分词作前置定语。例如：

the changing world = the world that is changing　正在变化的世界

the running water　自来水

注意：动名词作定语时与分词具有不同意义。动名词侧重表示与其所修饰的名词有关的动作，以说明该名词的用途。例如：

working people = people who are working（分词）

working method = method of working（动名词）

a sleeping girl = a girl who is sleeping（分词）

a sleeping car = a car used for sleeping（动名词）

②现在分词作后置定语。现在分词作后置定语时，要注意分词所表示的动作与句中谓语动词所表示的动作之间的时间关系。一般，只有两者所表示的动作同时发生，或分词所表示的是现在时刻正在进行的动作，或经常性动作以及当时所处的状态时，才用分词（短语）作定语，否则用定语从句。另外，分词是表示来去意义的词，如 coming，going，leaving 等时，分词可表示将来的动作。例如：

Tell the boys *playing* there not to make so much noise. （同时发生）

The comrades *working* in the countryside will come back the day after tomorrow. （现在时刻正在进行的动作，此时，分词动作和句中谓语动词所表示的动作不一定同时发生）

They lived in a room *facing* the south. （经常性动作以及当时所处的状态）

The boy *coming* to see you tomorrow is my brother. （将来的动作）

We shall arrive too late to catch the train *leaving* at eight. （将来的动作）

（2）过去分词作定语。过去分词作定语时，其所表示的动作处于句中谓语动词所表示的动作之前或没有一定的时间标识，相当于被动语态的定语从句。及物动词的过去分词表示被动的或已完成的意义。此时，被修饰的名词是分词行为的承受者。不及物动词的过去分词通常表示已完成的动作，且表示主动意义。此时，被修饰的名词是分词动作的执行者。

① 过去分词作前置定语。例如：

All the *broken* windows have been repaired. （及物动词的过去分词作前置定语）

the *risen* sun 升起的太阳 （不及物动词的过去分词作前置定语）

② 过去分词作后置定语。作后置定语的过去分词一般为分词短语。但有时为了强调分词的动作，或者由于分词仍保持着较强的动词意义，单个分词也可放在被修饰的名词后面。例如：

The experience *gained* will be of great value for us.

This is something *unheard of in history*.

2. 分词短语作状语

分词短语作状语时，句子的主语为分词的逻辑主语。此时，分词短语用以对谓语动词所表示的动作或行为发生的时间、条件、原因、让步、结果、方式或伴随情况等进行修饰说明。分词短语与主句之间一般用逗号隔开。通常，表示时间、条件、原因的状语位于句首；表示结果、方式、伴随情况的状语位于句末。另外，分词短语前可使用连接词，如 although，as，even if，if，though，unless，when，while 等。

（1）分词短语作条件状语。例如：

Working hard, you will succeed. （现在分词作条件状语）

Heating water, you will change it into steam. （现在分词作条件状语）

Unless heated, a body will have no tendency to expand. （过去分词作条件状语）

Considered from this point of view, the question under discussion is of great importance. （过去分词作条件状语）

（2）分词短语作时间状语。例如：

Hearing the noise, they immediately stopped talking. （现在分词作时间状语）

Pay attention to your grammar, *when speaking English*. （现在分词作时间状语）

Having arrived at a decision, they immediately set to work. （现在分词作时间状语）

When turned on, the radio still does not work. （过去分词作时间状语）

When combined with practice, theory becomes easier to learn. （过去分词作时间状语）

（3）分词短语作原因状语。例如：

Not knowing how to solve the problem, I asked the teacher. （现在分词一般式作原因状语）

Not having been told when to start, he came late. （现在分词完成式作原因状语）

Not given careful consideration, the work can not be easily completed. （过去分词作原因状语）

The book, *written in simple English*, is suitable for beginners. （过去分词作原因状语）

（4）分词短语作表示行为方式或伴随动作的状语。分词短语作此类状语时，一般居于后位，表明分词所表示的动作是次要的，从而用以说明主要的动作。在这种句型中，分词表示的动作一般与谓语动词的动作同时发生。例如：

They entered the room, *talking and laughing*. （现在分词作行为方式或伴随动作状语）

She stood here, *listening to the wind and watching the rain*. （现在分词作行为方式或伴随动作状语）

The teacher stood there, *surrounded by many students*. （过去分词作行为方式或伴随动作状语）

I sat until after eleven, *absorbed in a book*. （过去分词作行为方式或伴随动作状语）

（5）分词短语作结果状语。通常，只有现在分词作结果状语。例如：

Her husband died in 1945, *leaving her with three children*.

Their car was caught in a traffic jam, *thus causing the delay*.

（6）分词短语作让步状语。例如：

Although working his fingers to the bone, John still couldn't make enough money to pay off his debt. （现在分词作让步作状语）

Though warned of danger, he still went skating on the thin ice. （过去分词作让步作状语）

3. 分词短语作表语

现在分词作表语时，表示与主语的关系是主动关系，即主语是表语的分词动作的行为者；过去分词作表语时，表示与主语的关系是被动关系。

（1）现在分词作表语表示主语所具有的特征。此时，现在分词具有形容词的特征，不能带有自己的宾语，但可以被程度状语 very, much, quite 等修饰，有时也可以被表示比较意义的 more, most 修饰。例如：

It feels quite *refreshing* to take a bath after work.

The result of the experiment is *encouraging*.

（2）过去分词作表语表示主语所处的状态。但是，并非所有的过去分词都可以作表语，常见的可以作表语的过去分词有 broken, closed, completed, done, covered, dressed, finished, gone, illustrated, injured, killed, known, loaded, lost, married, prepared, shut, spent, surrounded, translated, won, wounded 等。这些过去分词已被看作形容词，一般用程度副词 very 来修饰。尚未形容词化的过去分词，如 changed, drawn 等用 much 来修饰。very much 则可以修饰所有的过去分词。例如：

They were very *upset* when they parted.

He got very *excited* when he heard the news.

4. 分词短语作宾语补足语，构成复合宾语

分词短语作宾语补足语时，在逻辑上与宾语之间存在主谓关系。现在分词作宾语补足语表示的意义为宾语正在进行的动作全过程还未完成；过去分词作宾语补足语表示的意义为宾语的状态。

（1）现在分词作宾语补足语时，句中所用的谓语动词可分为以下两类。

① 表示视觉、听觉、触觉、嗅觉等生理的动词，如 discover，feel，find，hear，imagine，listen to，look at，notice，observe，see，watch，smell 等。例如：

I felt somebody *patting* me on the shoulder.

Can you smell something *burning*?

注意：本句型中谓语动词后可用现在分词作宾语补足语，也可用动词不定式作宾语补足语，但二者在用法上有所不同。具体区别如下：

（i）现在分词作宾语补足语时，表示动作正在进行（还未完成全过程）；不定式则表示动作的完成。例如：

I *saw* him *crossing* the road. （看见他过马路，还未过完）

I *saw* him *cross* the road. （看见他过马路，已经过去）

（ii）宾语补足语由短暂性动作动词表示时，不定式中的动词表示一次性的动作，现在分词中的动词表示反复性的动作。例如：

I *heard* the door *slam*. （我听见门砰然一声关上了）

I *heard* the door *slamming*. （我听见门砰砰不断地响）

②具有"致使"意义的词，如 bring，catch，draw，get，have，keep，leave，send，set，start 等。例如：

A phone call *sent* him *hurrying* to London.

His remarks *left* me *wondering* about his real purpose.

（2）过去分词作宾语补足语时，句中所用的谓语动词可分为以下三类。

①表示感觉和心理状态的动词，如 consider，expect，feel，find，hear，like，observe，see，think，urge，watch 等。例如：

We *found* Beijing greatly *changed*.

He once *heard* the song *sung* in English.

②表示"致使"意义的词，如 allow，get，have，keep，leave，make，permit 等。例如：

On these questions, we *have* made our views *understood*.

Please *keep* us *informed* of the latest developments.

③表示"希望、要求"意义的词，如 like，order，want，wish 等。例如：

We *want* the work *finished* by Monday.

5. 分词短语作主语补足语

分词短语作主语补足语时，用以说明主语的动作和状态。主动句变为被动句后，原先作为主动句中的宾语补足语就成为主语补足语。因此，分词短语作主语补足语的句型都为被动句。例如：

She was never heard *singing* that song again. （现在分词作主语补足语）

Our views have to be made *known* to them all. （过去分词作主语补足语）

6. 分词的复合结构——独立主格

有时分词，可以在其之前用名词或代词来表明分词的动作由谁执行，即分词的逻辑主语。但这些名词或代词不是句子的主语或分词所修饰的中心词。这种结构称为分词的复合结构，即独立主格。分词复合结构可在句中作状语，表明时间、原因、条件、方式及伴随动作等。另外，with 复合结构还可作定语。分词复合结构的类型如下：

（1）"名词/（主格）代词 + 现在分词"结构。例如：
The teacher having left, the students resumed their discussion. （时间状语）
Weather permitting, the football match will be played on next Sunday. （条件）

（2）"名词/（主格）代词 + 过去分词"结构。例如：
The duty completed, he had three months leave. （原因）

（3）"名词/（主格）代词 + 形容词"结构。例如：
The commander was waiting, *his face white with anger*. （方式及伴随动作）

（4）"名词/（主格）代词 + 介词短语"结构。例如：
He stood at the door, *his hands in his pockets*. （伴随动作）

（5）"名词/（主格）代词 + 副词"结构。例如：
Class over, all the students went out from the classroom. （时间状语）

（6）"名词/（主格）代词 + 名词"结构。例如：
His first shot failure, he fired again. （原因）

（7）"with/without + 名词/（宾格）代词 + 分词/形容词/介词短语/副词/名词"结构。例如：
With the problem solved, the meeting came to its end. （原因）

（8）"There being + 名词"结构。例如：
There being no spare parts, the equipment could not be repaired at once. （原因）

（二）分词的时态和语态

1. 分词的时态和语态形式

分词的时态和语态的具体形式如表 12 - 3 所示。过去分词只有一种形式：规则动词由动词原形加词尾 ed 构成；不规则动词无统一的变化规则，需一一记住。

表 12 - 3　现在分词的时态和语态形式

形式	主动式	被动式	否定式
一般式	doing	being done	not (being) done
完成式	having done	having been done	not having (being) done

2. 分词的完成式

（1）现在分词一般式所表示的动作通常和句中谓语动词的动作同时发生；现在分词完成式所表示的动作在句中谓语动词动作之前发生，在句中主要作状语，表示时间和原因。例如：

Having sent the children to bed, she began to study. （表时间）

Having studied hard, he got high marks in the test. （表原因）

（2）单独的过去分词可以表示完成。例如：

He told us of the great wrong done to him. (= He told us of the great wrong which had been done to him.)

3. 分词的被动语态

（1）现在分词一般式的被动语态。表示一个被动动作时，如果这个动作是此刻正在进行的动作，或与句中谓语动词所表示的动作同时发生，就可以用现在分词的被动式来表示。现在分词一般式的被动语态在句中主要作定语、状语和宾语补足语。例如：

This is one of the experiments *being carried on*. （定语）

Being done in a hurry, the exercises were full of mistakes. （状语）

You'll find the topic *being discussed* everywhere. （宾语补足语）

（2）现在分词完成式的被动语态。现在分词完成式的被动语态在句中主要作状语，有时也可作定语。例如：

Having been trained for a year, we know how to operate the complicated system.

（3）单独的过去分词可以表示被动。例如：

He often hears the song sung in the next room. （一般时）

Weakened by the successive storms, the bridge was no longer safe. （完成时）

三、动名词

动名词由"动词原形 + ing"构成，具有名词和动词的特征，可带有自己的宾语和状语。动名词连同其宾语和状语一起被称为动名词短语，在句中作主语、表语、宾语、定语和补足语。

（一）动名词的句法作用

1. 动名词作主语

动名词作主语时，通常表示抽象的、习惯性的或经常性的动作，并且通常不与特定的动作执行者一起联用，多表示说话者多次做过所述的动作或对其有过经验。动名词作主语的常见句型如下：

（1）"主语 + 系动词 + 表语"句型。例如：

Walking, *running*, *rowing and cycling* are all healthy forms of exercise.

（2）"主语 + 谓语动词 + 宾语"句型。例如：

We don't allow smoking in the workshop.

（3）"There be + no + 动名词"句型。(= it is impossible to do sth. = No one can do sth. = we cannot do sth.) 例如：

There is no *knowing* when the rain will stop.

（4）"It is + adj. /n. + 动名词"句型。此类句型的应用范围比较小，主要在以 dangerous, hard work, no good, no point, not any help, not easy, no use, senseless, useless, worthwhile 等词作表语的句子中使用。例如：

It's no use buying books but not reading them.

It is hard work keeping the grass green at this time of year.

（5）用于布告形式的省略句中。例如：

No *smoking*！

2. 动名词作定语

（1）动名词作前置定语时，位于其所修饰的词之前，用以说明它所修饰的名词的用处及与之相关的动作，只能够单独使用，不能带有宾语或状语。例如：

This is a new type of *printing machine*.

Their *working plan* will be made next week.

（2）动名词作后置定语时，必须与其前面的介词一起构成介词短语。此时，动名词可以带有自己的宾语。"介词+动名词"构成的介词短语作定语时，相当于一种名词性定语，表示抽象概念，并不强调动作，而且其时间概念也不强。例如：

The importance of *learning English* is more and more evident.

I don't know the date of *opening the library*.

3. 动名词作表语

动名词作表语时，具有名词的作用，表示主语的内涵。因此，主语和表语在概念上必须一致（相同或相似）。另外，动名词作表语时，句子的主语有很大的局限性，一般为只限于表示工作、任务（duty，job，work，task）或精神状态（wish，happiness）的抽象名词。有时动名词作表语的句法作用相当于名词性从句。例如：

His greatest happiness is serving the people heart and soul.

Our task is building our country into a modern powerful socialist country.

4. 动名词作宾语

动名词作宾语时，通常表示一般的、习惯的、抽象的、经常性的行为。常见的句型如下：

（1）动名词作及物动词的宾语。在这种句型中，常见的及物动词有 acknowledge，admit，advise，advocate，allow，appreciate，avoid，complete，consider，contemplate，defer，delay，deny，discontinue，endure，enjoy，escape，evade，excuse，facilitate，fail，fancy，favor，fancy，finish，forbid，forgive，imagine，include，involve，keep，mention，mind，miss，omit，pardon，permit，postpone，practise，recommend，report，resent，resist，risk，save，stop，suggest，support，tolerate，understand，feel like，give up，leave off，look forward to，object to，put off 等。例如：

Tom always *defers doing* his homework till the last moment.

You certainly mustn't *miss seeing* this wonderful film.

注意：

①有些及物动词可以后跟动名词，也可以后跟不定式作为其宾语。通常，动名词作宾语表示的意义为一般的、习惯的、抽象的、经常性的行为；不定式则为特殊的、具体的、一次性的行为。常见的这类及物动词有 like，love，prefer，dislike，dread，fear，hate，intend，plan，begin，start，attempt，neglect，propose 等。例如：

He *prefers to* talk *rather than* take a bus.

I *prefer going* with you *to waiting* at home.

②有些及物动词虽然可以后跟动名词或动词不定式作为其宾语，但在这两种情形下，其表示的意义不同。这类及物动词主要有 chance, forget, help, learn, mean, regret, remember, try, want 等。例如：

Should we *chance getting* home before it snows?

He *chanced to find* his lost bike in front of a store.

（2）动名词作介词宾语。在这种结构中，动名词位于介词之后，与介词一起构成介词短语，在句中作定语和状语。例如：

I hope you don't *forget about posing* my letter.

His father has *stopped him from using* the car.

He did not *speak of having read* this book.

5. 动名词作补足语

动名词作宾语补足语或主语补足语时，其句法作用相当于名词，只有在少数情况下动名词才用作补足语。例如：

People call that *killing two birds with one stone*.

Telephoning a place outside your area is called *telephoning long distance*.

6. 动名词的复合结构

在动名词前面可以加上一个物主代词或名词所有格来表示这个动名词的逻辑主语。此时，动名词同其逻辑主语构成动名词的复合结构，在句中可作主语、表语、宾语。动名词复合结构的类型主要包括以下六种。

（1）"所有格名词+动名词"结构。例如：

My sister's falling ill worried Mother greatly.（主语）

（2）"通格名词+动名词"结构。当动名词的逻辑主语是非生命的名词或是一个词组时，动名词的逻辑主语通常用通格，特别是当动名词的复合结构作宾语时。例如：

Is there any hope of *your brother getting first place in the race*?（宾语）

（3）"物主代词+动名词"结构。例如：

We congratulated on *his being admitted to the national team*.（宾语）

（4）"宾格代词+动名词"结构。现代英语中，当动名词复合结构作宾语时，如果动名词的逻辑主语是代词，则用代词的宾格形式代替物主代词。例如：

I don't doubt *you being able to do it*.（宾语）

（5）"指示代词/不定代词+动名词"结构。例如：

We insist on both of *them coming in time*.（宾语）

（6）"There+being+名词"结构（本结构只作主语和介词宾语）。例如：

There being a bus stop so near the house is a great advantage.（主语）

（二）动名词的时态和语态

1. 动名词的时态和语态形式

动名词的时态和语态的具体形式如表 12-4 所示。

表 12-4 动名词的时态和语态形式

形式	主动态	被动态	否定式
一般式	doing	being done	not doing
完成式	having done	having been done	not having done

2. 动名词的完成式

动名词的完成式所表示的动作先于句中谓语动词的动作，在句中主要用作宾语。例如：

He is proud of *having written* such a good text book.

I regret *not having seen* the exhibition.

3. 动名词的被动式

动名词的逻辑主语同时也是动名词动作的承受者时，动名词用被动语态。例如：

Some plastics can be shaped without *being heated*.

They admitted to *having been influenced* by his ideas.

 Exercises

Ⅰ. Choose the best answer to complete each sentence.

1. _____ in this light, the matter is not as serious as people generally suppose.
   A. To see   B. Seen   C. Seeing   D. Being seen
2. Parts of an aircraft fell on to a village today, narrowly _____ a group of children.
   A. missed   B. to miss   C. having missed   D. missing
3. Everyone assumed what he said _____ on fact.
   A. Being based   B. having based   C. to base   D. to be based
4. I prefer the _____ eggs.
   A. boiled   B. to boil   C. boiling   D. having boiled
5. I can't understand why he goes on _____ the same, if he hates _____ in the office.
   A. doing; working   B. to do; to work
   C. doing; to work   D. to do; working
6. Did you remember _____ your appointment last night?
   A. keeping   B. to keep   C. having   D. to have kept
7. The man was accused of receiving the goods, _____ them _____.
   A. to know; stolen   B. having; to be stolen
   C. knowing; to have been stolen   D. knowing; being stolen
8. They clearly suspect him _____ the full truth about what happened.
   A. hiding   B. hidden   C. to be hiding   D. hide
9. He did quite well, _____ everything into consideration.
   A. to take   B. taking   C. taken   D. having taken
10. A lion escaped from the zoo, _____ fear and terror among the population.

A. to create B. to have created
C. created D. creating

11. _____ into the question of how much the holiday would cost, they decided to stay at home.
    A. Having gone   B. Going   C. To go   D. To be going

12. After _____ him better, I regretted _____ him unfairly.
    A. getting to know; to judge
    B. getting to know; to have judged
    C. getting to have known; judging
    D. getting to know; having judged

13. He turned down the job he was offered, _____ reluctant _____ himself to a long contract.
    A. to be; to commit
    B. being; to commit
    C. having been; to commit
    D. to have been; committing

14. The platform was crowded with people _____ goodbye to friends and relatives.
    A. to wave   B. waved   C. waving   D. to be waving

15. It would be no good _____ Tom to leave his camera at home. It would be like _____ a woman _____ without a handbag.
    A. asking; asking; to travel
    B. asking; to ask; travelling
    C. to ask; asking; travelling
    D. asking; asking; travelling

16. Your hair needs _____. You'd better have it _____ tomorrow.
    A. to be cut; do   B. cutting; doing   C. to be cut; done   D. cutting; to be done

17. The driver put on his brakes _____ the car in front of him.
    A. to avoid hitting
    B. to avoid to hit
    C. avoiding to hit
    D. to have avoided hitting

18. Anyone _____ a term in prison will not be hired by that company.
    A. serving   B. to be served   C. having served   D. being served

19. The boy came running into the room, _____.
    A. his face was dirty and his clothes torn
    B. his face dirty and his clothes torn
    C. his face was dirty and his clothes were torn
    D. his face dirty and his clothes were torn

20. _____ wrong with the motor, he stopped his car.
    A. Feeling something go
    B. Feeling something gone
    C. To feel something going
    D. Having felt something gone

21. It's almost impossible _____ boys _____ soldiers.
    A. to be preventing; from playing
    B. preventing; to play
    C. to prevent; being playing
    D. to prevent; playing

22. Weather _____, the picnic will be held as _____.
    A. permit; schedule
    B. permitting; scheduled
    C. permits; scheduling
    D. permitting; to be scheduled

23. The witness reported _____ a dark car _____ outside the bank at the time of the robbery.

  A. having seen; parking   B. seeing; having parked
  C. seeing; to have parked   D. seeing; parked

24. _____ a fine day, we decided to go fishing.
  A. Having been   B. There being
  C. Being   D. It being

25. Her only desire is _____ in good health.
  A. his family to be   B. for his family to be
  C. to his family being   D. his family been

26. He was happy _____ of some of his duties.
  A. to relieve   B. to have relieved
  C. to be relieved   D. having been relieved

27. It was considerate _____ me in the hospital.
  A. for you to visit   B. of you to visit
  C. to you to have visited   D. for you to have visited

28. Rather than _____ the vegetable _____ bad, he sold them at half price.
  A. allow; going   B. to allow; going
  C. allow; to go   D. allowing; to go

29. He reached children _____ only _____ that the train had just left.
  A. exhausting; learning   B. exhausted; to learn
  C. exhausted; learned   D. exhausting; to learn

30. I'll recommend Mr. Mark _____.
  A. consulting   B. for you to consult
  C. for you to be consulted   D. for you to have consulted

31. Peter walked away _____, the old book _____ beneath his arm.
  A. whistling; tucked   B. whistling; tucking
  C. whistled; tucked   D. whistling; to be tucked

32. The students must learn _____ word by word and, instead, _____ the general idea of the article.
  A. to stop to read; to grasp   B. stopping to read; grasping
  C. stopping reading; grasping   D. to stop reading; to grasp

33. According to the conditions of my scholarship, after finishing my degree, _____.
  A. my education will be employed by the university
  B. employment will be given to me by the university
  C. the university will employ me
  D. I will be employed by the university

34. We think it important for the accommodation _____ in advance.
  A. to be reserved   B. to reserve
  C. having been reserved   D. being reserved

35. _____ in pencil, the letter was difficult _____ out.

    A. Being written; in making   B. Written; to make
    C. Having written; to make   D. Having been written; making

36. _____ in such a way is not what we admire.
    A. Children being educated   B. Children to be educated
    C. For children to be educated   D. For children being educated

37. The fire that broke out in the factory during the night was still seen _____ a lot of smoke the next morning.
    A. to give off   B. to be giving off
    C. give off   D. giving off

38. _____ in her own affairs, she forgot _____ her son.
    A. Absorbing; picking up   B. Absorbed; to pick up
    C. Having absorbed; to pick up   D. To be absorbed; picking up

39. They need a room _____ sixty people.
    A. seated   B. be seated   C. being seated   D. seating

40. Her husband _____, she decided to get a job herself.
    A. out of work   B. gone out of work
    C. was going out of work   D. was out of work

Ⅱ. Identify the mistake in each sentence and then correct it.

1. It been Sunday, we had no classes.
2. The article to be read, a lively discussion began.
3. All hope is going.
4. Whenever asking about it, she would not say a word.
5. The policeman caught the boys steal the lady's purse.
6. There is not knowing how long we might be away.
7. With you being supporting me, I've got nothing to worry about.
8. You coming here will be of no help.
9. The girl deserves to praise.
10. Should we chance to get home before it rains?

第十三章

名词性从句

第一节 名词性从句的定义与连接词

一、名词性从句的定义

名词性从句（Noun Clause），是指在句子中起名词作用的句子。名词性从句的语法功能相当于名词词组，在复合句中可担任主语、宾语、表语、同位语、介词宾语等。因此，根据名词性从句在句中的不同语法功能，可分为主语从句、宾语从句、表语从句和同位语从句。

二、名词性从句的连接词

引导名词性从句的连接词可分为以下三类：

（1）连词（5个）：that, whether, if, as if, as though。这五个连词在从句中均不充当任何成分。that 本身无意义，引导单一的宾语从句时 that 常可省略，但引导主语从句、表语从句、同位语从句时 that 通常不能省略；whether, if 意为"是否"，表示从句内容的不确定性；as if, as though 表示"好像""似乎"。

（2）连接代词（10个）：what/whatever, who/whoever, whom/whomever, whose/whosever, which/whichever.

（3）连接副词（7个）：when/whenever, where/wherever, how/however, why.

第二节 名词性从句的分类及用法

一、主语从句（Subject Clause）

1. 主语从句的定义

主语从句是指在复合句中充当主语成分的句子。

2. 主语从句的引导词

主语从句通常由下列连接词引导。

（1）连词 that、whether 等。例如：

That she has just graduated from college is true.（that 位于句首不能省略）

It occurred to me that I would travel Europe.

Whether she comes or not makes no difference.

That China ranks first in the world in population is well known.（为避免头重脚轻，通常用形式主语 it：It is well known that China ranks first in the world in population.）

（2）连接代词 what, who, which, whatever, whoever, whom 等。例如：

What struck me was that they have all suffered a lot.

Whoever pollutes the environment should be punished.

（3）连接副词 how, when, where, why 等。例如：

How much we can spend must be agreed on.

When and where the meeting will be held is not yet decided.

3. 主语从句的用法及注意问题

（1）主语从句通常被认为是单数形式，因此主句的谓语动词用单数形式。例如：

Which country you are going to does matter.

That the famous actress is coming to our hometown is the best news to us.

Whether the conductor would support his son was a problem.

（2）What 引导的主语从句，其主谓一致问题较为复杂。这是因为谓语动词受其主语的数的影响，可以使用单数或复数的形式。当从句为带有复数意义的并列结构时，主句的谓语动词用复数形式。例如：

What I read and write are quite different.（What I read and what I write are...）

当主句的表语是复数名词时，主句的谓语动词通常用复数形式。例如：

What we bought were children's books.（这种情况下，美式英语也可用单数谓语动词。）

二、宾语从句（Object Clause）

1. 宾语从句的定义

宾语从句是指在主、从复合句中充当宾语，位于及物动词、介词或复合谓语之后的句子。宾语从句必须用陈述句语序。

2. 引导词

宾语从句的连词主要有 that, if, whether；连接代词主要有 who, whom, whose, what, whoever, whomever, whosever, whatever, whichever 等；连接副词主要有 when, where, why, how, whenever, wherever, however 等。

3. 宾语从句的用法及注意问题

（1）that 引导宾语从句时并无词义，不充当句子成分，多数情况下可以省略。例如：

I have found out that all the tickets for the concert have been sold out.

He assured me that he was able to do it.

注意：当句子中有 it 作形式宾语时，that 引导的宾语从句中的 that 不能省略。例如：

They thought it strange that we did not arrive at Guilin yesterday.

（2）动词 find, feel, consider, make, believe 等后面有宾语补足语时，需要用 it 做形式宾语而将 that 引导的宾语从句后置。例如：

We all find it important that we (should) make a quick decision about this mater.

但是，如果是由 wh - 引导的宾语从句，则宾语不可用 it 代替。例如：

We all consider what your friend said to be unbelievable.

（3）if, whether 在宾语从句中的区别。

if 和 whether 都表示"是否"时，两者可以互换。例如：

I doubt whether/if he is telling the truth.

介词后面的宾语从句只能用 whether，不能用 if。例如：

It all depends on whether we can get their cooperation.

whether 后面可以接 or not, if 不可以。例如：

I want to know whether it's good or not.

（4）宾语从句的时态。当主句是一般过去时时，从句必须用过去时态的某种形式。例如：

The boy was sorry that he hadn't finished his homework on time.

三、表语从句（Predicative Clause）

1. 表语从句定义

表语从句是一种由句子充当系动词的表语的结构。表语从句只能置于主句之后，且主句的动词只能是系动词。

2. 表语从句引导词

连接表语从句的连接词有：that, what, who, when, where, which, why, whether, how, whoever, whichever, whatever, because, as if, as though 等。例如：

The reason why he was late is that his car broke down.

What is troubling me is how we can get there on time.

She seems as if she had done a great thing.

3. 表语从句的用法及注意问题

（1）表语从句要用陈述句语序。例如：

My question is when he can take up the job.

（2）if 不能引导表语从句，只能用 whether 来引导。例如：

The question is whether John has finished his drawing yet.

（3）that 在表语从句中不可以被省略。例如：

The fact is that more than seventy percent of the earth's surface is covered by water.

The reason why he was dismissed was that he was irresponsible.

四、同位语从句（Appositive Clause）

1. 同位语从句的定义

一个名词（或其他形式）对另一个名词或代词进行修饰、限定或说明时，这个名词

（或其他形式）就是同位语。因此，同位语从句是指在复合句中充当同位语的句子。

通常同位语从句跟在一些"抽象"名词，如 news, idea, fact, promise, hope, message 等之后，用以说明该名词所表达的具体内容。

2. 同位语从句的引导词

同位语从句通常由下列连接词引导。

（1）连词 that, whether 等。例如：

The news that the team won the game is quite exciting.

The question whether the Prime Minister should resign must be decided soon.

注意：if 不能引导同位语从句。

（2）连接代词 what, who, whom, whose 等。例如：

I have no idea what size shoes she wears.

The question who should do the job requires consideration.

（3）连接副词 when, where, how, why 等。例如：

We haven't yet settled the question where we are going to spend our summer vacation.

 Exercises

Ⅰ. Choose the best answer to complete each sentence.

1. My question is _____ student is the best at math.
   A. what   B. why   C. whether   D. which
2. Information has been put forward _____ more middle school graduates will be admitted into universities.
   A. while   B. that   C. when   D. as
3. Miss White is angry at _____ you said.
   A. when   B. whether   C. what   D. that
4. When my friend just got off the bus, he gave me a good description of _____ in Hezhou.
   A. what he had seen   B. that he had seen
   C. which he had seen   D. he had seen what
5. Kate asked me if I knew _____.
   A. whose pen is it   B. whose pen it was   C. whose pen it is   D. whose pen was it
6. You must remember _____.
   A. what your teacher said   B. what did your teacher say
   C. your teacher said what   D. what has your teacher said
7. It is true _____ the man has made a great important discovery in chemistry.
   A. that   B. why   C. which   D. what
8. It is known to all _____ the gun powder was first invented by the Chinese.
   A. /   B. what   C. that   D. when
9. _____ he will join us won't make too much difference.
   A. Which   B. If   C. What   D. Whether

10. The reason _____ he was late is that his bike broke down.
    A. that   B. why   C. what   D. /
11. The trouble is _____ we are short of funds.
    A. that   B. why   C. what   D. /
12. _____ John wanted to do was different from _____.
    A. That; that you had expected   B. What; that you had expected
    C. That; what you had expected   D. What; what you had expected
13. It is a pity _____ we won't be able to go to the south to spend our summer vacation.
    A. what   B. why   C. that   D. /
14. _____ we can't get seems better than _____ we have.
    A. What; what   B. What; that   C. That; that   D. That; what
15. _____ they will have the sports meet _____ still a question.
    A. /; is   B. When; is   C. What; are   D. Where; are
16. _____ leaves the room last ought to turn off the lights.
    A. Anyone   B. The person   C. Whoever   D. Who
17. _____ he really means is _____ he disagrees with us.
    A. What; what   B. What; that   C. That; that   D. That; what
18. I've come from Mr. Smith with a message _____ he can't visit you this afternoon.
    A. is   B. /   C. why   D. that
19. She has no idea _____ size shoes her husband wears.
    A. which   B. what   C. how many   D. whose
20. We haven't yet settled the question _____ we are going to spend our summer vacation.
    A. that   B. what   C. where   D. if
21. When and why he came here _____ yet.
    A. is not known B. are not known C. has not known D. have not known
22. _____ is no reason for dismissing her.
    A. Because she was a few minutes late   B. She was a few minutes late
    C. The fact that she was a few minutes late D. Being a few minutes late
23. Along with the letter was his promise _____ he would visit me this coming Christmas.
    A. which   B. that   C. what   D. whether
24. I don't know _____ they have gone.
    A. where   B. that   C. what   D. which
25. She made _____ clear _____ she had nothing to do with him.
    A. /; that   B. it; /   C. it; that   D. what; /
26. _____ he finished writing the composition in such a short time surprised us all.
    A. Why has   B. /   C. How can   D. That
27. _____ one can succeed depends on _____ hard he works.
    A. Whether; how B. If; however   C. If; how   D. Whether; however
28. He lost way in this city, and _____ made matters worse was _____ he lost his cell

149

phone.

    A. what; /   B. that; that   C. what; that   D. that; /

29. Such is human nature that a great many consumers are often willing to go for _____ many others are buying.

    A. that   B. /   C. what   D. why

30. I rang them to see _____ I could cancel the appointment.

    A. when   B. if   C. as if   D. that

Ⅱ. Identify the mistake in each sentence and then correct it.

1. No matter what he has done has aroused the public attention.
2. It is clear she is good at English.
3. I didn't know whether they like the lecture.
4. What he wants and what he has is so different.
5. The boy kept quiet that the team had won the match.
6. My question is when will the CEO come to our school to give us a lecture.
7. If we will go for an outing tomorrow remains unknown.
8. I never make a promise I don't intend to keep, so when I say forever, forever is that I mean.
9. She told her sister she would come to see him, and she would never forget him.
10. The question is if it is safe to walk on the ice.
11. The fact why Jack was late for school made his mother angry.
12. I believe that they don't know how to do it.
13. We can see the building very well from we stand.
14. She was chosen as our monitor made us very happy.
15. This is a fact that English is being accepted as an international language.
16. Anyone comes to the classroom last will be punished.
17. In one's own home one can do which one likes.
18. She looked like she had looked five years ago.
19. It is quite clear the whole project is doomed to failure.
20. When we should have the party have not been decided.

第十四章

定语从句

第一节 定语从句的定义与结构

一、定语从句的定义

定语从句（Attributive Clause），是指跟在名词或代词（先行词）之后，对其进行修饰、限定的句子。通俗来讲，定语从句在整个句子中作定语，充当复合句中的定语成分。一般，定语从句位于所修饰的词之后，作后置定语。被定语从句修饰的词称为先行词。

二、定语从句的结构

定语从句由关系词（关系代词、关系副词、关系限定词）引导，且关系词位于定语从句句首。其结构为：

定语从句 = 先行词 + 关系词 + 从句

第二节 定语从句的用法及注意问题

如上所述，定语从句由关系词引导。关系词在定语从句中主要有3个作用：一是连接作用，即连接主句和定语从句；二是指代作用，即指代主句中的先行词；三是在定语从句中担当句子成分。另外，关系词包括关系代词（that, which, who, whom, whose）、关系副词（where, when, why）以及关系限定词（as）。

注意：关系代词有主语、宾语、定语之分。通常，who 作主语，whom 作宾语（口语中可用 who 代替 whom），whose 作定语。关系代词在从句中可作主语、宾语、定语等；关系副词通常在从句中作地点状语（where）、时间状语（when）、原因状语（why）。

一、关系代词引导的定语从句（who，whom，that，whose，which）

关系代词所代替的先行词为表示人或物的名词或代词，并在句中充当主语、宾语、定语等成分。关系代词在定语从句中作主语时，从句谓语动词的人称与数要与先行词保持一致。

（1）who，whom，that 用来指代人。例如：

He is a man who means what he says.（who 在从句中作主语，先行词为单数"a man"，因此，从句谓语动词用"means"）

The man (whom/that) you talked to yesterday is my teacher.（whom/that 在从句中作宾语，可以省略）

（2）whose 用来指代人或物（whose 在从句中只用作定语，当指物时，可以与 of which 互换）。例如：

They rushed over to help the girl whose car had broken down.

Shanghai is an international metropolis whose population is more than 21 million.

（3）which，that 用来指代事物，在从句中充当主语、宾语等。例如：

A prosperity which/that had never been seen before appears in the countryside.（which/that 在从句中作主语）

The points (which/that) you have stressed are important.（which/that 在从句中作宾语，可以省略）

（4）通常用关系代词 that，而不用 which，who（whom）的情况。

①当先行词为不定代词时，如 all，everything，nothing，something，anything，few，much，none 等。例如：

Is there anything that I can do for you?

②当先行词被序数词或形容词最高级修饰时。例如：

The first thing that she wants to do is to get a new car.

This is the most beautiful city that Mary has ever visited.

③当先行词为人和物的名词词组时。例如：

They talked about their respected teachers and the happy moment that they could recall in the school days.

④当主句是以 who 或 which 开头的特殊疑问句时，为避免重复用 that。例如：

Who is the person that is standing at the gate?

⑤当关系代词在从句中充当表语时。例如：

He is not the man that he used to be.

（5）通常用关系代词 which，而不用 that 的情况。

①当从句为非限定性定语从句时（非限定性定语从句的相关知识见本章第三节）。例如：

The film, which I am looking forward to seeing, is directed by Steven Spielberg.

②当从句位于介词后面，用于指代物或事时。例如：

We all like the program of which he is speaking. / We all like the program which he is speaking of.

There are many interesting books, some of which are familiar to us.

二、关系副词引导的定语从句（when，where，why）

关系副词代替的先行词为表示时间、地点或理由的名词，并在从句中作状语。另外，关系副词 when，where，why 的含义相当于"介词＋which"结构，因此常常与"介词＋which"结构交替使用，例如：

I still remember the day when (on which) I was elected as a monitor.
Nanning is the place where (in which) I live.
Is this the reason why (for which) he is not in favor of our plan?

判断从句中应用关系代词还是关系副词是学习定语从句的重点与难点。具体的判断方法如下。

（1）要用关系代词还是关系副词完全取决于从句中的谓语动词。当从句中的谓语动词为及物动词，且其后面无宾语时，必须采用关系代词，这是因为只有关系代词才能充当宾语。例如：

This is the school where they visited last year. （错）
This is the school (which) they visited last year. （对）
I will never forget the days when I spent with you. （错）
I will never forget the days (which) I spent with you. （对）

（2）通过判断先行词在定语从句中的成分，正确选择出关系代词/关系副词。通常，当先行词在从句中作主语、定语、宾语时，选择关系代词；当先行词在从句中作状语时，选择关系副词。例如：

I'll never forget the day when I entered the university. （将从句补充完整为：I entered the university on the day。由此可知，先行词在从句中充当时间状语，因此用关系副词 when）

三、as 引导的定语从句

as 引导的定语从句可以指代人或物，常见的搭配有 such...as，the same...as，as...as 等。as 在从句中可充当主语、宾语和表语等。

（1）such...as 结构。例如：
I lend you such books as will interest you. （as 指代物，作主语）

（2）the same...as 结构。例如：
This is the same book as I lost last week. （as 指代物，作宾语）

注意：区分"the same...as"与"the same....that"：两者都可引导定语从句，不同之处在于：that 引导的从句所修饰的名词与 the same 修饰的名词是同一个；as 引导的从句所修饰的名词与 the same 修饰的名词是同一类，而非同一个。例如：

This is the same pen that I lost. （这支钢笔就是我丢的那一支。）
This is the same pen as I lost. （这支钢笔跟我丢的那支笔一模一样。）

（3）as...as 结构。例如：
We bought as many books as we want to read. （as 指代物，作宾语）

第三节　非限定性定语从句

1. 非限定性定语从句的意义

限定性定语从句对被修饰的先行词有限定、制约的作用,以使该词的含义更为具体、明确(限定性定语从句不能被省略,否则句意不完整),而非限制性定语从句只是对先行词作补充说明,对其没有限定作用。它与先行词的关系比较松散,如果省略,原句的意义仍然完整。通常,非限制性定语从句与先行词之间用逗号隔开。例如:

The clock, which my grandfather bought, is still in good order.

2. 非限定性定语从句的关系词

引导非限制性定语从句的关系词有:who, whom, whose, which, when, where, 以及 as, 不可用 that 和 why。

3. 非限定性定语从句的用法

非限制性定语从句可以修饰整个主句或是主句中的一个部分,用 which 或 as 来引导。例如:

He passed the exam, which/as he hoped he would. (表示"正如……"意思时,从句放在主句后,which 和 as 可以互换)

注意:as 引导的从句可以放在主句之前,而 which 引导的从句只能放在主句之后。例如:

The rooms are painted in white, which makes them very bright.

As is known to all, Shanghai is the biggest city in China.

第四节　同位语从句与定语从句的区别

1. 引导词的类型不同

what, how, whatever 等可引导同位语从句,但不能引导定语从句。

2. 引导词的功能不同

that 引导同位语从句时,不充当句子成分;而引导定语从句时,其作为关系代词,充当定语从句的主语或宾语。例如:

The news that the team won the game is quite exciting. (同位语从句, that 在从句中不充当成分, 通常不能省略)

The news that he told me is quite exciting. (定语从句, that 在从句中充当 told 的宾语, 可以省略)

3. 被修饰的词语不同

同位语从句所修饰的名词比较有限,通常为 hope, wish, idea, news, fact, promise, opinion, suggestion, truth 等抽象名词;而定语从句所修饰的名词十分广泛。另外,定语从句的关系词与其修饰的先行词之间有较大关联;而同位语从句则没有。例如:when 和 where

引导定语从句时，通常只修饰表示时间和地点的名词，而它们在引导同位语从句时却并不一定（例如，I have no idea when we should go. 此句为由 when 引导的同位语从句，其修饰的名词并不表示时间）。又如，why 引导定语从句时，通常只修饰名词 the reason，而它在引导同位语从句时则不一定。

 Exercises

Ⅰ. Choose the best answer to complete each sentence.

1. He didn't know English, _____ made it difficult for him to work in a transnational corporation.
   A. that B. as C. this D. which

2. If you have a taste for exciting adventures, you may want to join the group of people _____ is to explore the mysteries of the sky.
   A. their work B. who work C. they work D. whose work

3. The audience, _____, like the film very much.
   A. most of them were students B. most of whom were students
   C. whom they were students D. they were mostly students

4. We went to the science museum, _____ we saw the man-made satellite.
   A. there B. which C. in the placed D. where

5. The book is for the students _____ native language is not Chinese, to study in a Chinese college or university.
   A. their B. that C. whose D. of whom

6. He never stopped trying to do anything _____ to do.
   A. that he had decided B. which he decided
   C. he decided D. what he decided

7. Do you remember the day _____ we graduated from the university?
   A. which B. that C. when D. in that

8. Her mother knew the reason _____ she was late yesterday.
   A. which B. what C. why D. that

9. They are talking about the teachers and schools _____ they have visited.
   A. which B. what C. where D. that

10. He became a well-known actor, _____ his father had expected.
    A. that was what B. it is what
    C. which was what D. and which was

11. You can see the trees _____ leaves open at sunrise and close at sunset.
    A. which B. whose C. as D. that

12. The train was crowded and I had to get into a carriage _____ there were already many people.
    A. where B. what C. that D. which

13. October 1st is the day _____ is celebrated by the Chinese people.
    A. when   B. what   C. it   D. which
14. Guilin is one of the most beautiful cities _____ millions of tourists every year.
    A. that attracts   B. that attract   C. which attract   D. where attracts
15. Collecting stamps is a hobby _____.
    A. which he finds real pleasure   B. which he gets much pleasure
    C. what he gets from   D. that gives him a great of pleasure
16. The boy found a place in the cellar _____ he used as his study room.
    A. which   B. what   C. where   D. in which
17. The highest temperature _____ in any furnace on earth is about 10,000 centigrade.
    A. we can get   B. that we can get it
    C. which we can get it   D. what we can get
18. The first step in preparing such a program is to draw a flow chart, _____ shown opposite.
    A. two examples of it is   B. two examples of which are
    C. whose two examples is   D. which two examples are
19. Edison used to live in the country _____ there are flocks of sheep.
    A. which   B. what   C. where   D. that
20. The girl was born in 1997 _____ Hong Kong was returned to her motherland.
    A. which   B. what   C. whose   D. when
21. Every morning, the first thing _____ both my sister and I did _____ to go out to see the rabbit.
    A. which; was   B. that; was   C. which; were   D. that; were
22. Penicillin is perhaps the medicine _____ has saved more lives than any other in the history of medicine.
    A. which   B. what   C. whose   D. who
23. We moved to the country so that the children would have a garden _____ they could play.
    A. which   B. what   C. where   D. that
24. The headmaster, _____ we spoke to yesterday, said that he would be glad to consider whatever suggestions we may offer.
    A. what   B. that   C. which   D. whom
25. The engineer _____ my father works is very famous in our country.
    A. to whom   B. on whom   C. with which   D. with whom
26. I am interested in _____ you have told me.
    A. all that   B. all what   C. that   D. which
27. The astronaut did many experiments in the spaceship, _____ much help for knowing space.
    A. which we think it is   B. which we think are of
    C. of which we think is   D. I think which is of
28. That's one of the reasons _____ I asked you to come.
    A. why   B. what   C. where   D. to which

29. _____ she hoped she would, she received the offer from Cambridge.
    A. Which   B. That   C. As   D. /
30. Such people _____ you describe are rare nowadays.
    A. like   B. who   C. as   D. that

Ⅱ. Identify the mistake in each sentence and then correct it.

1. The sun warms the earth, this makes it possible for plants to grow.
2. She is such a gracious girl who is ready to help others.
3. The hotel which he stayed during the vacation was well managed.
4. This is the reason why he explained for his absence.
5. The only thing that really matter the children is how soon they can return to their house.
6. What is well known, Nanning is famous for its "green."
7. The students are going to spend their summer vacation in Roman, which they have some friends.
8. He came up with four solutions to the problem, none of them are feasible.
9. This is the pet dog for that I paid six hundred dollars.
10. All what glitters is not gold.
11. The man with who you talked just now is my teacher.
12. There is a mountain it's top is always covered with snow.
13. This novel, I have read three times, is very touching.
14. It rained hard yesterday, it prevented us from going to the library.
15. The machine is such that I have never seen before.
16. The farm his uncle works is very big.
17. Charles Smith, whom was my former teacher, retired several years ago.
18. The package you are carrying it is about to come unwrapped
19. Listening is not such a simple thing which it appears to be.
20. Is he the man who he wants to see you?

第十五章

状语从句

第一节 状语从句的定义

状语从句（Adverbial Clause），是指用作复合句的状语起副词作用的句子。状语从句可以修饰谓语、非谓语动词、定语、状语或整个句子。根据其在复合句中所起的不同作用可分为时间、地点、原因、条件、目的、结果、让步、方式和比较等从句。

第二节 状语从句的分类及用法

一、时间状语从句（Adverbial Clause of Time）

1. 时间状语从句的引导词

时间状语从句常用的引导词有：when（在……时），as（当……时），while（在……期间），as soon as（一……就……），before（在……之前），after（在……之后），since（自从……以来），not...until（直到……才），until/till（直到……时）等。例如：

He had known the fact before I wrote to him.

Since he was a child he has lived in Nanning.

特殊的引导词有：the minute, the moment, the second, every time, the day, the instant（瞬间，顷刻），immediately, directly（不久，立即），no sooner...than（一……就……），hardly...when（刚……就……），scarcely...when（刚……就……／一……就……）。例如：

Her teacher recognized her the minute she appeared at the door.

2. 时间状语从句的用法及注意问题

（1）一般情况下，时间状语从句的谓语动词用"一般现在时"表示"一般将来时"；用"现在完成时"表示"将来完成时"。例如：

I will write to you as soon as I arrive in Guilin. （一般现在时表示一般将来时）

Our monitor will give her opinion when she has read our drafts. （现在完成时表示将来完成时）

（2）注意区别 when 和 while。具体的区分方法如下。

①when 引导的状语从句的谓语动词可以是延续性动词，也可以是瞬间动词。另外，when 有时可表示"就在那时"，而 while 没有这个意思。while 引导的状语从句的谓语动词必须是延续性动词，并强调主句和从句的动作同时发生。除此之外，while 有时还可以表示对比，when 则没有对比的意思。when 和 while 有时可以互换，有时不能。例如：

When she came in, her mother was cooking. （瞬间动词，只能用 when）

When I lived in the countryside, I used to carry some water for him. （延续性的动词，可以互换）

We were about to leave when he came in. （瞬间动词，表示"就在那时"，只能用 when）

He likes watching TV while his wife likes reading. （表示对比，只能用 while）

②when 后面接一般过去式；while 后面接进行时。例如：

The girl was doing her homework when she saw the superstar.

While the man was buying a souvenir, the boy called the police.

③when 除了表示主句和从句动作同时发生之外，还可以表示从句动词的动作在主句动词的动作"之前"或"之后"发生。而 while 用于强调两个动作同时进行。例如：

When Jack arrived at the station, the train had left. （从句动词的动作在主句动词的动作之后发生）

While the teacher was giving the lecture, the boy smiled. （从句动词的动作和主句动词的动作同时进行）

（3）hardly...when, scarcely...when, barely...when, no sooner...than 等引导的状语从句位于句首时，意思为"一……就"，且一般采用主谓倒装的结构。例如：

No sooner had the sport meet started than it began to rain heavily.

Hardly had I finished my words when he stood up.

Scarcely had he opened the door when a gust of wind blew the candle out.

二、地点状语从句（Adverbial Clause of Place）

1. 地点状语从句的引导词

地点状语从句常用的引导词有 where, wherever。例如：

Where there is a will, there is a way.

Wherever he goes, he always carries his umbrella.

2. 地点状语从句与定语从句的区别

通常，根据从句在句中充当的成分来判断其为状语从句还是定语从句。若从句充当主句中状语的成分，则为状语从句；充当修饰名词的定语成分，则为定语从句。另外，where 引导定语从句时，从句前应有一个表示地点的名词作为先行词；而状语从句前则没有先行词。例如：

You can go where you want to go. （where 引导地点状语从句）

你可以去你想去的地方。

You can go to the school where you want to go. （where 引导定语从句，修饰 school）

你可以去你想去的学校。

三、原因状语从句（Adverbial Clause of Cause）

1. 原因状语从句的引导词

原因状语从句常用的引导词有 because，since，as 等。例如：

He had to take a part-time job because he needed money for his tuition.

As I was late for class, I was punished.

Since dinner is ready, let's start.

其他的引导词有：seeing that，now that，in that，given that 等。例如：

Seeing that you have no time, I do it myself.

I am lucky in that I have got two sisters and a brother.

2. because，since，as，for 辨析

（1）because 语势最强，用以回答 why 提出的问题，说明人所不知的原因。当原因显而易见或已为人们所知，应用 as 或 since。例如：

——Why were you late?

——Because the traffic was too heavy.

Since/As the weather is so bad, we have to delay our journey.

（2）若 because 引导的从句位于句末，且前面有逗号，则可用 for 来代替。for 引导的是一个并列句，多用以对多种情况加以推断，或对前一分句进行补充说明。例如：

He is absent today, because/for he is ill.

He must be ill for he is absent today.

It must have rained for the ground is wet.

四、目的状语从句（Adverbial Clause of Purpose）

1. 目的状语从句的引导词

目的状语从句常用的引导词有 so that，in order that。例如：

I got up early so that I could catch the bus.

In order that he could pass the exam, he worked hard.

注意：当主、从句的主语一致时，可以用 in order to 结构代替 in order that 引导的从句。例如：

In order that I can afford a car I am saving money.

＝In order to afford a car I am saving money.

其他的引导词有：lest（以免，唯恐），in case（万一，以防），for fear that（that 可以省略，表示"以免"）等。例如：

She hid the toy for fear that/lest her sister should see it.

Take your dictionary in case you need it.

2. 目的状语从句的用法及注意问题

for fear (that), lest 引导的目的状语从句常用虚拟语气。例如：

They talked in low voice lest they (should) be heard.

The little girl took an umbrella with her for fear it might rain. (for fear 后面省略了 that)

五、结果状语从句（Adverbial Clause of Result）

1. 结果状语从句的引导词

结果状语从句常用的引导词有 so...that，such...that。其中，such 是形容词，修饰名词；so 是副词，修饰形容词或副词。二者具体的应用形式如下：

（1）"so + *adj.* / *adv.* + that；so + *adj.* + a/an + *n.* + that"结构。例如：

He speaks so fast that we can not catch him.

There is so rapid an increase in population that a food shortage is caused.

（2）"such + (a/an +) *adj.* + *n.* + that"结构。其中，名词可以是可数名词的单数或复数，也可以是不可数名词。例如：

He is such a good person that we all love him.

They are such fine teachers that we all respect them.

注意：so 与表示数量的代词 many，few，much，little 等可形成固定搭配，在此类结构中，so...that 结构不能换用为 such 对应的结构。例如：

Our country has so much coal that she can export large quantities.

其他的引导词有：so that，such that，to the degree that，with the result that，to such a degree that 等。例如：

I was cooking, with the result that I did not hear the telephone.

2. so that 用法辨析

so that 可引导结果状语从句，表示"因此，以至于"；也可引导目的状语从句，表示"为了，以便"。例如：

It was very cold, so that the river froze. 天气非常寒冷，以至于河水都结冰了。(so that 引导结果状语从句)

I went to school early so that I could clean the classroom.

= I went to school early in order that I could clean the classroom. (so that 引导目的状语从句)

六、条件状语从句（Adverbial Clause of Condition）

条件状语从句表示条件时，分为真实条件和非真实条件两种情形。(关于非真实条件的相关知识，详见"虚拟语气"一章。这里只讨论真实条件的情况。)

1. 条件状语从句的引导词

条件状语从句常用的引导词有 if，unless，whether（whether... or not）。例如：

If you go to the party, you will have a good time.

They won't attend the party unless they are invited.

其他的引导词有 as/so long as（只要，如果），only if（只有，除非），providing/provided that（假如，除非），supposing that（如果，假如），on condition that（在……条件下）等。例如：

So long as I need you, you will be there.

The fans will go only if their idols go with them.

We will accept the price on condition that the goods are of good quality.

Supposing that you have no money, what would you do?

2. 用法及注意问题

使用条件状语从句时，要注意正确使用时态。当主句为将来时时，从句要用一般现在时。例如：

If it rains tomorrow, I'll stay at home.

If you don't hurry up, you'll miss the bus.

七、让步状语从句（Adverbial Clause of Concession）

1. 让步状语从句的引导词

让步状语从句常用的引导词有 though, although, even if, even though 等。例如：

I will have a try even though I should fail.

注意：though, although 表示"虽然"，不能与 but 连用。例如：

Although she may have told you the truth, you still think it is impossible.

2. as, though 引导的倒装句

（1）as/though 引导的让步状语从句通常采用倒装结构，其中，as 必须用倒装，though 可用可不用。其倒装结构的形式为表语或状语提前。例如：

Child as/though he was, he knew what was the right thing to do.

Fast as you read, you can't finish the book in a day.

Much as we admire his courage, we don't think he was right.

（2）as/though 引导的让步状语从句采用倒装结构时需注意下列问题。

①句首名词不能带有任何冠词。例如：

Boy as he is, he can manage it.

②句首为实义动词时，其他助动词要放在主语的后面。若实义动词带有宾语和状语，则宾语和状语要随实义动词一起放在主语之前（详见第十七章"倒装句"）。例如：

Try hard as he will, he never seems able to finish it before the deadline.

Change your mind as you will, you can not gain our support.

八、比较状语从句（Adverbial Clause of Comparison）

1. 比较状语从句的引导词

比较状语从句常用的引导词有 as（同级比较），than（不同程度的比较），"the + 比较级"…"the + 比较级"。三者具体的用法如下：

（1）同级比较：as…as（第一个 as 为副词，修饰副词或形容词；第二个 as 为连词，后

接主谓结构。由于第二个 as 后面的句子的谓语通常与主句一样,所以往往省略其谓语)。例如:

He studies as hard as she does. (as 修饰副词)

The lecture is as important as that one. (as 修饰形容词)

as...as 的否定结构为 not so/as...as。例如:

I have never seen so much rain as fell that March.

It was not as cold as on the previous night.

(2) 不同程度的比较:than。例如:

Health is more important than wealth.

The bag is less expensive than that one.

The old man moves more slowly than the young man does.

(3) "the + 比较级"..."the + 比较级"表示越……越……。例如:

The harder he worked, the happier he felt.

The more you read the book, the more you understand what I mean.

2. 比较状语从句的用法及注意问题

使用比较状语从句时,比较的内容要一致。例如:

The weather in Nanning is warmer than Beijing. (错)

The weather in Nanning is warmer than that in Beijing. (对)

九、方式状语从句(Adverbial Clause of Manner)

1. 方式状语从句的引导词

方式状语从句常用的引导词有 as(按照,正如,像),(just) as...so...(正如……一样,……也……)引导。例如:

You should do as the teacher tells you.

As water is to fish, so air is to man.

2. as though,as if 引导的从句的时态辨析

as if 和 as though 引导的从句中的时态取决于说话者对所谈内容的态度。若说话者认为其看法是真的或可能会成为事实,从句中的谓语不用虚拟语气。若从句的内容是不真实的,或与事实相反,从句中的谓语要用虚拟语气。例如:

It looks as if it may rain soon. (发生的可能性大,用陈述语气。)

They talked as if they had been friends for years. (与事实相反,用虚拟语气。)

When a pencil is partly in a glass of water, it looks as if it were broken. (与事实相反,用虚拟语气。)

 Exercises

Ⅰ. Choose the best answer to complete each sentence.

1. It is hard to avoid mistakes. _____ you correct them conscientiously, it will be all right.

A. In case of B. As long as C. Although D. Despite
2. Jane always focus her attention on what her teachers say in class _____ she can get good grades in her assignments.
   A. so that B. in order to C. because of D. rather than
3. He explained everything about his sister _____ anyone should misunderstand her.
   A. since B. when C. lest D. as if
4. Unlikely _____ it might seem, I am tired, too.
   A. although B. even if C. that D. as
5. I'd lend the book to you _____ I could get it back.
   A. on condition that B. now that C. except that D. considering that
6. The thief told him that he had better keep silent _____ he wanted to get into trouble.
   A. if B. unless C. otherwise D. whether
7. No sooner had he sat down _____ he heard the knock at the door.
   A. when B. then C. than D. as
8. He went to work so late _____ his boss called him again and again before he arrived.
   A. as B. that C. for D. when
9. _____ we gave him anything, he would say "thank you" with a smile.
   A. When B. That C. Whenever D. What
10. _____, they could not find any useful materials in the room.
    A. As they would search B. Would as they search
    C. Search as they would D. They would search as
11. The fuel must have been finished, _____ the engine stopped.
    A. since B. because C. for D. as
12. Anyone can borrow books from the library _____ he returns them in time.
    A. as long as B. so that C. unless D. even if
13. There was such a long line at the exhibition _____ we had to wait for a long time.
    A. as B. that C. so D. until
14. He married _____ he loved her but because he loved her money.
    A. because not B. though C. for D. not because
15. The more civilized man has become, _____ he is limited by the disadvantage of his environment.
    A. the little B. the many C. the more D. the less
16. His mother watched him _____ he disappeared from sight in the distance.
    A. until B. unless C. since D. before
17. Some students spent _____ much time on their mobile phones that they could not finished their assignments.
    A. as B. so C. such D. very
18. _____ the experiment, he had not yet got any satisfactory results.
    A. How carefully he performed B. How he performed carefully

C. No matter how carefully he performed   D. No matter what he performed carefully

19. _____ the teacher came in, the girls were singing loudly.
    A. When   B. While   C. After   D. Before

20. The super star grew up _____ he was born.
    A. since   B. when   C. while   D. Where

21. _____ we run fast, we will catch the first bus.
    A. Unless   B. When   C. Though   D. If

22. This river is _____ that river.
    A. as long as three times   B. as long three times as
    C. three times long as   D. three times as long as

23. Table tennis is _____ an interesting game _____ people all over the world play it.
    A. so; that   B. such; that   C. so; as   D. such; as

24. _____ the weather was fine, we went for an outing.
    A. As   B. Because of   C. For   D. Until

25. The professor spoke in a loud voice _____ every one of us could hear him.
    A. such that   B. so   C. so that   D. such

26. I will buy a car _____ I have enough money.
    A. though   B. even if   C. if   D. unless

27. I thought of it just _____ you opened your mouth.
    A. when   B. while   C. since   D. for

28. Generally, air will be heavily polluted _____ there are factories.
    A. though   B. until   C. where   D. so

29. _____ to the cinema, the movie had already started.
    A. When went   B. I went   C. While go   D. When I went

30. _____, I can't agree to his proposal.
    A. As much I respect him   B. Much as I respect him
    C. Him as I respect much   D. As I respect him much

31. _____ difficult the task may be, we will try our best to complete it in time.
    A. No matter   B. No wonder   C. Though   D. However

32. Not until he finished his job _____ take a rest.
    A. he stops to   B. did he stop   C. did he stop to D. he stopped to

33. _____, there is hope.
    A. There is man   B. When man is there
    C. Man is there   D. Where there is man

34. After the war, a new school building was put up _____ there had once been a theatre.
    A. as   B. where   C. if   D. when

35. The child was _____ immediately after supper.
    A. tired to go to bed   B. too tired to go to bed
    C. so tired that he went to bed   D. very tired, he went to bed

36. I don't know why she's looking at me _____ she knew me. I've never seen her before.
    A. as　　　　　　B. although　　　　C. even if　　　　D. as if
37. _____ the ground is, _____ the air becomes.
    A. Higher; than　　　　　　　　　　B. The more high; the more thinner
    C. The higher; the thinner　　　　　D. More high; less thin
38. The couple worked in the laboratory _____ day had broken.
    A. not until　　　B. until　　　　　C. with　　　　　D. though
39. Our boss _____ the hotel until he has done all his business.
    A. will not leave　B. not leaves　　C. has leaved　　D. is not leave
40. We'll start our project _____ the president agrees.
    A. if　　　　　　B. whether　　　　C. that　　　　　D. no matter

II. Identify the mistake in each sentence and then correct it.

1. The temperature in Nanning is hotter than Guilin.
2. She gives her parents a call as soon as she arrives at the school.
3. He likes playing chess more than to watch TV.
4. Although she saw the film many times, but she still wanted to see it again.
5. He fell asleep while was doing his homework.
6. He is saving money so he can buy a house.
7. No sooner had he seen the policeman when he ran away.
8. The cat scratch you if you pull its tail.
9. When he entered the room, his sister has been eating for five minutes.
10. Whether you cheat in the exam, you'll never get away with it.

第十六章

虚拟语气

第一节 虚拟语气的定义

虚拟语气（Subjunctive Mood）是谓语动词的一种特殊形式，用以表示假设、主观愿望、猜测、建议、可能或空想等非真实情况。英语中有三种语气形式，即陈述语气、祈使语气和虚拟语气。陈述语气用以说明事实或就事实提出询问，可用于陈述句、疑问句和某些感叹句中；祈使语气用于表示请求、命令、建议或警告等；虚拟语气则用来表示假想，即并非客观存在的事实。例如：

He is honest.
他很诚实。（陈述语气）
Don't be late next time.
下次别迟到。（祈使语气）
If I were you, I would not go.
我要是你，我就不会去。（虚拟语气）
I wish I had a lot of money.
要是我有很多钱就好了。（虚拟语气）

第二节 虚拟语气的用法

一、虚拟语气用于非真实条件句中

虚拟语气用于非真实条件句中时的具体形式如表16-1所示。

表 16-1 虚拟语气用于非真实条件句

时态类型	主句谓语形式	条件句的谓语形式	例句
与现在事实相反	would/should/could/might + do	动词过去式 did；be 多用 were	1. If I were you, I should study English. 2. I would certainly go if I had time.
与过去事实相反	would/should/could/might + have done	动词过去完成式 had done	1. If you had taken my advice, you would not have failed in the test. 2. If I had left a little earlier, I would have caught the train.
与将来事实相反	would/should/could/might + do	①动词过去式 ②should + do ③were + to do	1. If you came tomorrow, we would have the meeting. 2. If it were to rain tomorrow, the meeting would be put off.

1. 虚拟语气的倒装结构

若条件句中有 had, should, were 时，可以把虚拟条件句中的连词 if 省去，而将 had, should, were 等词提到主语之前，即用倒装结构。另外，句中如果出现 not 等否定词，则需将否定词放在主语后面。例如：

If she had been here five minutes earlier she would have seen her old friend.
= Had she been here five minutes earlier she would have seen her old friend.
如果她早到五分钟，她就会看见她的老朋友了。

Were it not for the expense (= If it were not for the expense), I would go abroad now.
如果不是因为费用问题，我早就出国了。

Were I in school again (= If I were in school again), I would work harder.
如果我能再上一次学，我会学习得更努力。

Had you asked me (= If you had asked me), I would have told you.
如果你问我，我就会告诉你。

2. 混合型虚拟语气

有时，虚拟条件从句与主句所指的时间不一致。如果从句指的是过去，而主句指的是现在或将来，则应根据具体的语境情况，结合上面提到的三种时态类型对时态作出相应的调整。例如：

If it had rained last night, the ground would be wet now.（条件从句表达的时间是过去，因此用 had + 过去分词；主句表示的时间是现在，因此用"would + 动词原形"）
要是昨晚下过雨的话，现在地面就会是湿的。

You would be much better now if you had taken my advice.（条件从句用"had + 过去分词"，表示对过去的假设，而主句是表示对现在的假设，因此用"would + 动词原形"）
假若你当时听我的话，你现在就会好多了。

If you had followed the doctor's advice, you would be all right now.（条件从句表达的时间

是过去，因此用"had + 过去分词"；主句表示的时间是现在，因此用"would + 动词原形"）

如果你听从医生的建议，你现在就会好了。

I would never have been able to finish those two miles if I were you. （从句中用过去时，表示事实与现在相反；主句用"would + have + 过去分词"，表示事实与过去相反。）

如果我是你的话，我绝不可能跑完那两英里。

If the weather had been more favorable, the crop would be growing better.

如果当时的天气好一些，现在的庄稼还会长得更好。

If you were in better health, we would have allowed you to join them in the work.

如果你的身体好些，我们早就让你参加他们的工作了。

3. 含蓄型虚拟语气

具体的情形如下：有时，虚拟条件并非通过 if 引导的条件句来表示，而是暗含在上下文中。具体的情形如下：

（1）用 but for, with, without, in the absence of（如果没有）等来代替条件从句。例如：

Without electricity human life would be quite different.

= If there were no electricity, human life would be quite different.

如果没有电，人类的生活就会大不一样。

Without your help, I couldn't finish my work on time.

如果没有你的帮忙，我就不可能按时完成工作。

In the absence of water and air, nothing could live.

如果没有空气和水，一切生命都无法生存。

What would you do with a million dollars? (= if you had a million dollars)

如果你有一百万美元，你会用来做什么？

But for the rain (= If it hadn't been for the rain), we would have finished the work.

如果不是因为下雨，我们早就完成工作了。

（2）用 otherwise, or (or else), even though 等来表示与上文的情况相反，从而引出虚拟语气。例如：

I lost your address. Otherwise I would have visited you long before.

= I lost your address. If I hadn't lost your address, I would have visited you long before.

我弄丢了你的地址，要不然我早就拜访你了。

I was ill that day. Otherwise, I would have taken part in the sports meet.

那天我病了，否则我就会参加运动会了。

（3）虚拟条件通过 but 暗示出来。例如：

He would have given you more help, but he was too busy.

他本来会给你更多的帮助，但是他太忙了。（如果那时他不忙，他可以给你更多的帮助。句中的"but he was too busy"实际上暗示了一个虚拟条件——如果那时他不忙）

He would lose weight, but he eats too much.

他本来可以减肥的，但是他吃得太多了。（如果他吃得不多的话，他是可以减肥的。句中的"but he eats too much"实际上是说"如果他吃得不多"这一虚拟条件）

二、虚拟语气用于名词性从句

1. 用于主语从句

主语从句中的虚拟语气通常采用"should + 动词原形"的形式。在此句型中，主语从句由连词 that 引导，且其句型通常为"It be + 形容词/过去分词 + that...（should）..."。其中，常见的用于此句型的形容词或过去分词如下。

（1）用于该句型的形容词有表示"迫切，紧急，重要"的词，如 imperative, urgent, necessary, essential, important, vital 等；

表示"适当，较好"的词，如 appropriate, advisable, better, preferable, proper 等；

表示"可能"的词，如 probable, possible 等；

表示"好，坏，对，错"的词，如 good, bad, right, wrong 等；

表示"自然，有趣，吃惊"的词，如 natural, funny, strange, surprising 等。例如：

It's natural that he should feel hurt.

他感到疼是很正常的。

It was necessary that we (should) make everything ready ahead of time.

把一切提前准备好很有必要。

（2）用于该句型的过去分词有表示"要求"的词，如 required, demanded, requested, desired 等；

表示"建议"的词，如 suggested, recommended 等；

表示"命令"的词，如 ordered 等。例如：

It is desired that the building of the house be completed next month.

真希望这所房子在下个月前就能竣工。

It is required that nobody (should) smoke here.

要求每个人不许在这里吸烟。

It is advised that one (should) take plenty of boiled water.

有人建议每个人都应多喝水。

It is ordered that all the students should not carry a mobile phone with them while taking an exam.

根据命令，所有学生在考试期间都不能携带手机。

2. 用于宾语从句

（1）wish 后面所接宾语从句中的虚拟语气的时态应根据从句的意义来判断。具体的判断方法如下：

①当 wish 表示与现在和将来事实相反的愿望时，从句的谓语动词用过去时态。例如：

I wish they were not so late.

要是他们来得不是这么晚就好了。

I wish I were ten years younger.

但愿我年轻十岁。

I wish I could fly to the moon someday.

如果有一天我能飞到月球上就好了。

②当 wish 表示与过去事实相反的愿望时，从句的谓语动词用过去完成时态。例如：
I wished he hadn't done that.
我真希望那件事不是他做的。
I wish you had come to the lecture.
要是你来听报告就好了。

注意：wish 与 hope 所接的宾语从句的区别在于：hope 表示的希望，一般可以实现，因此其宾语从句用陈述语气。wish 表示的愿望通常难度很大或不大可能实现，因此其宾语从句用虚拟语气。例如：
We hope they will come. (We don't know if they can come)
We wish they could come. (We know they are not coming)
我们希望他们能来。

(2) 表示"要求，建议，命令"等动词后面的宾语从句中的谓语动词也会采用虚拟语气。通常，用于此句型的动词有：advise, direct, agree, ask, demand, decide, desire, insist, order, prefer, propose, request, suggest 等。并且，此句型从句的谓语动词要用 "should + 动词原形" 形式，其中 should 可以省去。例如：
I insisted that he (should) go with us.
我坚持让他和我们一起去。
He urged that they go to Europe.
他督促他们到欧洲去。
He suggested that we should leave early.
他建议我们早点动身。
He ordered that it (should) be sent back.
他命令把它送回去。
I ask that he leave.
我要求他走开。
He requires that I (should) appear.
他要求我出场。
I move that we accept the proposal.
我提议通过这项提案。
He arranged that I should go abroad.
他安排我去国外。
She desires that he do it.
她希望他做此事。
The general directed that the prisoners should be set free.
将军指示释放那些俘虏。

注意：当 insist 表示"坚持认为"，suggest 表示"表明，显示"时，不用虚拟语气。例如：
He insisted that she was honest.
他坚持认为她是诚实的。

（3）would rather 后面的宾语从句，其谓语动词习惯上也要用虚拟语气，表示"宁愿做什么"。具体的用法如下：

①用一般过去时表示现在或将来的愿望。例如：

I'd rather you came next week.

我宁愿你下周来。

I'd rather you went now.

我宁愿你现在去。

②用过去完成时表示过去的愿望。例如：

I'd rather you hadn't said it.

我真希望你没有这样说过。

3. 用于表语从句或同位语从句

在由与表示决定、主张、要求、建议、命令等的动词相对应的名词如 order，plan，suggestion，idea，proposal，advice，demand 等构成的表语从句或同位语从句中，也会采用虚拟语气，且其从句的谓语动词通常采用"should + 动词原形"结构，其中，should 可省略。例如：

Our suggestion is that you（should）be the first to go.

我们的建议是你应该第一个去。

My advice is that you（should）quit smoking.

我的建议是你应该戒烟。

I made a suggestion that you（should）stay here until the party was over.

我建议你待到晚会结束。

三、用于定语从句中

定语从句中的虚拟语气通常用于"It is time（about time/high time/the very time/right time）that... +（过去时或 should + 动词原形）..."句型中，其从句的谓语动词通常用过去式表示"早该干某事了"。有时，从句的谓语动词也可采用过去进行时或"should + 动词原形"（较少见，且 should 不能省略）。例如：

It is high time that you went home now.

＝It is high time I should go home now.

我该回家了。

It is high time that we went to school.

我们早该上学了。

It's time we left.

我们该走了。

It's about time that we put an end to this controversy.

现在该是我们停止这场争论的时候了。

四、用于 as if（as though），even if（even though）引导的从句中

as if（as though），even if（even though）引导的从句中所用虚拟语气的时态与 wish 后面

所接从句中谓语动词的时态情况一致，即当从句表示与现在和将来事实相反的愿望时，从句中的谓语动词用过去时态；当从句表示与过去事实相反的愿望时，从句中的谓语动词用过去完成时态。例如：

He acts as if he knew me.
他显得认识我似的。
They treat me as though I were a stranger.
他们待我如陌生人。
I really don't care for the way you're speaking to me.
It seems as if you were my father.
我真的不喜欢你和我说话的方式，好像你是我父亲似的。
He talks as if he had been abroad.
他说起话来好像曾经出过国。
It isn't as if he were poor.
他不像穷的样子。或：他又不穷。

注意：从句所表示的内容若为事实或可能成为事实，其谓语动词也可用陈述语气。例如：

It looks as if we'll be late.
我们似乎要迟到了。

五、用于 if only 引导的感叹句中

if only 表示"如果……就好了"，其与 wish 一样，也可用于表示与事实相反的愿望。并且，if only 所接从句中虚拟语气的时态与 wish 后面所接从句中谓语动词的时态情况一致，即当从句表示与现在和将来事实相反的愿望时，从句中的谓语动词用过去时态；当从句表示与过去事实相反的愿望时，从句中的谓语动词用过去完成时态。例如：

If only I were as clever as you.
要是我像你一样聪明就好了。
If only I were taller.
要是我再高一点就好了。
If only she would go with me!
她要是愿意和我一道去就好了！
If only he would come.
但愿他能来。
If only she had had more courage!
她再勇敢一些就好了！

六、用于表示祝愿的话语中

表示祝愿的话语中也可以用虚拟语气。其虚拟语气的形式为谓语动词用动词原形或"may + 动词原形"。例如：

Long live motherland.

祖国万岁。

Heaven help us.

愿老天保佑我们。

God bless you.

愿上帝保佑你。

May there never be another world war.

愿再也不发生世界大战。

May you be happy all your life.

祝你一生幸福。

May you enjoy many years of health and happiness.

祝您健康长寿美满幸福。

 Exercises

Ⅰ. Choose the best answer to complete each sentence.

1. If only he _____ quietly as the doctor instructed, he would not suffer so much now.
   A. lies   B. lay   C. had lain   D. should lie
2. How I wish every family _____ a large house with a beautiful garden.
   A. has   B. had   C. will have   D. had had
3. You did not let me drive. If we _____ in turn, you _____ so tired.
   A. drove; didn't get   B. drove; wouldn't get
   C. were driving; wouldn't get   D. had driven; wouldn't have got
4. _____ it rain tomorrow, we would have to put off the visit to the Yangpu Bridge.
   A. Were   B. Should   C. Would   D. Will
5. _____ the clouds, you would find the airplane in the sky easily.
   A. Had it not been for   B. If it were not
   C. If it had not been for   D. Were it not for
6. If my lawyer _____ here last Sunday, he _____ me from going.
   A. had been; would have prevented   B. had been; would prevent
   C. were; prevent   D. were; would have prevented
7. _____ hard, he would have passed the exam.
   A. If he were to work   B. Had he worked
   C. Should he work   D. Were he to work
8. _____ today, he would get there by Friday.
   A. Were he to leave   B. If he had left   C. Did he to leave   D. Had he left
9. Had you listened to the doctor, you _____ all right now.
   A. are   B. were   C. would be   D. would have been
10. I did not see your sister at the meeting. If she _____, she would have met my brother.

A. has come B. did come C. come D. had come

11. Mike's father, as well as his mother, insisted he _____ home.
    A. stayed B. could stay C. has stayed D. stay

12. It was requested that the play _____ again.
    A. should put on B. would put on C. be put on D. put on

13. She insisted that a doctor _____ immediately.
    A. had sent for B. send C. be sent for D. was sent

14. —Did you scold him for his carelessness?
    —Yes, but _____ it.
    A. I'd rather not do
    B. I'd rather not have done
    C. I should't do
    D. I'd better not do

15. If only I _____ my car.
    A. hadn't lost B. wouldn't lose C. didn't lose D. haven't lost

16. I would rather you _____ anything about it for the time being.
    A. do B. didn't do C. don't D. didn't

17. It is high time that we _____ a meeting to discuss this problem.
    A. hold B. held C. have held D. had held

18. If it _____ the snow, we _____ the Simian Mountain last week.
    A. were not; could have climbed
    B. were not; could climb
    C. had not been; could have climbed
    D. had not been; could climb

19. What do you think of his proposal that we _____ a play at the English meeting?
    A. had put on B. should put on C. have put on D. will put on

20. Supposing he never _____, what would happen then.
    A. come B. came C. would come D. will come

21. I'm surprised that he _____ in the exam.
    A. should fail B. would have failed C. may have failed D. should have failed

22. With so much work on hand, you _____ to see the game last night.
    A. mustn't go
    B. shouldn't go
    C. couldn't have gone
    D. shouldn't have gone

23. It is natural that he _____ his mind.
    A. changes B. changing C. change D. to change

24. If only I _____ to my parents' advice!
    A. listening B. listen C. am listening D. had listened

25. I wish it _____ spring all the year round.
    A. were B. is C. be D. will be

26. I suggested the person _____ to be put into prison.
    A. refers B. referring C. referred D. refer

27. When a pencil is partly in a glass of water, it looks as if it _____.
    A. breaks B. has broken C. were broken D. had been broken

28. Without the Communist Party of China, _____ New China now.
    A. there would be no   B. there will be
    C. there were not   D. there hadn't been

29. The doctor proposed that my brother _____ his right hand.
    A. avoid to use   B. should avoid to use
    C. avoid using   D. avoided using

30. It is very important that they _____ advice of others about their work.
    A. will ask   B. shall ask   C. have asked   D. ask

31. The TV play for tonight won't be interesting. Even if it _____, I might not have time for it.
    A. would be   B. be   C. had been   D. were

32. I was really anxious about you. You _____ home without a word.
    A. mustn't leave   B. shouldn't have left
    C. couldn't have left   D. needn't leave

33. You are late again. You _____ here earlier.
    A. should come   B. will come
    C. should have come   D. will have come

34. The two strangers talked as if they _____ friends for years.
    A. should be   B. would be   C. have been   D. had been

35. —If he _____, he _____ that food.
    —Luckily he was sent to the hospital immediately.
    A. was warned; would not take   B. had been warned; would not have taken
    C. would be warned; had not taken D. would have been warned; had not taken

36. I told Sally how to get there, but perhaps I _____ for her.
    A. had to write it out   B. must have written it out
    C. should have written it out   D. ought to write it out

37. He's always talking like that, as if the whole world _____ to him alone.
    A. had belonged   B. belonged   C. were belonging   D. were belonged

38. _____ the friendship between us last forever!
    A. Could   B. Will   C. May   D. Wish

39. —There were already five people in the car but they managed to take me as well.
    —It _____ a comfortable journey.
    A. can't be   B. shouldn't be
    C. mustn't have been   D. couldn't have been

40. _____ so busy, she would come to help you.
    A. Should my daughter   B. Was my daughter not
    C. If my daughter were not   D. If my daughter isn't

Ⅱ. Identify the mistake in each sentence and then correct it.

1. I made a suggestion that you stayed here until the party was over.

2. Jane's face suggested that she should be ill, and her parents suggested that she have a medical examination.
3. —If he had warned, he would not have taken that food.
   —Luckily he was sent to the hospital immediately.
4. Without the air to hold some of the sun's heat, the earth at night would be frozen cold, too cold for us to live.
5. —Have you ever been to Beijing?
   —No, but I wish I have.
6. If it hadn't rained last Sunday, we could go picnicking.
7. Everybody would be very happy if the hot summer finishes tomorrow.
8. If only I took your advice!
9. I wish I attend the meeting last week.
10. The TV play for tonight won't be interesting. Even if it had been, I might not have time for it.
11. The workers in France demanded that their pay would be raised from the following week on.
12. If it hadn't snowed yesterday, we could have played football on the sports ground now.
13. The monitor made a proposal that the whole class be discussed the matter.
14. Don't come this afternoon. I'd rather you come tomorrow.
15. John was very busy last week, otherwise, he would come to attend the meeting.
16. It was ordered that no smoking will be allowed in the library.
17. —Did you go to see the football match yesterday?
    —No, I didn't feel well, but I would have gone if I did.
18. Wish the friendship between us last forever!
19. —Where have you been?
    —I got caught in traffic; even though I could have been here soon.
20. She would rather pay more money on books than on clothes.

第十七章

倒 装 句

第一节 倒装句的定义与结构

一、倒装句的定义

倒装句（Inversion），是指由于语法结构的要求，或是由于修辞的需要而改变句子的自然语序，把一些本应置于主语之后的句子成分提到主语之前的句子。其中，因语法结构的要求而产生的倒装是必须的，否则就会出现语法错误；因修饰的需要而产生的倒装是选择性的，其目的或是强调，或是使上下文紧密衔接，抑或是保持句子结构的平衡匀称，因此倒装与否只会产生表达效果上的差异。根据句子中的谓语是全部还是部分置于主语前面，倒装可分为完全倒装和部分倒装两种类型。

二、倒装句的结构

主语和谓语是句子的核心，它们之间有两种语序：自然语序（Natural Orde）和倒装语序（Inverted Order）。英语的自然语序为"主语 + 谓语 +……"；英语的倒装语序为"谓语的全部或部分 + 主语 +……"。而倒装语序又可分为完全倒装和部分倒装两种类型。

1. 完全倒装

完全倒装是指句子的全部谓语置于主语之前，其结构为"全部谓语 + 主语 +……"。
例如：
Down jumped the prisoner from the top floor when the policeman pointed his pistol at him.
当警察把手枪瞄准那个囚犯时，"砰"的一下他就从顶楼跳了下去。
On the ground lay piles of red apples, which are to be shipped to some southern cities.
成堆的红苹果放在地上，等着用船运到其他南方城市去。
Here is the present with red ribbons you have been looking forward to.
你有一份盼望已久的系着红丝带的礼物在这儿。

注意：
(1) 完全倒装中，谓语动词的数要与其后面的主语的数一致。例如：

There is a growing tendency these days for many people who live in rural areas to come into and work in city.

农民进城打工正成为日益增长的趋势。

(2) 完全倒装的主语必须是名词，如果主语是人称代词则不用倒装。例如：

There are many blind paths now, but they are not standardized, and they were not built or designed by blind people.

现在有了很多盲道，但是并不标准，不是由残疾人修建或设计的。

Down came the rain and up went the umbrellas.

下雨了，伞都撑起来了。

Down it came.

它掉了下来。

2. 部分倒装

部分倒装是指只把系动词、情态动词、助动词等置于主语之前，谓语的主体部分仍位于主语之后，其结构为"系动词 be（am/is/are/was/were）/情态动词（can/could/should/may/must/will/shall）/助动词（do/does/did/have/has）+ 主语 + 谓语主体部分（动词原形/过去分词/现在分词）+……"。例如：

Only when the scientists have carried out a lot of experiments in the lab, can they arrive at a reasonable conclusion.

只有当科学家们在实验室进行大量的实验时，他们才能得出一个合理的结论。

Had it not been for the timely help from my friends, I would not achieve such a great success as it is.

要不是朋友们的及时帮助，我就不会像现在这样取得巨大的成功。

In no place other than the small mountain area, it had been said, can one experience four seasons in the course of a single day.

据说除了这片小山区，世界上没有哪个地方能让人在一天中感受到四季的变化。

第二节　倒装句的用法及注意问题

一、疑问句引起的完全倒装或部分倒装

疑问句可采用完全倒装或部分倒装语序。例如：

Will you attend the professor's lecture after ending these series of complex research works?

你在完成这一系列复杂的研究工作后还参加教授的课程讲座吗？

Was it the paper you had to submit to the tutor at the end of last semester?

这是你上学期末提交给导师的论文吗？

Are these two brothers working together to overcome difficulties they encountered in their lives?

这两兄弟有没有共同努力工作来克服他们在生活中遇到的困难？
Does knowledge render things more comprehensible, or more complex and mysterious?
知识使事物变得更加明了还是更加复杂和神秘了呢？

注意：以疑问词或疑问词修饰的名词作主语的疑问句要用正常语序。例如：

Who told you the news that homeless people had fled from their home because of this great hurricane?
这则关于无家可归的人们因为这场飓风逃离家园的信息，是谁告诉你的？
Which girl with excellent running performance won the first place at this track meeting?
哪位女孩以优秀的跑步成绩在田径赛中拔得头筹？

二、there be 结构引起的完全倒装

there be 结构中，主语位于 be 之后，属于完全倒装。在此结构中，可代替 be 的半联系动词有 exist, seem, happen, appear, live, rise, stand, come, lie, flow 等。例如：

There are crowds of people purchasing these fresh vegetables in the supermarket that in less than half an hour nothing is left.
成群的人在超市购买这些新鲜的蔬菜，不到半小时，蔬菜就被抢购一空。
There stands a spectacular pagoda in the southeast of this small village where few people live.
在这个很少有人居住的小乡村的东南方矗立着一座宏伟的宝塔。
There have been some small fluctuations in the past year, but by and large prices have remained stable.
去年物价虽然有一些小波动，但是整体仍保持稳定。
There have occurred many tremendous changes in my hometown since the policy on the improvement of people's living standards was carried out.
自从改善人民生活水平的政策落实以来，我的家乡发生了巨变。

三、表示地点的介词短语引起的完全倒装

为使句子的叙述或描绘更加生动形象，增加其语言效果，在以 here, there, now, then, in, out, off, up, away, under, down 等表示地点、方位的副词，以及表示地点的介词短语，如 in the distance, in the front of, in the middle/center of 等开头的句子中使用完全倒装结构。例如：

In the center of the square surrounded with green trees stood a soldier on duty.
绿树环绕的广场中央站着一位执勤的士兵。
Out rushed a ballistic missile from under the bomber.
从轰炸机下窜出一枚弹道导弹。
From down the hospital hallway came a blood-curdling scream.
从医院的走廊上传来了一阵毛骨悚然的尖叫。
As soon as the door of the theater was opened, in rushed a large crowd of audience who had been waiting outside for a long time.

剧院的门刚打开，在外等候已久的观众就冲了进去。
Then came the exciting hour at which our team has got the first place in the math contest we have been looking forward to.
我们的团队在这次数学竞赛中获得了第一名，这一我们期盼已久的激动人心的时刻终于来了。

注意：如果句子中的主语是代词，则只能将副词置于句首，主语和谓语动词的位置不变，即用正常语序。例如：

Ahead she sat with some kind of satisfactory facial expression for the excellent performance of her granddaughter on the stage.
她坐在前面，为孙女精彩的舞台表演感到满意。

四、表语或状语开头引起的完全倒装

为强调句子中的某种成分，以表语或状语开头的句子采用完全倒装语序。其结构为：
（1）"表语 + 系动词 + 主语 + ……"。
（2）"状语 + 谓语动词 + 主语 + ……"。

Present at this symposium in the summer are the most experienced experts and scholars in this research field.
来参加今年夏天的研讨会的都是这个研究领域中最资深的专家学者。
Seated on the grassland are a lot of tireless visitors after long hours of tour sighting.
坐在草地上的是一群长时间观光旅游后感觉到疲倦的旅客。
Of physical health or optimistic mentality she had almost none.
在健康的身体或乐观的心态这两样中，她什么都没有。
Standing on the platform for such an eloquent speech right now is dean of this academy.
现在站在讲台上作出如此精彩演讲的是这个学院的主任。
On the other hand is a compelling argument that education should be the given priority whether or not our economic conditions stay well.
另一方面，有个很有说服力的观点，认为无论经济条件处于何种状态，教育都要放在优先地位。
By what standard, then, should we decide which species are worth saving and which ones are not?
那么，我们该用何种标准来决定哪些物种值得被拯救，哪些又不值得呢?

五、直接引语中的完全倒装

直接引语的全部或一部分置于句首时，主句的主语和谓语次序要颠倒，采用完全倒装结构。例如：

"I shall not scold you." said the man, "you are punished enough now."
"我不会责备你的。"这个人说，"你现在已经得到了惩罚。"
"Perhaps he isn't a bad sort of chap after all." remarked David.

"他毕竟不是那种混蛋家伙。"大卫说。

注意：如果主句的主语为代词，或谓语另有宾语，则一般不用倒装。例如：

"Who's paying?" shouted the fat man at the corner. "You are," I answered.

"谁买单？"角落里一个肥胖的男人大声问道。我回答道："你买单。"

"I'm leaving for Hainan during the Spring Festival next month." Mary told me yesterday.

玛丽昨天告诉我："我下个月计划去海南过春节。"

六、as/though/although（尽管）引导的让步状语从句中的倒装语序

在 as/though/although（尽管）引导的让步状语从句中，当把表语或状语（名词、形容词、副词、分词、实义动词）提前时，会引起句子的倒装。其倒装结构为"名词/形容词/副词/名词/实义动词原形/分词 + as + 主语 + 谓语 +……"。例如：

Little boy as he is, he gets far away from his family and begins to make a living on his own by doing part-time jobs.

尽管他是个小孩，但他远离家人开始通过做兼职谋生。

Foolish though he looks, he always seems to make the wisest proposals.

他看起来样子傻傻的，可似乎总是能提出最聪明的建议。

Fast as you read, you can't finish the novel characterized with detailed and vivid narration in a week.

尽管你读得很快，你也不可能在一周之内将这本叙述生动而又翔实的小说读完。

Eating the apple as he was, he had got an eye for all David's movements.

他尽管咬着苹果，但仍警惕着大卫的一举一动。

注意：

（1）句首的名词不能带有任何冠词。例如：

Child as she is, she knows how to keep harmonious interpersonal relationship with the others.

她尽管是个孩子，但知道如何与他人维持和谐的人际关系。

（2）句首为实义动词时，其他助动词要放在主语之后。如果实义动词带有宾语和状语，则宾语和状语要随实义动词一起放在主语之前。例如：

Try hard as he will, he never seems able to achieve the goal which he has been fighting for.

他尽管工作很尽力，但似乎一直实现不了久久为之奋斗的目标。

七、否定或半否定意义的词或词组开头引起的部分倒装

含有否定或半否定意义的词或词组，如 never, not, no, neither, nor, nowhere, on no account, in no case, at no time, by no means, under/in no circumstances, in no conditions, hardly, scarcely, barely, rarely, seldom, little, few 置于句首时，句子要采用部分倒装。例如：

Under no circumstances should we do anything that will benefit ourselves but harm the interests of the state.

在任何情况下我们都不能做有损国家利益而利己的事情。

Never have these two good friends quarreled with each other since they established a close relationship in 1991.

这两个好朋友自1991年成为莫逆之交以来，彼此从未争吵过。

Never before has our country been as powerful and as prosperous as it is today.

我们的国家从未像今天这般强大而富强。

Seldom in all my life have I met such a selfish person who always takes his things into account without considering others.

我一生都很少碰到像这样自私至极，从来只想到自己而不为他人着想的人。

Nowhere will you find the answer to this question as you haven't taken any efforts in finding the solution.

因为你没有设法去寻找解决办法，所以无论如何你也不会找到这个问题的答案。

Nor can we alter facts by virtue of our inclinations or passions when it comes to history.

在历史方面，我们不能以自己的喜好或热情来更改事实。

注意：如果含有否定或半否定意义的词或词组并不置于句首，则不需要倒装。例如：

We should under no circumstances do anything that will benefit ourselves but harm the interests of the state.

在任何情况下我们都不能做有损国家利益而利己的事情。

八、Only 开头引起的部分倒装

副词 only 置于句首时，起强调作用，此时，句子要采用部分倒装形式。例如：

Only by making efforts to overcome all kinds of difficulties can we succeed in the end.

我们只有付出努力克服各种各样的困难，才能最终取得成功。

Only when I saw him did I realize that I forgot to prepare a birthday gift for him.

只有当我看到他的时候，我才意识到忘了给他准备一份生日礼物。

注意：如果置于句首的 only 修饰主语，则不用倒装结构。另外，在"only + 状语从句 + 主句"结构中，主句采用倒装语序，从句采用正常语序。例如：

Only David failed in the final exam in our class because of his laziness in his daily learning.

因为大卫平时学习懒惰，所以在我们班的期末考试中，只有他不及格。

Only when the patient recovered consciousness were these doctors finally relaxed.

只有在病人恢复意识时医生们才终于松了口气。

Only when educators help students establish correct fundamental values, do young people grow into successful working adults.

只有当教育者们帮助学生树立正确的价值观时，这些年轻人才能成长为成功的工作者。

九、省略了 if 的虚拟语气条件从句中的部分倒装

虚拟语气条件从句如果省略了 if，则要采用部分倒装的结构。此时，需将 were, had 或 should 放在主语之前。例如：

Were my mother here, she would give attendance to my daily life and keep everything in order.

我妈妈要是在这儿，她就会无微不至地关照我的生活，把任何事情都处理得井井有条。

Were politicians to fully disclose every personal foible, few of them would be elected.

如果政界领导们彻底暴露其私人弱点，那么他们当中几乎没有几个人可以当选。

Should you fail in this business investment, you could get encouraged again to get rid of the disadvantageous factors and regain prosperity you have created.

万一你生意投资失败，你要再次鼓起勇气摆脱不利因素，重拾你曾创造的辉煌。

Should we ever become so clever a species as to devise machines that can truly think for themselves and look out for their own well-being.

如果我们成了如此聪明的物种，以至于我们可以像它们一样设计真正为自身考虑并关心自身利益的机器。

Had it not snowed so heavily, the company would have held an annual gathering party yesterday.

要不是下了大雪，这家公司昨天就已举行了年度聚会活动。

Had these idealists concerned themselves with short-term survival and immediate needs, they might still be not recognized by the public.

如果这些理想主义者仅仅考虑短期的生存和即时的需要，他们也许就不会被公众所接受。

十、表示祝愿的句子中的部分倒装

表示祝愿的句子采用部分倒装时，谓语动词或谓语的一部分要放在主语之前。例如：

May the season's joy fill you all the year round.

愿节日的愉快伴你一生。

May the coming New Year bring you joy, love and peace.

愿新年为你带来快乐、友爱和宁静。

May the New Year bring many good things and rich blessings to you and all those you love!

愿新年带给你和你所爱的人许多美好的事物和无尽的祝福！

十一、频率副词及短语开头引起的部分倒装

以频率副词及短语，如 often, always, many a time, now and again, once a week, now and then, every other day 等开头的句子，要采用部分倒装的形式。例如：

Often did we advise them not to smoke in the public area because Nicotine is harmful to people's health.

因为尼古丁有害人体健康，我们经常建议他们别在公共场合抽烟。

Many a time have I helped her whenever she encountered misfortune and suffered sickness in her life.

她患病遭遇不幸时，我多次地帮助她。

Now and then did the old couple go outside for a walk after supper every day since they have developed this habit into part of their lives.

这对老夫妇时不时地在每天晚饭后外出散步，因为他们已经把这种习惯融为生活的一部分。

十二、so 开头引起的结构倒装

so 开头引起的结构倒装分为以下两种情况：

（1）在 so/such...that 结构中，当 so 或 such 位于句首时，句子可以构成部分倒装句，用于表示对 so/such 和 that 之间的部分的强调。例如：

So loudly did he speak that even people in the next room could hear him.

他讲话的声音那样大，以至于连隔壁屋子里的人都听得见。

Such an outstanding musician was Beethoven that still today many people highly appreciate his representative works.

贝多芬是一位如此卓越的音乐家，以至于现在仍然还有许多人高度认可他的代表作。

Such a successful merchant was in the architectural industry that he set up countless branches and accumulated large amounts of money.

他是一位在建筑行业取得成功的商人，已经开了众多的分公司，积累了巨额财富。

So beautiful is the scenery of my hometown that each year it attracts thousands of tourists from both home and abroad.

我的家乡风景很美，每年都会吸引来自国内外的上千名游客。

（2）在重复倒装句型"so/neither/nor + 助动词/be 动词/情态动词 + 主语"中，为避免句子中部分内容不必要的重复，通常以 so，nor，neither 作为开头，表示谓语所述的情况也适用于另一个人或另一事物。其中，so 用于肯定句，表示"也一样""也这样"；nor，neither 用于否定句，表示"同样也不，也不这样"。例如：

Nonstop waves of immigrants played a role too, and so did bigger crops of babies as yesterday's "baby boom" generation reached its child-bearing years.

不间断的移民浪潮也发挥了作用——而且随着昔日在"生育高峰期"出生的一代人达到生育年龄，婴儿的出生数量增加了，这同样起了作用。

My parents do not like eating chicken for they feel the taste disgusting. Neither/Nor do I.

我的父母亲因为觉得鸡肉味道不好而不喜欢吃。我同样也不喜欢吃。

十三、复合句或并列句中的倒装

在判断带有倒装句的复合句或并列句中的倒装位置时，应遵循如下规则。

（1）not only...but also 结构遵循"前倒后不倒"的原则，即在 not only...but also 引导的并列句中，当 not only 位于句首时，其所引导的位于前面的分句倒装，but also 所引导的位于后面的分句不倒装。例如：

Not only is the child good at figure calculation, but also he has talent for music and painting.

这个孩子不仅擅长于算术运算，而且在音乐和绘画上颇有天赋。

Not only can he dance very gracefully, but he can also play some musical instruments very skillfully.

他不仅跳舞很优雅，而且能够熟练地演奏乐器。

Not only did they design such a device but they had also managed to apply it into batches of industrial products.

他们不仅设计出这样一种装置，还成功地将它应用到成批的工业产品中。

（2）Neither...nor 遵循"前倒后也倒"的原则，即前后分句均用倒装。例如：

Neither do I know her personal information and family background, nor does he.

我不了解她的个人信息和家庭背景，他同样也不了解。

Neither is David willing to stay in the polluted countryside for a holiday, nor am I.

大卫不愿意待在环境受到污染的乡村度假，我同样也不愿意待在那里。

（3）not until..., hardly/scarcely... when, no sooner... than 结构遵循"主倒从不倒"的原则，即主句采用倒装，从句不倒装。例如：

Not until you lost all property you have once possessed did you realize how precious these things are.

直到你失去曾经拥有的所有财产，你才会意识到这些东西是多么的宝贵。

Not until Columbus discovered the new land, were bananas brought to Europe.

直到哥伦布发现新大陆，香蕉才得以运送到欧洲。

Hardly/Scarcely had the thief arrived at the train station when he was arrested by the policemen who tracked him beforehand.

这个贼刚到火车站就被早先跟踪他的警察们逮个正着。

No sooner had he stepped onto the stage for performance than a wave of warm cheer was heard.

他一上舞台表演就收到了一阵热烈的喝彩声。

Exercises

Ⅰ. Choose the best answer to complete each sentence.

1. From inside a wooden building _____ the sounds of laughter and the clink of glasses.

　　A. come　　　　B. comes　　　　C. is coming　　　D. did come

2. There _____ a bewildering selection of dishes for starter and main course, while the sweets are more varied than usual for a Chinese restaurant.

　　A. are　　　　　B. have been　　　C. is　　　　　　D. was

3. Along with these _____ of hip-hop culture such as language and fashion.

　　A. are other distinctive aspects　　　　B. other distinctive aspects are

　　C. have other distinctive aspects　　　 D. other distinctive aspects have

4. _____ the days when you simply went out for a night drinking with your friends before your wedding.

　　A. Going are　　B. Going were　　C. Were gone　　D. Gone were

5. There is a real possibility that we can solve this problem completely, _____ cooperation among all parties involved.

A. although there should be B. there although should be
C. there should be D. should there be

6. Splendid _____, the heart of the city, with its one hundred and more skyscrapers.
A. are the architecture of Manhattan B. is the architecture of Manhattan
C. the architecture of Manhattan is D. the architecture of Manhattan has been

7. Gone forever _____ when the Chinese people had to use foreign soaps due to China's backward industrial manufacturing.
A. were the days B. the days were C. was the days D. the days was

8. Not only _____ all our money, but we also came close to losing our lives.
A. had we lost B. we had lost C. we lost D. did we lose

9. So vigorously _____ that the authorities reconsidered his case and conducted another meticulous investigation.
A. he protested B. protested he C. did he protest D. he did protest

10. _____ change your mind, no one would blame you, for he is the supervisor behind such an issue.
A. You could B. Could you C. You should D. Should you

11. _____, there was no hope of her being able to fall asleep.
A. Exhausted if she was B. Exhausted though she was
C. Exhausted though was she D. Exhausted if was she

12. There _____ entertainment in a good book than in a month of typical TV programming.
A. are more B. is more C. is much D. more is

13. May the rest of your journey _____ unforgettable.
A. is B. has been C. will be D. be

14. _____ in the past, at the moment it is a favorite choice for wedding gown.
A. Unpopular has as white been B. White has been as unpopular
C. Unpopular has been as white D. Unpopular as white has been

15. The millions of calculations involved, _____ by hand, would have lost all practical value by the time they were finished.
A. had they been done B. they had been done
C. having been done D. they were done

16. Not until the early years of the 19th century _____ what heat is.
A. man did know B. man knew C. didn't man know D. did man know

17. Only when one is away from home _____ how warm and comfortable home is.
A. he realizes B. does he realizes C. does he realize D. he will realize

18. _____, I have never seen anyone to equal her in thoroughness, whatever the job is.
A. Much as I have traveled B. As I have traveled much
C. Much did I travel D. Much have I traveled

19. Nowhere _____ 1980 census statistics dramatize more the American search for spacious living than in the Far West.

A. do   B. were   C. does   D. have

20. To such length _____ in rehearsal that two actors walked out of the theatre.
    A. has she gone   B. she has gone   C. she did go   D. did she go

21. Rich blessings for health and longevity _____ my special wish for you in the coming year.
    A. have been   B. have   C. are   D. is

22. _____ in the accident that he had to stay in the hospital for treatment.
    A. Such badly was he injured   B. So badly was he injured
    C. So badly did he injure   D. So badly he was injured

23. Not only _____ a musical performance but also _____ a brief introduction to the history of western brass instrument.
    A. did they present; they gave   B. they presented; they gave
    C. did they present; gave they   D. did they present; did they give

24. _____ for the leadership of the Party, we should not have succeeded in enjoying today's happiness.
    A. Had not it been   B. Had it not been   C. There was   D. Was there

25. Typical of the new type of young people _____, who set a shining example to the whole nation.
    A. was Lei Feng   B. were Lei Feng   C. Lei Feng was   D. Lei Feng were

26. Hardly _____ he got out of the court _____ the reporters photographed and raised a lot of questions to him.
    A. had; when   B. had; than   C. did; when   D. has; than

27. Neither _____ up the treatment to his ankle, nor _____ up the chance to take part in the next race.
    A. will he give; will he give   B. he will give; will he give
    C. will he give; he will give   D. he will give; he will give

28. Nowhere else in the world _____ cheaper tailoring than in Hong Kong.
    A. a tourist can find   B. can a tourist find   C. a tourist will find   D. a tourist has found

29. Under no circumstances _____ first use nuclear weapons, which is a unchangeable diplomatic policy we have been sticking to for many years.
    A. will China   B. China will   C. does China   D. do China

30. Then, down the crowed thoroughfare _____ the University of Cambridge's most distinctive vehicle, bearing its most distinguished citizen.
    A. are coming   B. comes   C. did come   D. come

II. Identify the mistake in each sentence and then correct it.

1. Blessed does the person who is too busy to worry in the daytime and too sleepy to worry at night.
2. Housewife as is she, she teaches me by example and guides me to develop an optimistic attitude towards life.
3. It had not been for the timely investment from the general public, our company would not be so

thriving as it is.
4. Not only he refused the gift, he also severely criticized the sender who wished to give him a surprise beforehand.
5. Not until did he fail in the final test did he regret not having taken notes in class and worked harder in his every day's learning.
6. Only when he was 30 years old he realized how important English is as an international language and begin to learn English.
7. From 1930 to 1940 was there a significant rise, which, since 1940, has been followed by a steady fall.
8. So rapid has the change that a section can be transformed from morning to evening.
9. Down jump the burglar from the tenth floor when he heard someone shouted at him.
10. May everything beautiful and best is condensed into this card. I sincerely wish you happiness, cheerfulness and success.

第十八章

感 叹 句

第一节 感叹句的定义与结构

一、感叹句的定义

感叹句（Exclamations），是指用以表示喜、怒、哀、乐等强烈感情的句子。感叹句有多种表现形式，但主要的表现形式只有两种，即由 what 与 how 引导的感叹句。另外，还有许多特殊形式的感叹句。例如，在特定的语境中表达强烈情感的陈述句、疑问句、祈使句可作为感叹句；有时，一个不定式或者从句，甚至是一个短语或者单词也可作为感叹句。

感叹句的构成结构为"感叹部分＋陈述部分（主语＋谓语）"。其中，感叹部分由感叹词来引导（感叹词包括 how 与 what。其中，how 作状语，修饰形容词、副词或整个句子；what 作定语，修饰名词，名词前可以有形容词或冠词）；陈述部分则包括主语与谓语。例如：

Oh，first love，how unblemished and unforgettable it is！（How 句型）
Oh，what unblemished and unforgettable first love it is！（What 句型）
噢！多么圣洁的值得回忆的初恋啊！（《初恋》谢冰莹）
How flexible and user-friendly a system it is for beginners and advanced users alike！（How 句型）
What a flexible and user-friendly system it is for beginners and advanced users alike！（What 句型）
对于初学者和高级用户来说，这是一个多么灵活且用户友好的系统！

二、感叹句的结构

1. 由感叹词 what 引导的感叹句

由 What 引导的感叹句的结构如下：

What + a/an + 形容词 + 可数名词单数 + 主语 + 谓语!
What + 形容词 + 可数名词复数/不可数名词 + 主语 + 谓语!

2. 由感叹词 how 引导的感叹句

由 how 引导的感叹句的结构如下：
How + 形容词/副词 + 主语 + 谓语!
How + 形容词 + a/an + 可数名词单数 + 主语 + 谓语!

3. 感叹句的学习难点

（1）如何确定使用 what 还是 how？

通常，如果感叹句强调的是可数名词单数、可数名词复数或不可数名词，则由 what 引导；如果强调的是形容词、副词或整个句子，则由 how 引导。但"How + *adj.* + a/an + *n*"结构例外。

（2）如何判断是否使用冠词以及使用什么样的冠词？

通常，名词的复数形式和不可数名词之前不用冠词；以元音开头的词语之前用 an，以辅音开头的词语之前用 a。

第二节　感叹句的用法及注意问题

一、What 引导的感叹句

What 引导的感叹句包括以下三种。

（1）"What + a/an + 形容词 + 可数名词单数 + 主语 + 谓语!"结构。例如：

What an important historical turning point that day is since these two countries finally established the formal diplomatic relationship between them!

两个国家最终在那天建立了正式的外交关系，这是多么重要的一个历史转折点啊！

What an extraordinarily harmonious balance The Forbidden City displays between buildings and open space within a more or less symmetrical layout!

故宫蕴含着对称设计，建筑与空间之间的平衡是多么和谐啊！

What a pity it is that he was severely injured in the car crash and lost his ability to work!

他在这场车祸中遭受重伤，失去了工作能力，多可怜啊！

（2）"What + 形容词 + 可数名词复数 + 主语 + 谓语!"结构。例如：

What long-drawn cadences they are with crowds of people gathering to appreciate them and applauding!

这是何等悠扬绵长的节奏，成群的人们聚拢欣赏并为之喝彩！

What terrible earthquakes they were that countless people lost their homes and even some rescue team members sacrificed their lives!

多么可怕的地震啊！无数的人失去了家园，甚至一些救援队员也献出了生命。

What gorgeous decorations these Christmas trees have, among which people can sense more festival atmosphere!

从这些圣诞树极其豪华的装饰中，人们能够感受到更多节日的氛围。

（3）"What + 形容词 + 不可数名词 + 主语 + 谓语！"结构。例如：

What great progress in his studies he has made from the last place to the top one in the whole grade!

从学习成绩最后一名提升到年级第一名，他取得了多么大的进步呀！

What bad cough he has although he has already taken medicine for at least three days!

他尽管已经服药至少三天了，还是咳得好厉害！

What fantastic fun it will be when we all go on holiday together.

我们大家一起去度假，那可太有意思了。

二、How 引导的感叹句

How 引导的感叹句包括以下四种结构。

（1）"How + 形容词 + 主语 + 谓语！"结构。例如：

How well-known Jiangsu cuisine is for its careful selection of ingredients, its meticulous preparation methodology and its not-too-spicy, not-too-bland taste.

江苏菜系有其精选的原料、精细的准备和不辣不温的口感，多么闻名啊！

How excited he became when he heard the news that the first prize in the chess contest belonged to him!

当他听到自己在围棋竞赛获得一等奖这个消息时，他是多么激动啊！

How wearisome the players are!

这又是何等令人恹恹欲绝的戏啊！

（2）"How + 副词 + 主语 + 谓语！"结构。例如：

How passionately he looks at her since beauty is in the eyes of beholder!

因为情人眼里出西施，他多么深情地望着她！

How gracefully the moves displayed the body in the most elegant and beautiful manner possible!

这些动作以其优雅绝妙的姿态展现出体态之美，多么优美！

How well she remembered the first time she had seen him, which illustrated she cared him so much.

她把初见他的那幕情景记得好清楚呀，这说明她还是很在意他的。

（3）"How + 主语 + 谓语！"结构。例如：

How her mother worried because this was the first time she stayed away from home!

因为这是她第一次离开家，她母亲是多么担心啊！

How he wished for a drink when the area was cut off water and electricity by the demolition team!

这片区域被拆迁队断水断电了，他多希望能有点东西喝！

How news get around! Everyone must know you are in town.

消息传得多快！人们一定都知道你到城里来了。

（4）"How + 形容词 + a（an）+ 可数名词单数！"结构。例如：

Miss Langham arm in arm with Mr. Peabody——how astonishing a sight!

兰哈姆小姐挽着皮博迪先生的胳膊，看上去真叫人吃惊！
How passionate a man he is for whom being able to give the poor necessary aid is his upmost happiness.
对于他来说，能够给予穷人必要的帮助是他最大的幸福，他是多么有同情心的一个人啊！

三、感叹句的注意问题

(1) 当遇到表示数量的形容词，如 many, much, little, few 等时，感叹句要用 how。即使这些形容词后面跟有名词，仍要用 how，而不能用 what。例如：
How many books he has for he is the one who likes to crazily seek knowledge and spend large amounts of money buying them!
他是一个喜欢疯狂追求知识并为之一掷千金购书的人，他的书真多！
How much money he gave her otherwise she threatened to expose his scandal!
他给了她好多钱呀，不然她就威胁曝光他的丑事。
How little money I have for the reason that Mom did not send me a remittance for months!
妈妈好几个月没给我汇款了，我的钱多么少呀！
How few friends he has as he is seen as an introverted guy not fond of interacting with people!
被认为是一个不喜欢与人接触且性格内向的人，他的朋友真少！
(2) 口语中，感叹句中的主语和谓语往往略去不讲。例如：
What an honest boy!
多么诚实的孩子呀！
How wonderful!
精彩极了！
(3) What 引导感叹句时在下列情形中不能后跟形容词。
①当感叹句中的名词带有形容词的意味时。例如：
What luck!
真幸运！
②当表示批评时。例如：
What nonsense!
一派胡言！
③当表示强调或夸张时。例如：
What a mistake is to have come here!
来到这里真是个错误！
④当表示蔑视时。例如：
What a man he is!
那家伙算什么！

四、特殊形式的感叹句

(1) 只有一个单词的感叹句。例如：

Nonsmoking!（不要吸烟了！）Fire！（失火了！）Excellent！（太棒了！）Nonsense！（胡说！）Alas！（哎呀！）Oh！（啊！/哦！/哎哟！）Well！（好啦！）Why！［什么（话）！/嗯！/岂有此理！/好好！］

（2）由短语构成的感叹句。例如：

At last! At last!

终于盼到了！

Five seconds! Such a fleeting time!

5秒钟！多么转瞬即逝的时间呀！

The sunshine and the fresh air!

多么明媚的晨光，多么新鲜的空气！

（3）不定式短语引起的感叹句。不定式短语单独使用时，常用于表示惊异、气愤、祝愿等情绪。例如：

To trust such a liar without credit!

竟然相信这样一个毫无信誉的骗子！

To think that I shall get the signature of my superstar!

真没想到我能得到我喜欢的明星的签名！

To think of my leaving the purse in the taxi!

真没想到我把钱包落到出租车上了！

To think a scandal of this sort should be going on under my roof!

真想不到这种丑事竟然出在我们家里！

（4）So 与 such 引起的感叹句，其结构为"so + 形容词/such + 名词"。例如：

Weddings are so important in China! Couples are willing to fork out about many times their monthly income on getting hitched and everything that comes with it.

结婚在中国是件大事！新人们不惜花费约相当于收入数倍的"重金"来置办婚礼。

The lion in the zoo is such a fierce beast that it opened its mouth, stretched its paws and roared to people.

动物园里的狮子是多么凶猛的野兽，它张牙舞爪地对人们咆哮着。

（5）That 引起的感叹句。That 引起的感叹句，多用于表示愿望、遗憾。例如：

That it should ever come to this!

事情竟会弄到这种地步！

That she won the race!

她赢得这次比赛该多好！

（6）If 或 if only 引起的感叹句。例如：

If I were ten years younger!

我要是能年轻十岁就好了！

If only I had not chosen this way to go!

如果当初我不选择走这条路！

（7）Who 引起的感叹句。以 who 为首引起的感叹句多用于表示惊奇。例如：

Who would have thought it!

谁能想得到啊!

Who else could have done it!

还有谁会做这件事!

(8) 疑问句形式的感叹句。疑问句形式的感叹句包括肯定和否定两种形式。例如:

Am I silly!

我真傻!

Can he run!

他真会跑!

Was she angry!

她气极了!

Did he look annoyed!

他看来很烦恼!

Hasn't she grown!

她长这么大了!

Isn't it a lovely day!

天气真好!

(9) 以 off, in, away, here, there 为首引起的感叹句。例如:

Up to the cliff climbed a man!

那个人爬到悬崖上去了!

Here it begins!

来吧,开始啦!

 **Exercises**

Ⅰ. Choose the best answer to complete each sentence.

1. _____ hobby martial art is, for it challenges you mentally and physically.
   A. How exciting   B. How an exciting
   C. What a exciting   D. What an exciting

2. _____ very important and unique form of Chinese culture Chinese Kungfu is!
   A. How a   B. How   C. What   D. What a

3. _____ these social activities played a role in local communities!
   A. How   B. How important
   C. What important   D. What an important

4. _____ the Silk Road became a communication route between different parts of many countries!
   A. How significantly   B. How significant
   C. What significant   D. What a significant

5. What _____ the city is developing at!
   A. a breathtaking pace   B. breathtaking pace

    C. an breathtaking pace   D. the breathtaking pace

6. What _____ The Summer Palace is to Chinese architecture!

    A. monuments   B. the monument   C. monument   D. a monument

7. _____ these maps and guidebooks become as soon as they are printed!

    A. What an obsolete   B. What obsolete

    C. How obsolete   D. How obsoletely

8. _____ expression of the creative art of Chinese landscape garden design The Summer Palace is!

    A. What an outstanding   B. How an outstanding

    C. How outstanding   D. What outstanding an

9. _____ the large and priceless collection of cultural relics in the museum has been!

    A. How well-known   B. What well-known

    C. What well-known   D. What a well-known

10. _____ fascinating and mysterious Egyptian civilization it is in the history of mankind!

    A. What   B. What a   C. How a   D. How

11. _____ valley land it is because there is an abundance of water and sun, elements which the ancient ancestors believed were gods.

    A. What a fertile   B. What fertile   C. How fertile   D. How a fertile

12. _____ the magnificence of this palace is to everyone!

    A. How admirable   B. How admirably

    C. What admirable   D. What an admirable

13. _____ the phenomenon of young people riding a skateboard or showing off their cycling tricks in a park is!

    A. How commonly   B. How common   C. What common   D. What a common

14. What _____ yoga is to find peace of mind in a world that is anything but peaceful.

    A. way   B. a way   C. ways   D. the way

15. _____ increasingly important role the post 80s are playing in the modern society!

    A. What   B. What the   C. What a   D. What an

16. _____ these young people became compared with previous generations!

    A. What a self-centered   B. What self-centered

    C. How   D. How self-centered

17. _____ these young people have been to high-tech products and an advanced lifestyle!

    A. What open   B. What openly   C. How open   D. How openly

18. _____ learning Chinese characters can be for foreigners!

    A. What challenging   B. What challenge

    C. How challenging   D. How challenging a

19. _____ difficult language Chinese is for many foreigners, whatever their mother language.

    A. What a   B. What an   C. How a   D. How

20. _____ hip-pop music has been these days, from popular radio to TV commercials.

A. How ubiquitously   B. How ubiquitous   C. How ubiquitous a   D. What ubiquitous
21. _____ unrestrained and romantic that would be if you could go to a cinema with your lover on weekends.
   A. How   B. How a   C. How an   D. What
22. For those who have been working hard for a whole week, _____ time the weekend is!
   A. what happy   B. what a happy   C. How a happy   D. How happy
23. _____ process learning this style of dance is, while the results on stage are magical.
   A. What difficult   B. How a difficult
   C. What a difficult   D. How difficultly
24. _____ long, tough battle he fought against the lung cancer which eventually took his life!
   A. What a   B. What   C. How a   D. How
25. _____ large quantities of coffee seem to be in diabetes prevention!
   A. What helpful   B. How helpful a   C. How helpfully   D. How helpful
26. _____ it has become to see someone sitting at Starbucks listening to music or surfing the web on his or her laptop!
   A. How commonly   B. How common
   C. What common   D. What a common
27. _____ it is that tea has weaved itself into the fabric of our consumer-oriented culture.
   A. What a fact   B. What fact   C. How a fact   D. How fact
28. _____ the dish proves in the prevention and the treatment of hypertension, hyperlipemia, heart diseases and hypertrophy.
   A. How high effectively   B. How effective highly
   C. How high effective   D. How highly effective
29. _____ dish it is for lowering blood sugar, preventing aging and curing diabetes and poor appetite.
   A. What a good   B. What good   C. What good a   D. How a good
30. _____ it is to say grace before the meal begins in many Christian homes.
   A. What a customary   B. What customary
   C. How customary   D. How customarily

Ⅱ. Identify the mistake in each sentence and then correct it.

1. How skeptically I have always been about the taste in this restaurant because I often found it either too sweet, greasy and oily, over sauced or with the flavors unbalanced.
2. What innovative array the traditional tea snack is!
3. What an indispensable part of the Dragon Boat Festival Dragon boat racing are!
4. How so much fun some holidays are that they catch on outside of their culture.
5. How hugely the celebration of Thanksgiving Day is to express thanks for the year's bounty and continued blessings.
6. What a lot of funs children have for they dress on costumes and go on trick or treating on

Halloween Day.
7. What financially beneficial tourism has been to China, which needs more foreign currencies for its modernization program.
8. Foreign languages are such commonly used in some ethnic neighborhoods that visitors might think they are in another country!
9. How wide English is spoken around the world, so English training organizations appear one after another like mushrooms.
10. How possible it would be to prove him guilty for the reason that most of the evidence was destroyed in the fire.

参考文献

［1］Eastwood，J. Oxford Practical Grammar［M］.Oxford：Oxford University Press，2006.

［2］Dale E. Elliot. Toward a Grammar of Exclamations［J］.Foundations of Language，1974，11（2）：231－246.

［3］Douglas Biber，Stig Johansson，et al. Longman Grammar of Spoken and Written English［M］.Beijing：Foreign Language Teaching and Research Press，2009.

［4］Hogue，A. The Essentials of English：A Writer's Handbook［M］.New York：Pearson Education，2003.

［5］Hornby，A. S. Oxford Advanced Learner's English-Chinese Dictionary［M］.Oxford：Oxford University Press，2014.

［6］Murfy，R. English Grammar in Use：A Self-Study Reference and Practice Book for Intermediate Students［M］.Cambridge：Cambridge University Press，2011（2）.

［7］Zanuttini，R，Portner，P. Exclamative Clauses：At the Syntax-Semantics Interface［J］.Language，2003，79（1）：39－81.

［8］雷切尔·芬尼，卡罗尔·费雷恩，等. 国际英语语法大全（汉译版）［M］.北京：北京语言大学出版社，2015.

［9］薄冰. 高级英语语法［M］.北京：高等教育出版社，1990.

［10］薄冰. 高级英语语法［M］.北京：世界知识出版社，2000.

［11］薄冰. 薄冰实用英语语法详解［M］.太原：山西教育出版社，2008.

［12］薄冰，赵德鑫. 英语语法手册［M］.北京：商务印书馆，1978.

［13］董国忠. 英语倒装句的翻译［J］.中国科技翻译，1994（03）：16－18，55.

［14］冯大德. 英语语法详解［M］.成都：成都科技大学出版社，1994.

［15］宫守伟，刘冬梅. 星火英语高考突破［M］.北京：中国社会出版社，2007.

［16］侯宁海. 英语感叹句构成及应用［J］.大学英语，1996（08）：67－69.

［17］霍荣全. 语法表解大全［M］.北京：首都师范大学出版社，2012.

[18] 金立鑫. 语法的多视角研究 [M]. 上海：上海外语教育出版社，2000.

[19] 朗文当代高级英语辞典 [Z]. 北京：外语教学与研究出版社，2014.

[20] 刘科成，彭爽. 中国学习者英语感叹句习得特点研究 [J]. 外语学刊，2012（06）：124-128.

[21] 刘晶. 高中英语语法一本通 [M]. 上海：华东理工大学出版社，2014.

[22] 秦裕祥. 英语语法专题研究 [M]. 长沙：湖南师范大学出版社，1999.

[23] 孙锋. 英语语法大全 [M]. 北京：外文出版社，2012.

[24] 孙德玉，王桂英. 现代英语解疑语法 [M]. 大连：辽宁师范大学出版社，1996.

[25] 360 百科. 介词 [EB/OL]. https：//baike. so. com/doc/3855164-4047635. html.

[26] 360 百科. 数词 [EB/OL]. https：//baike. so. com/doc/6166229-6379459. html.

[27] 苏秦. 从零开始学英语语法 [M]. 北京：化学工业出版社，2014.

[28] 吴志福. 全国高等学校实用英语语法 [M]. 成都：电子科技大学出版社，2006.

[29] 徐李洁. 英语倒装句再研究 [J]. 外语与外语教学，2003（08）：11.

[30] 徐盛桓. 英语倒装句研究 [J]. 外语教学与研究，1995（04）：28-37，80.

[31] 许国璋. 英语 [M]. 北京：商务印书馆，1989.

[32] 新东方在线 [EB/OL]. 高考英语短文改错专项训练：介词类错误. http：//gaokao. koolearn. com/20140928/829172. html.

[33] 杨才英. 论感叹句的功能语义特征——对感叹句形式逻辑分析的质疑 [J]. 外语与外语教学，2010（02）：45-48.

[34] 袁懋梓. 大学英语语法 [M]. 北京：外语教学与研究出版社，2006.

[35] 英语网. 2015 高考备考：高中英语常用介词短语上 [EB/OL]. http：//yingyu. xdf. cn/201509/10348248. html.

[36] 英语语法网. 2016 情态动词考点精确模拟训练 [EB/OL]. http：//www. yygrammar. com/Article/201606/4878. html.

[37] 英语语法网. 2007 数词用法英语语法 [EB/OL]. http：//www. yygrammar. com/Article/num/

[38] 英语语法网. 2015 英语主谓一致专项考点模拟训练 [EB/OL]. http：//www. yygrammar. com/Article/201509/4174. html.

[39] 曾红霞. 英语倒装句的认知研究 [D]. 长沙：湖南师范大学，2007.

[40] 翟象俊，余建中，陈永捷，梁正溜. 21 世纪大学实用英语（U 版）综合教程（1）[M]. 上海：复旦大学出版社，2016.

[41] 张道真. 实用英语语法 [M]. 北京：商务印书馆，1992.

[42] 张道真. 实用英语语法 [M]. 北京：商务印书馆，1994.

[43] 张道真. 最新张道真大学英语语法（全能版）[M]. 济南：山东科学技术出版社，2008.

［44］张福元. 英语语法精讲与测试［M］. 上海：华东理工大学出版社，2007.
［45］赵俊英. 现代英语语法大全［M］. 上海：上海交通大学出版社，2008.
［46］章振邦. 新编英语语法［M］. 上海：上海外语教育出版社，1997.
［47］郑长木. 应用英语语法精要［M］. 沈阳：辽宁教育出版社，2015.
［48］中华文本库. 数词练习及答案［DB/OL］. http：//www.chinadmd.com/file/csziaiisseupixiwiswaxcev_14.html.
［49］中华资源库. 2016 语法填空和短文改错：情态动词［DB/OL］. http：//www.ziyuanku.com/g1234184.html.